SCOFIELD THAYER AND *THE DIAL*

E. E. Cummings *S. T. at The Dial*

SCOFIELD THAYER

AND

THE DIAL

An Illustrated History

by Nicholas Joost

SOUTHERN ILLINOIS UNIVERSITY PRESS

CARBONDALE AND EDWARDSVILLE

FOR

FRANCIS TAYLOR

PREFACE

IN THE SUMMER OF 1956, Francis Henry Taylor asked me to write a book about *The Dial*, as an appendage to the first major exhibition of art that he planned after his retirement from the Metropolitan Museum of Art and his return to the Worcester Art Museum. The exhibition would be in the spirit of his earlier shows of the 1930's, exhibitions that brought the Worcester Art Museum and himself to international notice: Carolingian art, Rembrandt, the Dutch masters. The Bollingen Foundation subsidized the book project, and Mr. Scofield Thayer's collection of the Dial Papers was made available. As the Dial Collection of pictures and objects had been already secured for some years by Francis Taylor on long-term loan to the Worcester Art Museum, my part in the proposed exhibition was to emphasize the literary aspects of the Dial venture—to write about *The Dial* and its Editor.

Compilation of data, ordering of the mass of papers in the Thayer collection, reading, looking at works of art, getting to understand *The Dial* and its background: these agreeable tasks occupied most of 1957. Then, early in November 1957, Francis Taylor suddenly and tragically died, at the height of his professional powers. "*The Dial* and the Dial Collection," as the exhibition came to be known, was only one of the projects brought to a halt by that untimely and irreparable death. Fortunately the Trustees and the staff of the Worcester Art Museum carried on with the plan. A new museum director of eminence came to Worcester, Daniel Catton Rich, and in May 1959, he brought to fruition the Dial exhibition. The concrete result of that most brilliant show is the catalog, "*The Dial* and the Dial Collection," which lists the entire Dial Collection on loan at the Worcester Art Museum and includes such supplementary matters as data on pictures and objects not in the Dial Collection but pertinent to it and illustrated in *The Dial* and the folio *Living Art;* there were also essays by Henry McBride and Daniel Catton Rich.

Despite the inclusive nature of the catalog and of this book, neither more than superficially scans *The Dial* in its decade. The available evidence is so rich that a rather spare selectivity must be exercised to order the material. Whether, in the present instance, the selectivity has been justified by the result is of course necessarily a reader's judgment. I alone am responsible for the use here made of any information, books, documents, photographs, and objects, but I now thank those persons and institutions to whom I am essentially indebted: Mr. and Mrs. Francis Henry Taylor; Scofield Thayer's representative, Walter A. Edwards; the Trustees and staff of the Worcester Art Museum, especially the Librarian, Alice Mundt, the Curator, Louisa Dresser, the Curatorial Assistant in 1957–58, Horst Vey, and the Director, Daniel Catton Rich; the American Antiquarian Society; Hermann P. Riccius, for his knowledge and unfailing help; Vernon Sternberg and his staff of the Southern Illinois University Press; Donald Gallup and his staff at the Sterling Library, Yale University; the Worcester (Mass.) Public Library; the English Institute of the University of Nijmegen; the Houghton Library, Harvard University; the Newberry Library; the Boston Public Library; the New York City Public Library; the Library, Edwardsville Campus, Southern Illinois University; the St. Louis Public Library; the late Henry McBride; T. S. Eliot; Marianne Moore; Gilbert Seldes; George Dillon; Henry Goddard Leach; Harley A. Stephenson; Charles Smutny; Doris Roth; Charles P. Williamson; and Kenneth Burke. For its generous grant of funds, I thank the Bollingen Foundation, and for released time from teaching duties, I thank Assumption College and Southern Illinois University (the latter, also, for research and travel funds). I thank the following persons and institutions for the permissions that I have obtained from all known owners of objects and pictures reproduced in this volume: for *The Peacock*, by Gaston Lachaise, Vizcaya, Miami, Florida; for *Spring Thaw*, by Charles Burchfield, Addison Gallery of American Art, Phillips Academy, Andover, Mass.; for *St. Séverin*, by Robert Delaunay, Mr. and Mrs. John McAndrew, Wellesley, Mass.; for *St. Francis*, by Alfeo Faggi, the Albright-Knox Art Gallery, Buffalo, N. Y.; for *Voyagers*, by Rockwell Kent, The Phillips Collection, Washington, D. C.; for *E. E. Cummings*, by Gaston Lachaise, Mrs. E. E. Cummings, New York City; for *Maltese Family*, by Jules Pascin, and for *James Sibley Watson*, by Gaston Lachaise, Dr. James S. Watson, Jr., Rochester, N. Y.; for *Harlequin with Clarinet*, by Jacques Lipchitz, the artist, Hastings, N. Y.; for *Two Horses*, by Franz Marc, the Museum of Art, Rhode Island School of Design, Providence, R. I.; for *Madonna and Child*, by Ivan Mestrovic, Mrs. Ivan Mestrovic, Notre Dame, Ind.; for *Pierrot*, by Pablo Picasso, Collection, The Museum of Modern Art, New York City, Sam A. Lewisohn Bequest; for *Mother and Child*, by Pablo Picasso, The Art Institute of

Chicago; for *Gesture*, by Max Weber, Dr. and Mrs. F. H. Hirschland, Harrison, N. Y.; and for *Stravinsky*, by Stuart Davis, The Downtown Gallery, New York City. Finally, for permission to quote, as well as to make use of, the Dial Papers—comprising manuscript and printed materials—and to reproduce pictures and objects in the Dial Collection—from plates made for *The Dial* and for "*The Dial* and the Dial Collection," and from plates made for this book—I thank Walter A. Edwards; and I thank the Worcester Art Museum for permission to use plates originally made for "*The Dial* and the Dial Collection." My work could not have begun nor would it thus have ended without the continuing sponsorship and co-operation of Walter A. Edwards and the Worcester Art Museum. I owe yet another debt to my wife: *exprimi non potest*.

Nicholas Joost

Southern Illinois University
24 JUNE 1964

CONTENTS

LIST OF ILLUSTRATIONS

In the following list of illustrations, the sign [1] designates a picture or object reproduced by the use of one of the copperplates made originally for *The Dial*, not all of which had been used when publication ceased and some of which are now first published; [2] designates previous reproduction in *The Dial;* [3] designates previous reproduction in the catalog of the exhibition "*The Dial* and the Dial Collection" held in the Worcester Art Museum, April 30–September 8, 1959; and [4] designates a version of the work here reproduced that differs from the version reproduced in *The Dial*.

SCOFIELD THAYER AND *THE DIAL*

ONE

Toward the Twenties

O N JUNE 20, 1918, *The Dial* printed an announcement of some importance. It did not concern the war, much as that great event occupied men's minds and the magazine's pages; and its importance was merely journalistic and, perhaps, literary—of restricted interest in those hectic summer days of distant but engrossing slaughter. The announcement was, at the time, important to a few persons directly connected with the operation of the magazine, to some contributors, to some readers.

The Dial briefly announced its move from Chicago to New York, another stage in a painful and prolonged metamorphosis that had been going on for several years. Francis F. Browne, a transplanted Vermonter, northern Democrat, and Union veteran, had founded *The Dial* in Chicago in 1880. Until his death in 1913, Browne had edited and published the magazine as a fortnightly and had made it the leading critical review in the Midwest, a journal serious enough to attract the talents of Professor Woodrow Wilson and Chief Justice Melville Weston Fuller. As an outpost of the New England tradition in its more liberal and literary aspects, *The Dial* prospered. The only grave financial blunder of Browne's publishing career came late in life, when in 1910 he secured local backing to establish Browne's Bookstore. With its interior designed by Frank Lloyd Wright, whose first commission it was for such work, the bookstore endured for a short three years as the most beautiful shop in America and a commercial failure.

The Dial survived its founder, and in the memorial issue of

June 1, 1913, William Dean Howells eulogized him with the assertion that none of Browne's "friends was more truly and proudly his friend than I, or could have valued him more for those spiritual, intellectual, and moral qualities which in their peculiar concord rendered him unique in his time and place." Other survivors of the genteel tradition lauded *The Dial* as "the purest literary journal in this country," established as it was "in the camp of the Philistines." Now the Philistines would triumph; despite the hard-earned and well-intentioned superlatives, *The Dial* must abandon Chicago in defeat.

Since Francis Browne's death his sons had given the magazine uncertain guidance; they had sold it, left it, returned, and left again. Then a young decorator named Martyn Johnson, recently from the East where he had had experience on *The New Republic*, somehow purchased *The Dial*. Announcing himself as Publisher in July 1916, he set the magazine on a liberal, even increasingly radical course in politics and the arts as well as in literature.[1] The last of the old guard had vanished; the new publisher's board of contributing editors was the one link with the time when the Brownes had controlled policy. Most of these men—among them Randolph Bourne, Padraic Colum, Henry Blake Fuller, Horace M. Kallen, and J. C. Squire—had contributed to the old *Dial*, but they had not previously been on the staff, which indeed had been a largely family group. Nor had they set the dominant tone of the old *Dial*. Of them only Fuller had been long and closely connected with the literary circle active in Chicago since the 1880's. Except for Squire, who lived in England, the others had always lived in the East or had gone there to better their fortunes. The traditional Midwestern influence in *The Dial*, which had anyway been cosmopolitan in isolationist Chicago, no longer counted. There was good reason for *The Dial* to move to New York, in response to its new orientation.

At this juncture, George Bernard Donlin, Johnson's editor of less than a year, had to go West on account of his tuberculosis, and the search was on for still another editor. Having traveled to New York to look for Donlin's successor, Johnson met a young reporter named Harold Stearns through somebody's recommendation, and the two men had several conferences at Ike's Bar on Sixth Avenue, the chief question between them being not so much that of Stearns's professional qualifications for the post as his immunity from the draft.

Stearns wrote in his memoir *The Street I Know* (1935) that he was living in a state of semihysteria in those days "when it seemed as if the war would never, *never* end, as if it were going on for an eternity with madness and death and unreality." At last, Johnson hired Stearns, who later confessed he had not had a regular job since his days on the *New York Post* in 1914. The inducements Johnson offered were a good job as an editor with a well-known periodical; the prospect of moving with *The Dial* to New York soon; a weekly salary of fifty dollars, part of which Stearns might send home to his mother in Boston; a favorable status in the draft, because he would be supporting his mother; and the rather stimulating idea of going to Chicago for a while. With the issue of January 3, 1918, Harold Stearns began his official duties as Associate Editor.

Needing somebody to assist him in getting out *The Dial*, Stearns persuaded Clarence Britten to throw up teaching in the Department of English at the University of Wisconsin for a working literary life as an assistant on *The Dial*. Britten, urbane and understanding, acted as anchor man in the editors' office. His appointment to *The Dial* took effect at the same time as did Stearns'.

Early in the spring of 1918 Johnson informed Stearns that he had accomplished the purpose he had set for himself, of bringing *The Dial* to New York "bag, baggage, and traditions of 40 years, on the first of July." This was good news for Stearns, who could not abide the flatness of Chicago and welcomed the aim of transplanting the magazine from its native Midwestern prairie to a city with hills by a big river. Now the publisher had made his preparations to move to that city and had even acquired a charming office in Greenwich Village at 152 West Thirteenth Street, the offices of *The Dial* for the remainder of its publication. With his new backing Johnson had formulated an ambitious program for "the new 'Reconstruction' *Dial*," as he liked to call it.

Later that spring a Harvard acquaintance of Harold Stearns came to Chicago for what Stearns guilelessly took to be a social visit of a fortnight or so. This young man, Scofield Thayer, had actually come to Chicago because he was interested in backing Johnson, but to Stearns' innocent eye, Thayer at this time did not have any intention of buying *The Dial*. All the same, Thayer not only was the cause of Johnson's optimism but was to be as deeply affected by the decision he had made to support *The Dial* as was the publisher.

Scofield Thayer was one of the remarkable persons of his time and milieu; his friend Henry McBride could vividly recall him as a lofty and superior nature—as more than a gentleman, a prince.[2] Mildly radical in his ideas and inclinations, he was too wealthy to have to work for a living and too interested in the arts to want to increase his inheritance by engaging in business. The elder Thayer had made a fortune in the woollen trade in Worcester, Massachusetts, and the son thus was able to prepare for Harvard at Milton Academy, and to spend some time traveling, accompanied by his tutor, in Europe. At Harvard Thayer met many of the men who later became his associates on *The Dial* and contributors to it; he was on the board of *The Harvard Monthly*. After graduation *cum laude* in 1913, Scofield Thayer attended Magdelen College, Oxford, for further study in classics and philosophy. The War disrupted his scheme of study, and he returned to the United States apparently without any definitely formulated plans. The Army draft had rejected him, and as he did not fit in precisely with the predominantly business tone of his class, he was at loose ends. His interest in ideas and the arts, his typically American desire to center his life around an improving substitute for business, and Johnson's search for a rich backer for *The Dial* nicely coincided.

Under the uncertain circumstances of the war years, Thayer and Johnson had met at the home of a mutual acquaintance, Merrill Rogers, who had just become business manager for Johnson. Thayer was looking for a congenial occupation; Martyn Johnson was looking for a congenial backer. More specifically, the attraction *The Dial* held for Thayer was not merely that it was congenial but that Johnson told him Randolph Bourne, whom Thayer greatly admired, was to be one of the editors of *The Dial* when it should be reorganized and moved to New York. Later in the winter of 1917–18 Thayer bought stock and entered on a series of transactions by which *The Dial* would gain his financial support. His understanding was that the stock he was buying from Johnson and the money he was lending *The Dial* constituted practically a gift, and he believed Johnson also held this understanding. Thayer further assumed he would share control of policy with Johnson, but apparently the only understanding the two men held mutually was that the sums advanced by Thayer were not loans and that they would never be paid off.

Thayer's visit to Chicago just prior to June 1918 thus was no sociable fortnight but was a business trip to look over a property he was interested in. Before going, he had already made arrangements to help Johnson financially. In the late spring of 1918, not only did Scofield Thayer think he would secure the future of *The Dial;* also he would help the publisher direct that future, and he would contribute reviews and critical essays to the issues. Just as importantly, Randolph Bourne would now have a journal in which to express his pacifist views about the War and his progressive views about American life.

The Dial announced in its "Notes and News" for June 20, 1918, that in accordance with its custom since becoming a fortnightly it would issue only one number in July and one in August and would resume fortnightly publication with the Fall Educational Number of September 5 and the Fall Announcement Number of September 19, 1918. At the beginning of this summer lull, on July 1, 1918, its publication offices would be moved to New York, and with the first "Reconstruction" issue—October 5, 1918, was the actual date, although "Notes and News" here announced it for October 3—*The Dial* would begin publication as a weekly. Acclaimed as *The Dial* was in its native Chicago, its removal was a real and, in the event, an irrecoverable loss to the cultural life of the city. The removal was symptomatic, too, of Chicago's gradual failure to fulfill its earlier promise of becoming a great American cultural center independent of New York and the East. Chicago could not support commercial publishing houses like Stone and Kimball; it could not support experimental journals like *The Chap-Book* and *The Little Review;* nor, despite the national prestige and circulation of *The Dial*, could Chicago as a community furnish the necessary financial backing to keep its one distinguished critical journal. Margaret Anderson's reason for moving *The Little Review* to New York, in March 1917, may also serve as Martyn Johnson's reason for soon following her example: it was time to touch the greatest city of America. Johnson realized that by staying in Chicago *The Dial* would become a provincial counterpart of *The New Republic*, and his desire to operate the magazine at the center of events, in New York, as well as the pinch of financial need, prompted him to make the move. Harold Stearns thought that many good citizens got up one morning and read in their *Tribune* "with surprised regret" that *The Dial*, so long a Chicago institution, had fled to New York. (But in 1958 Charles Smutny, librarian of that paper, was sorry to report that his office could not find any reference to *The Dial* or to Martyn Johnson in the *Tribune*.)

What would the New York *Dial* become? When Martyn Johnson remarked to Harold Stearns that he did not want *The Dial* to become "just another Liberal weekly" imitating *The New Republic* and *The Nation*, neither man could have taken the statement very seriously, for in those days of final hysteria just prior to the Armistice *The Dial*, with its Reconstruction issues, proceeded to make itself over in the image of its two liberal contemporaries. The process was no doubt abetted by the fact that Stearns and Britten were in these weeks practically getting out the magazine by themselves, and the future editor of *Liberalism in America* was no man to disguise his prejudices. Presumably aiding the two working editors was a group that had been "hooked" by Johnson—Stearns particularly recalls Randolph Bourne, John Dewey, Helen Marot, and Thorstein Veblen—and that made up a "curious 'advisory' board of contributing editors."

When *The Dial* moved to New York and tried to resume its regular schedule of publication, the editors found that, because of an acute paper shortage, they could not achieve the promised weekly periodicity. Consequently the editorial page of the first "Reconstruction" issue announced a change in schedule from semi-monthly publication, with one issue in July and August, to a straight fortnightly basis—twenty-six numbers a year—for which the old subscription rate of three dollars a year continued in force. To co-operate with the War Industries Board, the editors cut off exchanges with other periodicals, dropped departments, reduced the size of type, and cut down margins: "In fewer pages the new DIAL will carry more text than before. If at first it meets the eye strangely—c'est la guerre."

The issue of October 5, 1918, also announced a new staff for the magazine. The publisher remained Martyn Johnson, of course. The principal backer, Scofield Thayer, became Secretary-Treasurer of the Dial Publishing Company; he replaced Willard C. Kitchel, who remained in Chicago but kept his Dial stock to the end, in 1929. The editors were divided in two groups, one group of four with no special title and a second group "In Charge of the Reconstruction Program." The former was comprised of Clarence Britten, George Donlin, Harold Stearns, and Scofield Thayer; the latter was made up of John Dewey, Thorstein Veblen, and Helen Marot. In an accompanying leading article that set the tone for the new regime, Stearns wrote that the function of these three people was disinterestedly and deliberately to plan for reconstruction of the world—to plan for "a new world, a world of democracy in which wars will be made impossible, or at least more difficult than they have ever been in the past." Liberals must not allow this planning to be done entirely by the interested classes; business and industry would contribute their technical and scientific knowledge, but they must not be allowed to dictate policy, which must be adjusted to the interests of the whole community. A multiplicity of exciting and urgent-sounding questions must be answered: "Shall federal control of transportation and other public utilities be abandoned after the war? . . . How shall the war debt be paid? . . . How shall industry be reorganized and what hereafter shall be the status of labor? . . . Are we willing to abandon some of our claims to complete sovereignty and have our investments in weak and disorganized countries, if not directed, at least subject to the control of an international authority?" To these insistent questions, Professors Dewey and Veblen and Miss Marot would no doubt supply the sufficient answers.

Looking back in 1935 on his days at *The Dial* during its "Reconstruction" phase, Harold Stearns confessed that everybody had a peace scheme of his own, and nearly everybody was quite willing to tell the whole world what the proper scheme was, precisely and in detail, even though most of the complicated ethnographical, political, and economic perplexities of Europe—war-weary Europe, as Stearns would have it—were in cold fact a complete mystery to most Americans, even intelligent Americans. In the offices of *The Dial* its Associate Editor and his friends and colleagues must have rearranged the whole map of Europe at least two or three dozen times and at least a hundred different ways. They were not alone. All the liberal groups, all the radical groups, whether or not they had organs of their own in which to publish their opinions and beliefs, all sorts of business and women's clubs, fraternal organizations, religious bodies, innumerable persons with enough money to buy enough space in the newspapers to advertise their views—all had plans for establishing a permanent peace. To Harold Stearns, the slightly earlier Peace Ship of Henry Ford was the most grotesque symbol of this pathetic and wasted flood of good will. Peace, when it came, would be made in private by the bankers, politicians, and diplomats. The small, self-conscious, and voluble groups such as that comprising the staff of Martyn Johnson's *Dial* had no, or at most very little, influence over public opinion in America or abroad, in Harold Stearns' later and perhaps jaundiced view of his past. Most people who had been away to the War were trying to make a difficult adjustment to American civilian life, which had changed greatly in the short space of two years from the prewar America they had known. Peace-making was the sport of the privileged few with the leisure and the taste for it, not for the deluded liberals.

Other groups in American journalism may have been more deluded but certainly few were more liberal then than the board of editors of *The Dial* in late 1918 and in 1919, though not all its members encouraged Harold Stearns in his pacifist views. Randolph Bourne had notoriously opposed the entrance of the United States into the First World War, whereas John Dewey occupied a "mediatorial" position similar to that of *The New Republic*. Robert Morss Lovett wrote in his autobiographical *All Our Years* (1948) that in consequence of the opposition between Dewey and Bourne, Johnson refrained from placing Bourne's name with the other contributing editors.

The plans formulated during the course of 1918 by Thayer and Johnson did not eventuate, because of this increasingly serious difference. By September, considerable friction had arisen between the two men. Thayer felt that Johnson had not kept to the idea of *The Dial* he had originally outlined and according to which it was to be a magazine that would be primarily critical—critical in the literary, the scientific, and the political spheres. Thayer here was responding to the influence of Randolph Bourne, who because he opposed a war that America was fighting anyway—a war that, thought Bourne, the liberals were opportunistically supporting—advised his readers to turn their energies to promoting what was truly best in American life. Artists must turn to their pictures, writers to their books, critics to their analyses not in an attempt to escape reality but rather in rejection of a fruitless reality.[3] The activist position could not accept this argument, which, even though its proponents might not admit the fact, possessed dangerous affinities with the aestheticism of the Nineties. Bourne was by no means an aesthete, as Thayer admittedly was; yet practically they shared much in their attitudes toward the relation of the arts to the American milieu, if for widely differing reasons. Both men held their limited common position against the developing opposition of the group on the *Dial* staff headed by Dewey and Johnson.

Thayer felt that his money was being used to finance an undertaking that was essentially propaganda. As one who made no secret of the fact that he always voted the Socialist ticket,[4] Thayer was entirely sympathetic to the aims of the propaganda in question; however, he felt that such propaganda was being handled far better by *The Liberator, The New Republic*, and *The Nation*. His disagreement with Martyn Johnson was based merely on what he considered the publisher's unfairness in obtaining a backer's money under a certain understanding and then spending it in a different way. In contradistinction to Johnson, Thayer saw his own interests as being almost purely aesthetic, and both he and his friend Bourne felt that a magazine such as they originally intended was the journalistic venture America most needed. Nearly four decades later in 1957, in his memoir *Days of the Phoenix*, Van Wyck Brooks ironically agreed with Thayer's words about himself: "the editors of *The Dial* were aesthetic or nothing." [5]

Randolph Bourne died of pneumonia, in Paul Rosenfeld's apartment only six weeks after the Armistice of 1918; his sudden passing was a terrible blow not just to the friends who loved him but to thousands of the younger liberals who thought of him as containing a force resistant to the flood of reaction, "a force so intense, that like Greek fire, it flamed the fiercer for the water hurled upon it." [6] For this embattled group, Bourne was the artist-fighter in the drab American streets, the great bearer of moral authority while America was at war. Yet John Dewey pragmatically espoused the entry of America into the war and carried most of his disciples along with him. Inevitably they opposed Randolph Bourne, who had been, as Paul Rosenfeld described him, Dewey's most brilliant pupil and who now believed on principle that the War was unjust. It was a fatal mishap that befell *The Dial* in 1918–19 when Bourne and his old teacher became so opposed over the question of America in the War that the magazine was used by them as a means of forwarding their ideological feud rather than as a means of compromising their differences and thus of enunciating a less partisan Reconstruction program. Had Scofield Thayer had his way, *The Dial* might have joined political and social interests to its espousal of the arts. In the former two areas, it almost certainly would have been Bourne's organ of expression; instead, the feud among the staff between the adherents of John Dewey and those of Bourne and Thayer wrecked Martyn Johnson's erratic career as a publisher, and almost wrecked the magazine itself.

Thayer's attitude toward Johnson's aims for *The Dial* was, then, quite as ambivalent as was Bourne's. Both as friends and as

journalists the two young men may have gotten along so well together because Bourne's theory of American "transnationalism" had
a practical formulation closely akin to Thayer's views as an avowed
cosmopolitan. Actually, when Bourne wrote of American transnationalism, he equated it with the cosmopolitan outlook–an outlook
that had always been peculiarly attractive to the various *Dial* groups,
in New England and the Midwest. While Bourne thus had overtly
formulated a set of principles that he repeated through the war years
in *The New Republic*, *The Seven Arts*, and *The Dial*, Thayer
obliquely intimated his attitude toward the War in the essays and
reviews he contributed to *The Dial* in the latter seven months of 1918.

Write as he wished for *The Dial* and finance it as he could,
Thayer was not to direct general policy. The divergence of Martyn
Johnson's views and Thayer's became critical when the publisher
continued to assume "that he carried *The Dial* in his pocket" and
that the new backer had no say in its control. When *The Dial* for
December 14, 1918, published the Original Decrees of the Soviet
Government in its department "Foreign Comment" simultaneously
with their publication by *The Nation*, Thayer's disapproval was so
vehement that he "threatened a law suit 'to protect his name,' "
according to Robert Morss Lovett. This further breach between
Thayer and Johnson came just at the time of Lovett's appointment by
Johnson as Editor of *The Dial*, at the beginning of 1919. Lovett
temporarily left his post teaching English at the University of
Chicago to follow *The Dial* to New York; it may be that he had been
attracted to it as early as the time that Martyn Johnson became
publisher, for Stearns noted his name along with others such as
Janet Fairbank and Waldo Frank in the artistic and academic sets in
Chicago. But not only did Lovett become Editor too late to heal the
split between Dewey and Bourne, who had just died, also the new
Editor added to the bitterness by openly favoring the Bolsheviks
and, away from the magazine, making speeches in favor of tolerating
them.[7]

The cabal some members of the staff formed against Bourne
and Thayer permanently affected the publication of *The Dial*. Although Bourne had been on the editorial staff of *The Dial*, he was
not invited to editorial conferences and was snubbed in other ways.
More serious was the affair of the publication of the Soviet Decrees,
coinciding as it did with Bourne's last days and resulting, too, in

Thayer's protest to the publisher. With Bourne's death, Thayer withdrew from actively participating in *The Dial*. Henceforth *The Dial* of Martyn Johnson would be engaged in a losing struggle for survival, deprived as it would be of Thayer's support and indebted as it already was to his purse.

All told, the struggle lasted over a year before Johnson and his colleagues lost. They were defeated because they lacked sufficient financial backing and also because Johnson's plans for *The Dial* lacked the clearcut formulation of Thayer's. Johnson's manifestoes rang strong, but his editorial and publishing policy was not consistent. This state of affairs was apparent to a good many others besides the principal backer and the publisher. When Robert Morss Lovett became Editor, he saw that *The Dial* was hanging on a shoe-string, with Scofield Thayer as the only resource. The magazine was top-heavy, overstaffed, and underfinanced. Johnson had, moreover, contracted for articles to which *The Dial*'s limited space was mortgaged, such as the serialized *Conversations in Ebury Street* from George Moore in London. Thorstein Veblen arrived fresh from Washington where he had refused a $4,800 job with the War Labor Board, to pre-empt still more of *The Dial*'s inadequate space, with the series "Bolshevism and the Vested Interests in America." When Lovett edited out portions of Veblen's articles, the proofs returned with the cuts restored and a note of admonition to let them run. As Veblen's admirers outside the magazine office were paying him $2500 as a contributing editor of *The Dial*, he was independent of editorial authority. But the magazine itself had to pay for John Dewey's series of three articles on "Liberalism in Japan," which ran concurrently with Veblen's on Russia, in October and November 1918. *The Dial*'s reason for existence, thought its Editor, was the book market, but he could keep even with this essential source of patronage only with difficulty, on account of the publisher's inconsistency. Incautiously Lovett remarked to Thayer on the anomaly of putting up money for a paper and letting others have the fun of running it.

Somehow things rocked along during most of 1919. The Dial Publishing Company inaugurated a short-lived series of booklet reprints from *The Dial*, thus returning to the extraperiodical activity of the old Dial Company of Chicago when Francis Browne was owner and Editor. Bertrand Russell's *Democracy and Direct Action*, a collection of *Dial* material on Russia entitled *A Voice Out of Russia*, and Thorstein Veblen's *Sabotage*—this last had originally appeared in *The Dial* as "On the Nature and Uses of Sabotage"—were advertised in the issue for July 12, 1919. Geroid Robinson's *Collective Bargaining—or Control?* was also published in the series and seems to have been the last such booklet to be issued; only one other item of much importance besides *The Dial* itself was afterwards published by the Dial Publishing Company, the great folio of reproductions *Living Art* of 1923.

The Dial organization bumbled along with a lack of system, but it partially made up for this failing by putting out the issues. The wretched typescripts of George Moore, despite an editorial oversight transmuting Franz Hals to Frank Hall ("Rembrandt and Frank Hall"), did get printed. John Gould Fletcher's "Rational Explanation of Vers Libre" saw publication even though the author changed in his proof the system of accents and caesuras that provided the rationale for the critic's explication. Fortunately, Lovett had one professional person on his staff who coped with such problems. Miss Florence Haxton put together and got out the fortnightly *Dial* with the exceptional and unsuccessful assistance of the Editor himself.

If Lovett's statement is accurate, that in order to deal with the flood of new poetry the staff made Conrad Aiken the arbiter of verse, it is curious that Aiken apparently was unable to attract distinguished work to the magazine. Indeed his name disappeared from the masthead with the move to New York, though he had been an editor since June 1917. Whatever the facts, the poetry *The Dial* published in 1919 approaches the palest, most feminine verge of Imagism, and many of the poems are frankly nineteenth-century in diction and attitude. Babette Deutsch, Amy Lowell, and Maxwell Bodenheim continued to favor the editors with their inspirations, and such contributors as Cuthbert Wright, Leonora Speyer, Stephen Vincent Benét, Eden Philpotts, Eunice Tietjens, Carl Sandburg, and Lola Ridge made their appearances; none of the major poets who appeared in *The Dial* of the Twenties was being printed. The verse generally contrasts to that printed by *The Dial* in the latter six months of 1918, before Thayer left the magazine, a period in which Edna St. Vincent Millay, John Hall Wheelock, and Conrad Aiken were published, as well as Louis Untermeyer and Alice Corbin.

That Lovett may have suffered from a lapse of memory about just who did help him edit *The Dial* is understandable. Nobody could possibly remember with complete accuracy the complicated and seemingly haphazard changes in staff during the fifteen months from September 1918 through November 1919. The fact that in these months twelve issues out of thirty-one announce changes, important or minor, in the lists of editors, publisher's staff, and Dial stockholders, suffices to exemplify the instability of *The Dial* before Martyn Johnson sold his Dial stock.

Although Johnson lacked money to run *The Dial* and thus possessed little bargaining strength, he had tried with some temporary success to change the terms of an agreement by which Thayer would have given twenty thousand dollars to *The Dial* in September 1918. After a discussion over lunch at the old Brevoort one day, the two men agreed to the proposition advanced by Johnson: Thayer took ten thousand dollars' worth of Dial stock and took back from *The Dial* notes for another ten thousand, "which were invested in paper," i.e., paper stock. The altered settlement solved nothing, and with the issue of December 14, 1918—the pro-Soviet issue about which he protested to Johnson—Thayer resigned from his posts as Secretary-Treasurer of the Dial Publishing Company and as an editor of *The Dial*. He generously insisted, however, on going through with his original agreement and indeed actually gave *The Dial* thirty thousand dollars and completed his payments with a third installment of five thousand dollars on January 1, 1919. Thayer was now out of *The Dial*. Within ten months of his resignation, the inevitable happened. Johnson was not able to meet the notes for ten thousand dollars that he had borrowed from Thayer for the buying of paper stock, when on delivery of the paper Thayer requested payment. Johnson could maneuver no further, and he offered his Dial stock for sale.

Scofield Thayer now brought forth a partner, Dr. James Sibley Watson, Jr., of Rochester, N. Y., to aid in consummating the transaction. In 1917 and 1918 Watson had contributed reviews dealing with Samuel Butler and George Moore to *The Dial*, and the column "Notes and News" had described him as, after studying at Harvard and spending some time abroad, "now devoting himself to writing." He was also a medical student in New York University at the time but, like Thayer, had no financial need to earn a living. A man of extraordinarily wide interests ranging from teaching radiology to translating Rimbaud to the production of avant-garde cinema, Watson had a central role in, to use E. E. Cummings' words, transforming a do-gooding periodical into a first-rate magazine of the fine arts. Many years after the sale of *The Dial*, Charles Norman recounted, in a study of E. E. Cummings (*The Magic-Maker*),[8] what Watson told him about the event: "Thayer said he would either start a magazine or set up a fund for artists. If he started a magazine, would I come in with him? The answer was 'yes.' Then came the question–should we start a new magazine or get hold of an old one? Because I had written for the fortnightly *Dial* I suggested we get hold of it. But we did not want to approach Martyn Johnson, the owner, directly. So Thayer wrote a check for $10,000, I wrote one for $2,500, and we gave the money to Harold Stearns, who was to act as go-between. Time passed, and nothing happened. Harold simply disappeared. He afterwards returned the entire sum. . . . About a year later, we heard that the magazine was on the point of suspending. This time we approached Johnson through our lawyers, and the deal was closed." With characteristic generosity, Watson bought Johnson's Dial stock for more than Johnson could obtain for it from any other of the many other people whom he had consulted before selling out to the Thayer-Watson representatives.

The "Casual Comment" column of *The Dial* for November 29, 1919, announced the fateful and final change of ownership of the magazine: "the resignation of Martyn Johnson, Oswald W. Knauth, and Helen Marot from The Dial Publishing Company and from the editorial staff; and of Robert Morss Lovett, Thorstein Veblen, Lewis Mumford, and Geroid Robinson from the editorial staff." The election of James Sibley Watson, Jr., as President of the Dial Publishing Company and of Scofield Thayer as Secretary-Treasurer–the post he had held briefly the previous year–was announced. And with that issue, the usual box enclosing names of the editorial staff listed Scofield Thayer as Editor and Stewart Mitchell as Managing Editor of *The Dial*. Of the former staff Clarence Britten alone stayed on, still as Associate Editor. The others scattered. Lovett returned to the University of Chicago. Martyn Johnson disappeared with the jocular remark to Lovett, "I have got my sixpence and am off for the moon," and more immediately Carmel, California.

"Casual Comment" also announced an equally sweeping change in policy. By merging the two fortnightly numbers for December

THE DIAL

A FORTNIGHTLY

| VOL. LXVII | NEW YORK | NO. 804 |

NOVEMBER 29, 1919

THE DIAL (founded in 1880 by Francis F. Browne) is published every other Saturday by the Dial Publishing Company, Inc.—J. S. Watson, Jr., President—Scofield Thayer, Secretary-Treasurer—at 152 West Thirteenth Street,
New York, N. Y. Entered as Second Class matter at the Post Office at New York, N. Y., August 3, 1918, under the
act of March 3, 1897. Copyright, 1919, by The Dial Publishing Company, Inc. Foreign Postage, 50 cents.

$3.00 a Year   *($4.00 after Jan. 1, 1920)*   *15 Cents a Copy*

The Last of the Old *Dial*

1919 into a single issue, *The Dial* would become a monthly. More
importantly, it would diverge from *The Dial* of the preceding year
and a half—since the arrival of Scofield Thayer and the move to
New York, and the ensuing struggle for control—particularly in its
greater emphasis on art and literature. The new owners would publish fiction and drawings in addition to the critical essays so typical
of the old *Dial*. They avoided the manifesto that the occasion would
have elicited from Johnson and contented themselves with assuring
all concerned that their choice of material would "be independent of
the conventional considerations, independent, that is, 'jusques au feu
exclusive.'" The strident tone of the years after 1916 had meta-
morphosed into the urbanity so admired in the early Twenties.

The situation when Thayer and Watson assumed control of
The Dial gave small occasion for optimism although it did call for a
good deal of urbanity. Eventually to break even as publishers the
owners must first sink a lot of money into what had been ever since
the fiasco of Browne's Bookstore in 1912 an enterprise at best of
uncertain profits and usually of considerable losses. Both young men
had inherited wealth; the prospect of spending substantial amounts
of their own money did not discourage them. On November 15, 1919,
Thayer and Watson entered into an agreement to take control of the
management of *The Dial*. In May 1920 another conference was held
by the two principals and their legal and financial advisers, for a
final settlement. According to this, Thayer held 441 shares, coming
to 35.9 per cent of the total; Watson held 451 shares, coming to 36.7
per cent of the total; and all other stockholders—Marion C. Ingersoll,
Mr. and Mrs. Henry Goddard Leach, Willard C. Kitchel, Gustave K.
Carus, and Frederick Lynch—held 335.5 shares, coming to 27.3 per
cent of the total.[9] The official, legally required "Statement of Ownership" published annually in *The Dial* listed these stockholders in the
Dial Publishing Company in the issue for January 1920 and listed no
subsequent changes. The face value of Dial stock had increased from
about $75,000 in 1912, the date of the closing of Browne's
Bookstore, to $122,750 in 1920, even though during those eight
years *The Dial* consistently lost money for its investors. Francis
Browne's profitable touch, unique in the history of various *Dials*, had
by now vanished, save for the statement still carried in the colophon
of *The Dial* of the Twenties that the magazine had been "founded in
1880 by Francis F. Browne."

What did Thayer and Watson receive for their money spent in acquiring a major portion of Dial stock? They acquired a means of publishing the kind of art and literature they liked. Thayer at any rate had no illusions about profiting financially from this indulgence of his tastes. He hoped to provide for America the journal it most needed, and by bringing in a partner, he hoped to keep *The Dial* going until eventually it might become self-supporting, but it was never expected to be able to pay back the stockholders. His aims— and, it may be supposed, those of Dr. Watson as well—were complex perhaps, but they were definite. They seemed reasonably attainable, and reasonably altruistic.

To set about accomplishing their objectives, the new owners not only had to reorganize the ownership of the Dial Publishing Company, they also had to reorganize the business office of the magazine itself. The Business Manager they first employed, W. B. Marsh, was also Secretary-Treasurer of the Dial Publishing Company. By January 23, 1920, Marsh had drawn up for the new owners a five-page "Report on the Condition of the Dial Magazine." He reported the obvious, that the condition of the business office of the magazine was "extremely bad" when he first went to work on a full-time basis, New Year's Day of 1920. The former business management had had to cope with an inadequate force and had not been able to keep the records of the concern in efficient fashion. The past record of performance of *The Dial* therefore could not be closely ascertained.

The system that had been instituted to keep advertising records and circulation records was both inadequate and out of date. Under Johnson the advertising rates had been cut indiscriminately, and Marsh could not find sufficient account of old contracts and agreements. The subscription files were in very bad shape; and subscription correspondence had not been filed during much of 1919, and the subscription stencils were full of duplication and error. Moreover, no daily cash statement had ever been used by Johnson, and he had no method by which to keep in daily contact with the financial situation of the magazine.

In Johnson's regime, promotion of *The Dial* had been very casual, and the management had entirely overlooked many excellent fields for promotional work. This situation was probably due largely to the financial straits the Company had gotten into. Practically no substantial circulation or advertising promotion had been attempted, and the decades of careful labor in these areas carried on by the Browne family counted for little by the time Thayer and Watson bought the controlling shares of Dial stock.

Although Johnson's *Dial* cost only about $750 per issue to print, or about $1500 per month, it lost money. By Scofield Thayer's estimate, its running deficit amounted to almost four or five thousand dollars every month. Obviously the greatest portion of this considerable sum must have been paid to staff and contributors. Revenue from subscriptions and advertising had catastrophically declined —in contrast to rises in salaries, payments to contributors, office upkeep, and general printing costs.

On the other hand, the books of the Dial Publishing Company were in fairly good shape when Martyn Johnson turned it over to Thayer and Watson. The new Business Manager found that he could strike a balance for the year 1919, and his records for January 1920 were, in consequence, all right. Johnson had left *The Dial* to the two new owners with a firm foundation upon which they might build the reconstituted magazine. He had, after all, found a rich and interested backer, even though that person had ousted the publisher. *The Dial* was, for all its weaknesses, a going concern with forty years of sound reputation behind it. And over such recently established journals as the liberal *New Republic* and the conservative *Review*, it had the decided advantage of a circulation of about 10,-000 per issue.

There was then hope for the new *Dial;* by an irony of circumstance, its "Reconstruction" program would differ radically from the program dear to Veblen, Dewey, and Helen Marot. Yet the cultural reconstruction directed by Thayer and Watson was as essential an undertaking as that proposed by the reformers.

TWO

The New Dial

JANUARY 1920 marked the resumption of the monthly *Dial*, after three decades as a fortnightly; but this was by every intention an entirely different magazine that Scofield Thayer edited and that James Sibley Watson, Jr., published as President of the Dial Publishing Company. To the political liberals, the economists, the sociologists of the old *Dial* (not to mention businessmen generally!) January 1920 heralded a depression as well as a curious unwelcome era of official snooping for Reds, Bolsheviks, members of the I.W.W., and other persons menacing the Republic. It was a measure of its difference that the new *Dial* would largely ignore those aspects of the early Twenties; its attitude would be nothing if not aesthetic.

Artistically, the Twenties had begun, though the Jazz Age had not quite yet been officially ushered in; *This Side of Paradise* was not published until March 1920. But *The Dial* rather than Scott Fitzgerald's first novel was, anyway, the more significant harbinger of the decade. It preceded and outlasted the vogue of Fitzgerald's fiction and ignored his work until April 1922, when the then Managing Editor, Gilbert Seldes, as "Vivian Shaw," reviewed *The Beautiful and Damned*. Seldes condescended to Fitzgerald: "The impression Mr Fitzgerald's work makes on his elders is so intense that one is grateful for the omission of the name of the Deity from his new title." To his youthful contemporaries, "interested only in ourselves and Art," his revelations were of quite secondary importance, and he had neither the critical intelligence nor the profound vision that might make him an imposing figure. Certainly *The Dial* considered

Fitzgerald neither significant nor outstandingly excellent as an artist; Seldes treated *The Beautiful and Damned* as a novel amateurishly written *à la* Edith Wharton and at least by intention damned it as being, in the title of his review, "This Side of Innocence." A degree of malice and of ribbing a merely popular success is detectable here; yet the review remains an impressive negative testimonial to Fitzgerald's superficial mass appeal in the early Twenties and his failure to impress the more advanced circles in New York. *The Dial*, then, is more than a mere seismograph mechanically and passively recording what went on. It expressed certain tastes, a certain view, and these fundamentally affected the American cultural milieu, so that because of the existence of this magazine, American arts and letters changed and public acceptance of them also changed by 1929 in a given direction. No more discriminating record remains than this month-by-month account of what the Twenties looked like to a group of intelligent men and women who lived through those febrile years.

To repeat, *The Dial* was more than a seismograph–to use Edmund Wilson's phrase–of the American Earthquake, the revolution in American culture that had begun among the artists and writers and scholars around 1910–13, that had shown its full force during 1917–18 in New York, and that would during 1920 begin to affect the whole country. The publication of such a journal as *The Dial* evinced the existence of a small but influential company of people in the United States, ten thousand or so men and women–and their institutions–receptive to the new doctrines and to the new works that the new doctrines were all about.

The artistic and literary changes *The Dial* recorded have to do with the continued struggle to consolidate a position. The course this struggle took is exemplified by *Dial* criticism of Eliot. In 1920 T. S. Eliot was a young bank clerk whose work was famous to a few and infamous to some. Eliot's *Poems* were reviewed in the June 1920 issue by a then quite inconspicuous and even younger poet named E. E. Cummings, who wrote of "this peppy gentleman" that, insofar as he had been responsible for possibly one-half of the most alive poetry and probably all of the least intense prose committed, during the previous few years, in the American and English languages, he merited something beyond the incoherent abuse and inchoate adoration that had become his daily breakfast-food–merited in fact "the

doffing of many kelleys"; that insofar as he was one of history's greatest advertisers he was an extraordinarily useful bore, much like a
riveter that, whatever you may say, asserts the progress of a skyscraper; whereas that insofar as Eliot was responsible for the over-
pasting of an at least attractive manifesto, "Ezra Pound," with
an at least pedantic war-cry, "Vorticism," he deserved to be drawn
and quartered by the "incomparably trite brush of the great and the
only and the Wyndham and the Lewis—if only as an adjectival
garnish to that nounlike effigy of our hero by his friend The Hieratic
Buster," Ezra Pound. The last review in the last number of *The Dial*,
in July 1929, was Conrad Aiken's appraisal of Eliot's *For Launcelot
Andrewes* as filled with "the presence of a spirit which is inimical to
everything new or bold or generous," despite the fact noted by the
reviewer that earlier essays by Eliot "helped materially to restore,
for a literary generation which had lost its bearings, a sense of tradition as a living and fruitful thing." The disparate tones of the two
reviews echo the artistic changes *The Dial* recorded and helped
bring about, from enthusiastic and rambunctious battling for Eliot's
poems in 1920 to acidulous antipathy toward him as a literary law-
giver in 1929.

As in literature, so in sculpture and painting and music,
through *The Dial* the revolution was consolidated, and what had
seemed shatteringly novel in 1920 was acceptably orthodox in 1929.
The frontispiece of the first *Dial* in 1920 was a photograph of Gaston
Lachaise's bas-relief, *Dusk;* the frontispiece of the last *Dial* was a
reproduction of Picasso's early self-portrait, then owned by Hugo
von Hofmannsthal. In *The Dial* for January and February 1920,
Paul Rosenfeld published his essays on Charles Martin Loeffler and
Richard Strauss; the last essay about a modern musical figure was
the conclusion, in the number for July 1929, of Boris de Schloezer's
series of essays about the art of Igor Stravinsky, translated by Ezra
Pound. Thus emphasizing in a consistent manner the contribution of
the new artists and writers, by the end of the Twenties *The Dial* had
played an essential part in consolidating and in gaining widespread
acceptance for what had been at its start in January 1920 a revolution only less frightening in its implications to most *bienpensants*
than the Revolution of October 1917 itself.

The Dial managed much more than merely consolidating the
revolutionary position, of course, and making it acceptable to most

American artists and to the prosperous middle class of the Twenties. It actively led the very forces whose side it fought on; it directed, in part, the movement it propagandized for. *The Dial* was more than a journal of the revolution. That "inevitable" revolution, as Frederick Lewis Allen termed it in *Only Yesterday*, was to be sure by 1920 well under way for the staff and the contributors and for a goodly portion of the readers of *The Dial*.[1] But Thayer and Watson re-formed *The Dial* on lines more inclusive than antitraditional, more selective than revolutionary. By 1920 the literary and journalistic tradition that had initiated and supported various *Dials* for eighty years seemed to have withered. Its creative figures—Emerson, Margaret Fuller, Thoreau, and Bronson Allcott—had been dead for at least a generation, and even most of the secondary personages, such as Francis F. Browne, those who had been no more than conservators and interpreters of the tradition, had died. Still, the archetypes both personal and literary that the New England tradition had furnished America remained alive at any rate as memorials in the academy, in the official life of letters, and to a certain extent even among the rebellious younger generation of American artists and writers. Van Wyck Brooks might use *The Dial* in March and April 1920 to inveigh against the "humbug" of the nineteenth century and its deleterious effects on Mark Twain, and in June Ivan Opffer might impudently caricature Six Harvard Worthies, but the two young men who controlled *The Dial* were nonetheless well aware of the positive values of the American tradition in which they participated by blood, training, position, and choice.

Thayer and Watson themselves were not revolutionaries in any aesthetic or political sense. Rather, they were the *philosophes* of a new, and aesthetic, Enlightenment. Scofield Thayer wrote George Santayana (February 5, 1922) concerning Harold Stearns' famous anthology of opinion *Civilization in the United States*, "This book has just appeared after protracted heralding, and is (not only by the Thirty [contributors]) said to do for God's Country what the encyclopedists did for the ançien régime." Thayer of course approved the liberalism of the volume and knowing Santayana's disapproval of liberals, told his former teacher that he could "imagine nothing more 'amusing' (in the Jamesian sense) than your reactions to this new 'Thirty.' " The result was Santayana's "Marginal Notes on *Civilization in the United States*," published in the June 1922

Dial. The notion that the writers of *Civilization in the United States* constituted a group analogous to the *encyclopédistes* of the old regime in France seems to have originated with Paul Rosenfeld, the magazine's music critic, for Gilbert Seldes wrote Thayer (September 22, 1921) about "the Stearns book, the authors of which Rosenfeld has referred to as the modern *encyclopédistes.*"

One of the earliest *Dial* advertising circulars, probably circulated before July 1920, makes the bias clear, perhaps too clear to be to the liking of some prospective readers. By intention, there was to be no "advertising punch" in this circular. The publishers of *The Dial* merely wanted to tell the persons to whom they sent out the circular that they were publishing a highly interesting magazine, one that intelligent men and women could find stimulating and entertaining. It was as far removed from the stodgy instructive moralizing monthly as it was from the little sheets issued by propagandists for special "isms" in art.

The Dial did not aim to educate, but its editors honestly believed, so they asserted, that the publication of fine creative and critical work was an enterprise in civilization that would do something to stir America from the apathy of the imagination that had fallen upon it. This task was to be performed by transforming *The Dial* from a fortnightly magazine of radical tendencies—so reads the verbiage of the circular—into a literary magazine without precedent in America. America, at the close of 1919, possessed no magazine that, in *The Dial*'s point of view, was trying to set free the imagination of American authors and artists and that was willing to publish the best work available in both the accepted and the unconventional forms of expression without prejudice to either. There was thus no magazine that put the best of both the new and the old produced in America side by side with the best of both the new and the old produced abroad.

Superficially this declaration of policy was, among other things, a part of the rebellion against the genteel tradition popularized by *The Atlantic Monthly* and instituted by the stodgy instructive moralizing side of Emerson's *Dial.* The editors declared that their new policy would actually provide a literary magazine without precedent in America, and in one way they were quite right in staking out their claim as literary pioneers, for the Boston *Dial* of the 1840's was not altogether literary but was, rather, a journal that combined letters with an ideology and its propaganda in much the manner of the early *Partisan Review* of the 1930's.

On the other hand, Thayer and Watson were repeating some of the verbiage and many of the leading ideas of Emerson, Margaret Fuller, and Elizabeth Peabody. In the first issue of the original *Dial*, Emerson welcomed those readers aware of a new "strong current of thought and feeling," which manifested itself not only as Transcendentalism but also as the great flowering of letters in New England between 1840 and 1860. Emerson was determined, like Thayer and Watson, to deny control of *The Dial* to the "Humanity and Reform Men," who trampled on letters and poetry; still, the activists were allowed their say in both magazines. Like the editors of the original *Dial*, Thayer and Watson were interested in "an organ whereby the Free may speak," though to be sure their organ ignored what another *Dial* advertising circular of 1920 termed "the fumy scene of contemporary politics." For *The Dial* of the Twenties was, at least in the intention of its two young owners, the magazine that was trying to set free the imagination of American authors and artists. Like Emerson and Margaret Fuller, Thayer and Watson sought to create a publication in which the American poet and the American artist would not only exhibit their works freely but also would be able to compare the best of both the new and the old produced in America side by side with the best of both the new and the old produced abroad. Each age in America, it would seem, must create again its image of the scholar, the artist, and the poet.

The thinking of Thayer and Watson was also more specially directed to the example furnished by Margaret Fuller and Emerson. Scofield Thayer's monthly editorial "Comment" of *The Dial*, at the start of its second year under the two new owners, overtly established the line of literary succession from *The Dial* of Francis F. Browne on back to *The Dial* of Emerson and Margaret Fuller: "When Margaret Fuller and Ralph Waldo Emerson edited their DIAL, they met with little encouragement from that alien thing, the American public. . . . Each hamlet rose *en masse* to sling its brave quota of mud, while Philadelphia, as always to the fore, asserted through its Gazette that these editors were 'considerably madder than the Mormons.' This last was surely a hit below the Transcendental belt. After four thin Transcendental years THE DIAL cashed in." In the same vein, "Comment" outlined the passing of the succession to the

Chicago *Dial* and the vicissitudes of that journal through its ultimate decline in New York.

Speaking for the editors, Thayer (the manuscript in the Dial
papers is in his hand) reviewed what to them had been "an amusing
year," and he restated their policy of giving "exponents of both the
accepted and the unaccepted an agreeable carpet whereon they
could fitly and cheek by jowl and in their very different ways perform." But, "Comment" confessed, despite "some really lovely letters" the editors had received, "to fill the cup of our contentment to
overflowing we want somebody (he doesn't have to come from or
stay in Philadelphia) to step right up and to say in a fine clear
tipstaff voice: 'considerably madder than the Mormons.'" Thayer
concluded by deploring the lack of "sane tipstaff subscribers"; the
only letters *The Dial* received were the tiresome ones "from foreign
and domestic pundits who say we are the best shot at a civilized
journal yet fired in English."

This portion of the January 1921 "Comment" was a jaunty
revision of the typescript for an unpublished advertising circular
composed about December 1920, which treated the linear succession
of the various *Dials* more openly, much less ironically, and with less
accuracy. According to it, in "the year 1853 a group of New England intellectuals striving for the liberation of the American mind
from the blight of puritanism, founded at Cambridge, a journal of
art and letters," *The Dial*. "Associated in this venture were some of
the finest minds that America has produced. The versatile but erratic Margaret Fuller was its first editor, and Emerson its second.
Much of the work that appeared in its pages is now accounted the
richest heritage of American letters." Such an unabashed tribute is
rather different from "Comment's" more ambiguous discription of
the original *Dial* as "that lavender publication."

The difference in tone between Thayer's "Comment" and the
unpublished typescript is probably due to the editorial desire, attuned to the *Zeitgeist* as it was, not be caught admiring a nineteenth-
century achievement. "Comment" referred to the emergence of a
renovated *Dial* in the metaphor of an aging lady acrobat: "More
or less coming up on her more or less renovated feet, clad in reas-
suringly genteel tights, she smiled stiffly at the world." The once
modish brittle irony does not, for all its banter, disguise the Editor's
consciousness of his debt to the Boston and Chicago *Dials* and their

editors. Equally revealing is the word "genteel." The very fact that the new *Dial* insisted on printing "both the accepted and the unaccepted" would place it beyond the pale of Bohemia despite the physical location of the editorial offices at 152 West Thirteenth Street, and "Comment" tacitly acknowledged, if unwillingly so, the spiritual home of the latest *Dial*.

The verbiage of the typescript is much more forthright. Here we learn that Emerson's effort "to emancipate the American imagination" was frustrated by the "severe ascetism and narrow intolerance of Puritanism, abetted by the gross materialism of our rising commercial civilization" and, indeed, that "these two forces have frustrated every like effort to the present day." The Chicago *Dial*, "dedicated to much the same policy as its New England predecessor," suffered a fate as a creative medium "hardly more successful"; for it "too finally succumbed after a worthy effort to establish itself as the voice of creative America." The long career of a third of a century enjoyed by the Chicago *Dial* and its publisher-editor Francis F. Browne together with its resolute eschewal of any role as the voice of the creative arts in America are here ignored in the anonymous writer's determination to place the new *Dial* of the Twenties as the rightful successor to its purchased title. He says, rather, that two efforts to give America "a literary and art periodical worthy of her creative possibilities and comparable to the best in the old world have failed." Another effort was made, however, and "for the third time THE DIAL has undergone an imaginative renaissance and is sponsoring the creative artist regardless of his reputation or the commercial value of his product." For twelve months, then, the "hopeful and forward looking editors" of *The Dial redivivus* had "given America a magazine whose quality is without peer or precedent in our literary history."

This ebullient claim was never circularized; nevertheless, in its published form in "Comment" the essence of the assertion remains. The tradition was acknowledged and—albeit ambiguously—adhered to. However willful its partial view of the Transcendentalist and Fourierist ferment, "Comment" agreed with the unpublished typescript in linking *The Dial* of Thayer and Watson to *The Dial* of Emerson and "the versatile but erratic" Margaret Fuller. The first *Dial* was properly understood as having been largely belletristic in its interests, and as having thereby created the model for its successor of the Twenties; and the insistence on the necessity for imaginative freedom in America was sympathetically seen as a continuing problem for every generation of intellectuals and artists. The conservative and primarily journalistic purpose of Browne's *Dial* was grievously misapprehended, but at any rate his magazine was viewed, to an extent, correctly, as having kept alive the tradition of a *Dial* devoted to letters and humane culture, one that served as a worthy link between the "group of New England intellectuals" of "1853" and the "group of hopeful and forward looking editors" of 1920. Indeed, an adequate understanding of *The Dial* and the taste of the Twenties is impossible until the magazine and its decade are seen as perhaps greatly modifying but nonetheless consciously perpetuating the values of the American past.

Appearance as well as content of the new *Dial* mattered. A file of *The Dial* in the original wrappers shows no major changes; the first issue as a monthly journal in 1920 is little different in appearance from its final number in 1929. The paper stock used for the wrappers varied slightly from the initial dusty rose to a light salmon to a light tan just as the paper also varied slightly in flexibility; in general, however, there seems to have been a studied attempt to reproduce consistently both the size (about six and three-eighths by ten inches) and the color of the wrappers of the Transcendentalist *Dial*. Bruce Rogers, then the most distinguished designer of books and magazines, collaborated with Scofield Thayer in producing the cover, which, when all is said and done, ranks as the outstanding American work of its genre—the cover for a periodical of arts and letters. Henry McBride, the art critic for *The Dial* of the Twenties, did not exaggerate when he remarked Mondrian did not go through half the trouble in making a picture that Rogers and Thayer went through in designing this cover.

Beneath the title of *The Dial* on the front cover were listed in order, from top to bottom, the essential informative data: date of the issue, here "January 1920"; list of contents, for there was, otherwise, no page of contents; volume, together with number of the issue in its volume; and price of the individual issue. As it sequentially occurred in the issue, each work was listed by title; in case of the reproduction of a picture or object, the medium also was indicated; and to the right were listed names of authors and artists followed by page numbers marking the beginning of an essay, story, poem, or regular feature, such as the editorial "Comment." Works of art were listed without page numbers. The only variable elements in this design were data pertaining to dates and contents and the price of an issue. This last was thirty-five cents for the first five months of 1920, forty cents from May through December of that year, and fifty cents thereafter. No extraneous element unconnected with information about *The Dial* obtruded itself on this plain, elegantly simple outside front cover. The design was absolutely functional, and its harmonious appearance resulted from the disposition of the functional elements within the framework of the cover's oblong.

Verso of the front cover contained at the top the names of the Editor, Scofield Thayer, and his assistants. In January 1920, Thayer was assisted by Stewart Mitchell, as Managing Editor, and Clarence Britten, as Associate Editor. The next month Gilbert Seldes' name appeared as the second Associate Editor. In April 1920, the name of Britten was dropped, and with Mitchell's resignation at the end of the year, his name also disappeared from the editorial roster with the issue of December 1920. For the next six months, Seldes was listed simply as Associate, after which he was denominated Managing Editor through the issue for January 1924. Then his name disappeared, and in the issues from February 1924 through June 1925 Alyse Gregory was named as Managing Editor. After this date, Marianne Moore appeared with the title of Acting Editor and later with the issue for January 1927, full Editor, with Scofield Thayer's name appearing as Adviser. No other changes occurred in this space.

Most of *verso* was taken up by "Notes on Contributors"— brief identifications of writers and artists whose work was listed on the outside front cover. The majority of these little sketches were a couple of sentences in length, but they varied greatly. One might, on occasion, occupy most of the space for the "Notes," and it might be followed by another sketch consisting of a single simple sentence. This was the case with the "Notes" in the issue for May 1925, in which a fairly detailed account was given not of Auguste Rodin but of his statue of Honoré de Balzac, a photograph of which was reproduced as the frontispiece for the issue; and the note on Rodin was followed by a spare statement that "The drawing by JEAN COCTEAU entitled Le Voyageur Dans les Glaces is a portrait of the artist himself." "Notes on Contributors" was selective rather than exhaustive;

THE
DIAL

JANUARY 1920

VOLUME LXVIII   NUMBER 1

35 cents a copy

not only did it barely identify the writers and artists, it customarily identified contributors new to *The Dial* or those about whom the editors deemed it best to set down some pertinent additional information. Occasionally staff changes might be noticed in this space, too, as for example in the issue just quoted from, where "Notes on Contributors" includes: "THE DIAL regrets to announce the resignation of SOPHIA WITTENBERG as Assistant Editor. THE DIAL announces the appointment to this office of ELLEN THAYER." Despite the care and expense that went into the compilation of "Notes on Contributors" as an accurate factual record—and it remains to this day a largely unexploited source of information about writers and artists, their works, and the milieu of the Twenties—the Editor himself was wont to refer to the feature for the excellence of which he was mainly responsible as "the funny page."

In a typical issue, the first and last pages, eight or twelve of them usually, were numbered in roman numerals, unlike the other pages of text, and were taken up with slick-paper pages of advertisements. Generally publishers' announcements about books and periodicals occupied the front pages of advertisements, while announcements of typists and booksellers and the like concluded the issue; these pages also were taken up with house advertising by *The Dial* and the Dial Press, though this latter enterprise was not connected with the magazine. The outside of the back cover was occupied by a full-page spread of some publisher such as Frank-Maurice or Harper or Houghton Mifflin.

Invariably the mat-paper text of *The Dial* was preceded by the reproduction, on slick paper, of some work of art. Beginning with Franz Marc's *Horses*, in the issue for September 1922, three of the frontispiece pictures were reproduced in color by Herwarth Walden's Der Sturm press in Berlin; beginning with Chagall's *Market Place*, in the issue for February 1924, color reproductions were made for *The Dial* by Julius Meier-Graefe's Ganymed Press in Berlin. Thence they were mailed to America and tipped in *The Dial* by the printers, the Haddon Press of Camden, New Jersey. These pictures, the work in prose or verse that followed them, and the concluding "Comment" usually represented, in the Editor's opinion, the most important contents of an issue. Many times these three portions of the issue were related in theme or in subject.

After a good deal of trial and error, the format of *The Dial* was regularized. The agonies of experiment with format and makeup that were undergone in gradually formulating editorial rules were mostly experienced by Scofield Thayer and Gilbert Seldes during the latter months of 1921 and most of 1922. Before Thayer and Alyse Gregory permanently left *The Dial* to be edited by Marianne Moore, Miss Gregory compiled a typed set of detailed "General Instructions for Editorial Department"; for the years of Miss Moore's incumbency, the magazine adhered to these rules. The text of each issue consisted of ninety-six pages. Breaks for slick-paper reproductions of works of art occurred at intervals of sixteen or thirty-two pages, and in every issue on the mat paper used also for printed text there were reproduced pictures that had been made in mediums in which line or strong contrasts of black and white predominated—lithographs, woodcuts, and ink or charcoal drawings. Usually verse and pictures were used to break up long prose stretches, but when the staff could arrange the contents of an issue in any other fashion, they did not place verse just before or just after an illustration. The rare exception to this rule would be the poem that began an issue, such as *The Waste Land*.

The pictures were carefully placed throughout the first two-thirds of an issue. As many as four pictures might occur as a set, between two prose works. If possible, one or more pictures preceded the foreign letter in each issue, or they preceded whatever preceded the letter; by this method the pictures were dispersed in the issue and were not bunched at the front of the magazine. Usually, however, no picture appeared farther to the rear of an issue than the heading "Book Reviews"; very occasionally an exception occurred, as when *The Dial* published a photograph of Gaston Lachaise's head of his friend Henry McBride, the art critic of *The Dial*, who in his monthly critique, "Modern Art," for March 1928 related the story of the execution of this work. When several pictures were used together, the photographs of sculptures were placed last among the art in an issue, but if the pictures were reproductions of drawings, the more important drawings were placed last. Great care was exercised to see that the art in each issue was appropriate and when possible that it be by an artist discussed authoritatively in the issue and thus illustrate the critical text. Obviously, the Editor took pains to dispose pictures throughout the text in each issue. As Scofield Thayer wrote on October 15, 1921, to Gilbert Seldes regarding *The Dial* for that month—

made up by Seldes—editorial custom at the magazine was carefully to "ordinate" the order of contents: "Of course we have often been forced to publish verse either just before or just after an illustration, but, as you know, this is always unfortunate, as verse like illustrations should be used to break up long prose stretches. . . . Also we try to have an illustration either immediately preceding the foreign letters or when that is not possible preceding whatever precedes the foreign letters, thus not having all our illustrations together in the front of the magazine. . . . It is also our good custom to have the pictures on regular [mat] paper preceding the last insert thus giving more variety as one turns the regular paper reproductions as though one had no more insert [slick] paper left. . . . One should always run the larger group [of pictures] last," although when the last group of drawings were about the same in number as ones of a preceding group, the more important drawings should come last.

Thayer arranged the text as carefully as he arranged the illustrations. *The Dial* had a twofold purpose in publishing as it did: to display new writing to the best advantage, whether the form of expression was accepted or unconventional, and to publicize appreciations of both new and old writing without any stodgy instructive moralizing. By editorial rule the text of an issue was 96 pages in bulk, but in editorial practice the printed matter in any single issue might vary from as little as 76 pages to as many as 120. The greater part of every issue was taken up with fiction, verse, biography, essays on various topics, and review-essays; pictures were interspersed with this portion of the text. Approximately the final quarter of every issue was devoted to book reviews, briefer mention of current books, the three monthly columns about the theater, the fine arts, and music, and the editorial "Comment."

Although critical prose of high quality was not always available in needed quantity, *The Dial* customarily used it as the staple reading matter in the proportion of about two to one over verse and fiction combined. "WE NEED ESSAYS," Gilbert Seldes implored the Editor on July 29, 1921: "Fiction we have much of, essays none. . . . At the moment of writing we are expecting an Irish letter but none too hopefully, and of course the arrangements for other foreign letters, except England and Italy, we confidently expect you to carry through. It would be a great blessing to have a Paris letter for the October number." So by the middle of August the Editor duly set about sending over a batch of essays and arranging for future foreign letters.

The Dial called itself a review, but that noun was qualified by the important adjective *literary*, and in contrast to American literary reviews of the 1950's and 1960's, a large quantity of the text of *The Dial* in every issue was given over to verse, fiction, memoirs, and essays dealing with ideas. Such works as Yeats's chapters of autobiography and Santayana's various *Dialogues in Limbo*, which are certainly "critical" prose, are of course to be distinguished from the review-essays, book reviews, and monthly chronicles of the arts. The crude proportion of two to one, according to which the critical prose of *The Dial* dominates its verse and fiction, is deceiving if no distinction is made between work that is independent and creative in its own right and the lesser work that directly depends for its very existence upon the appearance of new verse, fiction, memoirs, and philosophical writing. In sum, the greater portion of the text of *The Dial* consists of critical prose that is creative as well as journalistic writing; but the Editor and his staff intended readers to see that the magazine is consistently divided into two unequal parts, of which the larger by far consists of work of original creation—pictures, verse, fiction, memoirs, essays dealing with ideas, and, occasionally, review-essays—while the lesser consists of journalistic writing entirely—book reviews, brief paragraphs reviewing the current publishers' output, monthly chronicles of the theater, the fine arts, and music, and "Comment."

Few issues of *The Dial* are typical, however, and the proportion of critical prose of all kinds to verse and fiction and pictures combined varied widely, depending on what the editors had on hand to publish. The latter portion of each issue, given over to the journalism of the arts and literature, was less subject to these fluctuations than was the major body of an issue, for journalism can always be produced on demand. One issue might contain as many pages of fiction and verse as of critical prose; alternatively another issue might contain sixty-five pages of critical prose and only eleven pages of verse and fiction. Ordinarily, though, the creative work published in *The Dial* was of a quality sufficient to impress the reader with the fact that the magazine generously opened its pages to new, original writing—verse, fiction, memoirs, and essays.

The writing was disposed throughout an issue according to a

few simple rules. The Editor did not permit verse to occur in *The Dial* just before or just after an illustration, except when a poem introduced an issue. Two groups of verse were never juxtaposed, and as with illustrations, verse was customarily used to break up long prose stretches. With fiction, the main rule was never to juxtapose two pieces, but always to separate them with other matter. With all the writing in the front of an issue, the aim in general was to vary both content and appearance on the pages, to interest readers by avoiding monotony of form and subject. In achieving this aim, beauty and elegance of presentation invariably took precedence over any considerations of economy.

The first pages of text in each issue were ordinarily devoted to prose. William Butler Yeats might appear here in June 1921 with "Four Years," a portion of his autobiographies, or in February 1922 Sherwood Anderson might here publish one of his most famous stories, "I'm a Fool"; in March 1925, George Santayana might expatiate on self-government in one of his *Dialogues in Limbo;* or in January 1925, to celebrate her new Dial Award, Glenway Wescott might enthusiastically recommend Marianne Moore's *Observations*. Only very exceptionally a play would pre-empt these first pages, as was the case with Leonid Andreyev's *He, the One Who Gets Slapped*, which in Gregory Zilboorg's translation began the issue for March 1921. Equally rare was the issue that began with verse; in the first two years of Thayer's editorship, he placed verse at the beginning of an issue on but two occasions, when he published James Sibley Watson's translation of Rimbaud's poem, *A Season in Hell*, in July 1920 and Thomas Hardy's "The Two Houses" in August 1921.

The format and makeup of *The Dial* underwent remarkably few changes, in fact, during the entire decade of its publication. For one volume, LXIX (July–December 1920), Thayer and Watson experimented with a section entitled "Modern Forms." The italicized and explanatory subtitle states that *"This department of The Dial is devoted to exposition and consideration of the less traditional types of art";* but it was abandoned, and from the beginning of 1921 to the end, *The Dial* separated its special departments of Henry McBride's "Modern Art," Paul Rosenfeld's "Musical Chronicle," Gilbert Seldes' "The Theatre," and the Editor's "Comment" from the body of the magazine with the department of "Book Reviews," which included the longer, signed reviews as well as the inclusive "Briefer Mention" with its twelve to eighteen unsigned paragraphs. Perhaps no other periodical of similar quality and longevity can boast of greater consistency of physical appearance, not even the Chicago *Dial* of Francis F. Browne from 1880 to 1913.

Certainly no other American magazine of similar aims has even approached *The Dial* of Thayer and Watson in keeping to such a high level of excellence. If toward the latter Twenties *The New Republic* would with seeming justice voice complaints that *The Dial* was not opening its pages to new talent, these strictures were wrongheaded.[2] *The Dial*, to the best of its editors' abilities, always welcomed new talent, and if by 1927 the new talent was not evident in its pages, the lack was not due to editorial hostility so much as to the failure of new talent to come to *The Dial* in these years. Surely *The Dial* insisted on printing the best it could find both in America and abroad to the end of its days. Even more to its credit is the incontrovertible fact that in America it, and it mainly, published and publicized and found acceptance for the work of E. E. Cummings, Wallace Stevens, Marianne Moore, Hugo von Hofmannsthal, Paul Valéry, T. S. Eliot, Ezra Pound, Pablo Picasso, Marc Chagall, Gaston Lachaise, Aristide Maillol, Marie Laurencin, and many others. The great achievement of *The Dial* was that it displayed to a comparatively wide and usually receptive audience the coruscating fireworks explosions of the arts and letters in artistically the most creative, and bountifully productive, few years our century has yet seen, the years 1920–22.

Look at the record. The first issue of the new *Dial* published recognized writers and artists, true—Edwin Arlington Robinson, chiefly—but also it introduced E. E. Cummings, with "Seven Poems" —among the group are "Buffalo Bill's defunct" and "when god lets my body be"— and four line drawings caricaturing the "National Winter Garden Burlesque"; and it printed the work of then younger writers such as Paul Rosenfeld, Walter Pach, Evelyn Scott, John Gould Fletcher, Maxwell Bodenheim, Carl Sandburg, and Thomas Craven. The leading essay that significantly opened the text of the issue was Randolph Bourne's "An Autobiographic Chapter," as if to show that *The Dial* would carry on where Bourne had left off. Artists whose work was reproduced were Gaston Lachaise, Ivan Opffer, Boardman Robinson, and Charles Demuth. In the next issue *The*

Dial reproduced pictures by Odilon Redon and Carl Sprinchorn, with further examples of work by Lachaise and Opffer. In March 1920 appeared Van Wyck Brooks's "Mark Twain's Humour," the first of a series about Twain that Brooks brought out later in the year as his famous *Ordeal of Mark Twain;* Sherwood Anderson's "The Triumph of the Egg"; and a *Head of a Polish Girl* by Djuna Barnes, then, according to "Notes on Contributors," a young American artist and writer whose drawings were for the most part unpublished. In April *The Dial* published work of Cézanne, James Stephens, Marianne Moore, Van Wyck Brooks, Djuna Barnes, Kahlil Gibran, Llewelyn Powys, Hart Crane, William Butler Yeats, Edmund Wilson, Witter Bynner, Charles Burchfield, Kenneth Burke, Thomas Craven, Robert Morss Lovett, Malcolm Cowley, James Sibley Watson (as "Sganarelle"), Louis Untermeyer, and Gilbert Seldes as well as the "Comment" of the Editor. The issue of June 1920 contained an array of names and work equally impressive and exciting—James Stephens, John Dewey, Ezra Pound's "Fourth Canto," Amy Lowell, Arthur Schnitzler's "Crumbled Blossoms," James Sibley Watson (as "W. C. Blum") on "Rimbaud as Magician," Conrad Aiken, John Dos Passos, Ananda Coomaraswamy, and Paul Rosenfeld's short story "Fräulein," with book reviews by Robert Morss Lovett, E. E. Cummings ("Mr. T. S. Eliot inserts the positive and deep beauty of his skilful and immediate violins"), Lincoln MacVeagh, and Louis Untermeyer.

Yet, unprecedentedly brilliant as was the publication of *The Dial*, in these earlier months of 1920 it was only feeling its way. Except for the pictures and verse of Cummings and Djuna Barnes, the editors had not yet made discoveries, even though they published the work that would mark *The Dial* of the Twenties as an international leader among journals hospitable to the New Movement in arts and letters. But by July 1920, the editors were surer in practice if no bolder in their aims. James Sibley Watson's translation of *Une Saison en Enfer* and James Joyce's poem "A Memory of the Players"; Watson's translation of Rimbaud's *Illuminations* and William Carlos Williams' group of "Six Poems," among them "Portrait of a Lady" and "The Desolate Field"; D. H. Lawrence's story "Adolf" and Ezra Pound's truncated "H. S. Mauberly"—the first six parts were printed from the English edition of the Ovid Press—preceded by Wyndham Lewis's line drawing of Pound; a photograph of the

American Museum of Natural History's stone Chac-Mool, a work of chthonic power that has influenced the course of modern sculpture; Marcel Proust's "Saint-Loup: A Portrait," introduced by Richard Aldington's essay "The Approach to M. Marcel Proust"; T. S. Eliot's initial appearance with "The Possibility of a Poetic Drama" and William Butler Yeats's group of "Ten Poems," among them "Michael Robartes and the Dancer," "Easter 1916," and "The Second Coming"; Osbert Sitwell's poem "Malgré Lui," T. S. Eliot's essay on "The Second-Order Mind," Joseph Conrad's prefaces to "Three Conrad Novels," and Vincent Van Gogh's line drawing *Village of St Marie*, followed by Henry McBride's "Van Gogh in America" ("it does not now appear likely that the Metropolitan Museum will ever own as representative a group of his paintings as it does, say, of Manet"): these were among the works with which, each month from July through December of 1920, *The Dial* astonished and enchanted readers in America and abroad. And the play of fireworks burst and scintillated above a group of onlookers that grew issue by issue.

That burgeoning achievement was the result of unremitting labor by the staff of *The Dial* and of the financial generosity of the Editor and the Publisher. They tried to secure the aid of others in America who were known to be interested in the arts, but meanwhile they supported *The Dial* by themselves. On July 24, 1920, Scofield Thayer wrote his partner of a plan whereby they might approach someone to pledge ten thousand dollars or, failing that, ten people to pledge a thousand dollars apiece, to help "young art." *The Dial* would also double its rates of pay to contributors; thus, the Editor felt, either of these measures would be much better than to try to get money for the expenses of *The Dial*. The prospective donors were listed by Thayer simply as Chapman, Warren, Morgan, Lamont, Vanderlip, Astor, Chatfield-Taylor, Quinn ("I fancy not good for more than Pound's salary" as foreign editor for *The Dial;* "you and I might try him for that alone; I should want your help"), Barnes, Warburg, Kahn, Hearst, Riis. Thayer thought he could not see more than half the men listed, and of these Lamont, Barnes, and Hearst looked the best bets. The September 1920 number of *The Dial* was to be put out as the "millionaires' number," with a great deal of French material in it to attract patrons who would support literature so long as their doing so might be rationalized as furthering international good will—the inter-allied relations idea, as Watson phrased the notion, in his reply of July 27. But nothing came of the scheme, and the two young backers of *The Dial* went their way *à deux*, Thayer back to the *Dial* offices and Watson presumably to his final year of medical school.

On September 26, 1920, Scofield Thayer told Ezra Pound—as a cautionary hint to his foreign editor—that "We need ten times more circulation than we'll ever get to clear expenses. Present deficit about $84,000 annually. What we are about to save in overhead expenses (salaries) we lose by new rates." Thayer's forecast proved correct. Writing to the Editor on February 23, 1923, Samuel Craig, then the Business Manager for *The Dial*, estimated the actual cash deficit for 1920 as slightly over $100,000, with cash receipts of about $24,000. By the end of 1922, total cash receipts were $45,000, but the deficit for the year was about $65,000, despite strenuous efforts by the backers and the business staff to economize and to increase efficiency of operation. The increase in the editorial and manufacturing departments accounted for more than eighty-five percent of the deficit, and as both Thayer and Watson were in accord about rates of pay to writers and artists and as they both insisted on such niceties as the best paper stock and colored reproductions—the latter being initiated in September 1922—Craig foresaw a continuing deficit unless the circulation of *The Dial* could be increased to 30,000. But even the effort to increase circulation, determined as it was, brought up costs, actually doubling staff salaries because of the necessity of additional clerical help in handling subscriptions and circulars.

Late in December 1921 or early in January 1922, the business office reported on one of its periodic attempts to increase circulation by the commonly used method of mailing a circular to selected lists of names. In this instance, 30,000 copies of the "Peacock Folder"—anonymously compiled by Gilbert Seldes and thus called because a photograph of Gaston Lachaise's stone peacock was reproduced on the front—went out between November 20 and December 10, 1921. Half the addresses were on the list of prospects compiled by *The Dial;* 10,000 were on a list of names furnished by the publishers Boni and Liveright; and Robert Morss Lovett furnished four small lists totaling 5,000 names in the Chicago area, most of them members of such clubs as the Cliff Dwellers. The undated statistics reporting results of this campaign gave the disappointing return of only 100 favorable replies to the 30,000 circulars mailed, with the encouraging qualification added that these returns from the Peacock Folder had been "doing better in the last few days than at any time previously." The total cost of getting out the Peacock Folder was $981, and the money realized, by the date of the statistical report about the campaign, was $433. Two similar reports based on "No. 54–Booklet" and "the [Anatole] France Card" were equally discouraging. As they fully realized, Thayer and Watson were subsidizing, to a not insignificant extent, American arts and letters during these years.

Samuel Craig also submitted to Scofield Thayer an analysis of circulation figures for 1920–22, to show the rise in the circulation of *The Dial*, and thereby to encourage the Editor, who had grown restive about the sizeable sums of money he was expending. Sales at newsstands during 1920 dropped off slightly from about 3,500 in January to about 3,400 in December; but in November 1922 such sales reached just over 4,500, and, perhaps as the result of the publication of Eliot's *The Waste Land* in the November issue, *The Dial* for December 1922 sold at newsstands a total of 6,261 copies. But these sales ordinarily varied between no more than four and five thousand copies a month. Similarly, subscriptions numbered only 2,945 in 1920 and increased to 6,374 by the end of 1922. Even more encouraging was the fact that in February 1923 the net paid circulation further increased to 7,440. All in all, according to the rules of the Audit Bureau of Circulations, in early 1923 the business manager of *The Dial* assured the Editor that they were permitted to quote to potential advertisers a circulation of about 13,440; this figure did not include, however, the considerable burden of free copies, totaling 600 a month, which were mailed to contributors, advertisers both secured and potential, and friends of the magazine.

Despite the signal improvement in the fortunes of *The Dial*, advertisers in its most precious field were divided in their regard for it, according to Craig. Scribner, Putnam, Henry Holt, and Dutton he cited as prejudiced against the magazine's editorial policy, and he thought it would be difficult to get these firms, for a long time at least, to advertise regularly. Certain other publishers—particularly Appleton, Little Brown, Stokes, and Houghton Mifflin—would not advertise regularly because of the types of books they published.

But *The Dial* had managed to secure as advertisers Boni and Liveright, Knopf, Harcourt Brace, Doubleday Page, Huebsch, Macmillan, and Seltzer, all on regular contracts, even though Huebsch and Harcourt Brace had been hard to convince.

Craig believed that the money invested by Thayer and Watson in 1920–22 would begin to show definite results in revenue in 1923. From a printing of 14,500 copies for the issue of November 1922, the order was increased for December to 17,500 copies, so that the foreign demand might be satisfied. The January 1923 printing was 18,000 copies; but February saw the order decreased to 16,000 copies, with a slight rise to 16,500 copies for the issue of March 1923. What the business manager did not realize—as the Editor himself did—was that no future issue of *The Dial* would ever again print any work that caused quite the furore *The Waste Land* caused.

It was in this context of large sums dispensed; of a growing but limited circulation; of an inimical and powerful group of publishers; of the arts and letters brilliantly, but nervously, responding to a kaleidoscopically shifting American society; and of the advanced and fastidious tastes of its staff and patrons that Thayer and Watson continued their publication of *The Dial*.

THREE

Editorial Attitudes

Ascertaining and evaluating the editorial attitudes of *The Dial* involve making a distinction between the work it published that remains interesting primarily to specialists in the period and the more central body of work that has continued to interest, more generally, readers and critics over the years. The latter constitutes a link between the taste of later times and that of the Twenties and sets a standard by which to distinguish merely timely elements from the more enduring in the taste of the early Twenties.

The Peacock Folder that the business office of *The Dial* distributed at the end of 1921 furnishes a means of observing the contrast. Two facts about the folder merit emphasis; it was distributed at the conclusion of the two years, 1920–21, that the staff of *The Dial* looked on as critically formative for the magazine; and it was carefully composed as a circular publicizing the taste of *The Dial*. It is the staff announcing: here is what we have evolved, here is what we have accomplished, the best we are capable of.

The Peacock Folder came about as a part of the drive by *The Dial* for a larger circulation. Once the two patrons and their colleagues had established the routine, the editorial policy, and the aesthetic criteria for their magazine, they could turn their attention to means for getting it into the black. They did not aspire to sizeable profits and mass circulation, but they were optimistic that the large annual deficit *The Dial* was saddled with might be cut substantially, even, perhaps, eventually eliminated.

Nevertheless the expense of publishing *The Dial* kept increasing because the attempt to increase circulation necessitated a larger business staff. Editorial costs, moreover, were not sufficiently declining, for much of the Editor's business had to be conducted away from his offices in New York. In July 1921 Scofield Thayer sailed to Europe, leaving Gilbert Seldes as Managing Editor of *The Dial* to put out the magazine each month, with the aid and advice of Dr. Watson and the Business Manager, Samuel Craig. Not until August 1923 did Thayer return to New York to assume again the daily editorial responsibilities of *The Dial*, which from Europe he directed by cable and post. On the Continent he passed most of his time in Vienna, where he took an apartment.

As the Editor of *The Dial* wrote Stewart Mitchell on July 27, 1921, while he was in Europe he looked up the large fry of literary Germany in Berlin and Munich, and these meetings resulted in his obtaining for his magazine much of the best writing then being done in Middle Europe. A second set of results, just as important, had to do with European art dealers and the artists themselves. In the course of 1921 and 1922 *The Dial* would publish the work of the European artists that Scofield Thayer encountered and was attracted to, and by exhibiting their productions, together with those of the writers Thayer sought out, to an English-reading public, *The Dial* surpassed its own hitherto unequaled achievement. This feat Thayer and Watson would bring off by the excellence of the contributors they attracted to *The Dial* and also by their announcement of the Dial Award in the June 1921 issue and by the first of these annual awards, given to Sherwood Anderson and announced in the January 1922 issue.

In summarizing what *The Dial* stood for, then, the Peacock Folder publicized the superiority of the work *The Dial* published, the importance of the contributing artists and writers, the significance of the new Dial Award, and the favorable reception a certain type of reader was according the whole enterprise. In the middle of July, just a few days away from New York, Scofield Thayer began planning the folder. He wrote Gilbert Seldes that "I append the list of pictures for the illustrated pamphlet you are getting out. You remember I insist on seeing the proofs and OK-ing them before the pamphlet is sent to press. . . . I will cable you my OK provided I accept what you submit." Thayer went on to insist that of the ten titles for pictures he submitted to Seldes for inclusion as illustrations in this projected advertising circular, six titles he asterisked be included in the pamphlet. From the other four, Watson, Seldes, and Samuel Craig were to choose what they wanted: "But I dare say six pictures will be all for which appropriate space will be found. You will note that among the asterisked pictures there are three half-tones and three line cuts, and among the four extras there are two half-tones and two line cuts. . . . The understanding at any rate is that you will include absolutely no picture which is not in the list, the making up of which I have spent many hours and days considering. I have looked at the list from every point of view." The list given by Thayer consisted of pictures by Stuart Davis, Rockwell Kent, William Gropper, C. R. W. Nevinson, Gaston Lachaise, Hunt Diederich, Pablo Picasso, and Boardman Robinson and the Mayan sculptured Chac-Mool, all of which had appeared in *The Dial* and were to be reproduced in the pamphlet, and James Earle Fraser's sculptured *Mask*, previously photographed in the January 1921 *Dial* but rejected by the staff at the New York office for reproduction in the Peacock Folder. At the end of August 1921, Seldes submitted proofs of the folder to Thayer—along with proofs of a smaller, less thoroughly discussed folder—with the comment that he had "been afflicted with a hundred doubts about them in the process of getting them together, but they both look better to me than I thought they would."

What Seldes compiled is a four-page folder; the front is occupied by a photograph of Gaston Lachaise's stone peacock, underneath which is the quotation from Keats' *Endymion:*

> *A thing of beauty is a joy forever;*
> *Its loveliness increases; it will never*
> *Pass into nothingness.*

In a letter accompanying some proofs of the large folder, Craig had offered Thayer the alternative of a text by Santayana to this by Keats, but on September 17, 1921, the Editor cabled his choice of the first lines of *Endymion.* As he explained to Seldes two days later by letter: "In my cable I indicated Keats as being more popular." Thayer also complimented Seldes on his authorship of the folder and his supervision of its appearance: "The large pamphlet looks very well, particularly as always the bull fight. I think you have also written entertainingly and that the arrangement of type is excellent."

The following three pages of the Peacock Folder give pictures, lists of contents, and advertising matter, together with suitably commendatory passages about *The Dial* selected from periodicals and newspapers ranging from *The New Republic* and *The New York Times* to *The Duluth Herald* and *The New Witness* of London. Of *The Dial*, Gilbert Seldes repeated earlier editorial assertions that it was the only journal in America devoted exclusively to art and literature, "to beauty and ideas." *The Dial* tried as nearly as possible "to occupy the central point in this field," printing as it did the work of established writers like Thomas Hardy "side by side with that of men hitherto unrecognized except by a small, discerning public," for to do otherwise "would be an injustice to its readers." Thus Seldes merely restated what Thayer and Watson had already written, but the next paragraph gives for the first time a public statement about the art of *The Dial*, which constituted a basic contribution of the magazine: "THE DIAL prints not illustrations but pictures–drawing, painting, sculpture–reproduced for their own sakes." The prose of the folder continued with repetitions of previous editorial and advertising matter, again asserting, among other things, that *The Dial* had nothing to do "with the swaddling of the mind by the genteel tradition in American letters."

Seldes' writing here shows that after two years Thayer and Watson were keeping pretty consistently to their original aims, "without any intention of making money, of truckling to popular prejudice, or of undertaking propaganda for any school of art," but it is still more interesting because it also shows the publishing achievements that *The Dial* prided itself on and considered important and attractive enough to stand by. These have to do with the reproductions of drawing, painting, sculpture; the work by new and established writers; the foreign letters giving monthly "literary intelligence" and the monthly chronicles of arts and letters; and the institution of the annual Dial Award.

Besides the photograph of the Lachaise peacock, eight other works of art were reproduced, symmetrically arranged around the prose of the circular, all nine being cuts of illustrations that had appeared in *The Dial*. Besides the stone peacock, there were the great Mayan stone Chac-Mool in the American Museum of Natural History, William Gropper's line caricature *The Conductor*, Picasso's painting *Woman at a Table* of his blue period, Stuart Davis's line drawing of Fyodor Dostoevsky, Hunt Diederich's ink silhouette *Spanish Bull Fight*, Boardman Robinson's drawing *His Excellency the American Ambassador at the Court of St. James*, C. R. W. Nevinson's painting *New York: An Abstraction*, and Rockwell Kent's lithograph *Father and Son*. The Lachaise sculpture, according to "Notes on Contributors" in *The Dial* for April 1921, in which issue a photograph of it appeared, was part of the garden decoration of the James Deering estate, Villa Vizcaya, in Miami. It is suavely decorative and, coupled with the quotation from Keats, indicates sufficiently the intentions of *The Dial*. Of the eight small pictures on the margins of the second and third pages of the folder, the major reproductions decidedly are the two of the Picasso *Woman in Blue* and the Mayan Chac-Mool. The rest range from the slight if clever drawings of Gropper and Robinson to those of Diederich and Kent; here the early Twenties self-importantly were displaying themselves to themselves through this group of pictures and objects, reasonably advanced but not radically innovational. The art of the Peacock Folder is representative of the pictures in *The Dial* in the very early Twenties, but not after about the middle of 1922, when reproductions of Scofield Thayer's collection of modern art, which he bought specifically to be reproduced in *The Dial*, began appearing in each issue.

Calling itself "the leading review in the English language" with pardonable expansiveness, *The Dial* proceeded in the Peacock Folder to list some of its better known contributors: Sherwood Anderson, Julien Benda, Max Beerbohm, Johan Bojer, Robert Bridges, Van Wyck Brooks, Joseph Conrad, Benedetto Croce, Charles Demuth, André Derain, Hunt Diederich, T. S. Eliot, Anatole France, Jean Giraudoux, Thomas Hardy, James Joyce, Gaston Lachaise, D. H. Lawrence, Reinhold Lepsius, Wyndham Lewis, Vachel Lindsay, Robert Morss Lovett, Amy Lowell, Henry McBride, John Marin, Thomas Mann, Henri Matisse, George Moore, J. Middleton Murry, Pablo Picasso, Ezra Pound, Marcel Proust, Edwin Arlington Robinson, Romain Rolland, Paul Rosenfeld, Bertrand Russell, Carl Sandburg, G. Santayana, Arthur Schnitzler, May Sinclair, James Stephens, Arthur Symons, and William Butler Yeats. Not all forty-three of these names had significance for the magazine. Joseph Conrad and Romain Rolland, despite their inclusion, had no personal connections with the Dial group, nor does one easily associate T. S. Eliot, a leading member of the group, with the Poet Laureate, Robert Bridges. It is a company of writers and artists obviously compiled to catch the eye rather than to inform a potential reader as to just who consistently was favored by *The Dial*. More informatively, the folder went on to list seven books the complete texts of which *The Dial* had published: Julien Benda's *Belphegor;* Johan Bojer's *The Prisoner Who Sang;* Remy de Gourmont's *Dust for Sparrows*, as translated by Ezra Pound; William Butler Yeats's autobiographical *Four Years, 1887–1891;* Leonid Andreyev's, *He, the One Who Gets Slapped;* Sherwood Anderson's *Out of Nowhere into Nothing;* and Anatole France's autobiographical *La Vie en Fleur*—"two significant novels, a great Russian play, the chief work of contemporary criticism, two masterpieces of autobiography, and the posthumous epigrams of one of the most delicate minds of our time." On the fourth and last page of the Peacock Folder the names of three writers appeared, with brief descriptive paragraphs relating them to *The Dial:* Anatole France, G. Santayana, and William Butler Yeats. France was "the greatest of contemporary French writers"; Santayana, "poet, critic, philosopher," wrote essays that were "notable examples of clarity and profound thought . . . distinguished by wit, irony, and a deep, detached, unprejudiced understanding of human nature"; William Butler Yeats's "chapters of autobiography, Four Years, were the literary sensation of the summer [of 1921]." Besides the "work of many men and women who have never been published before"—and who were not named here—*The Dial* in this folder listed two other categories of writing, with names of contributors given—the letters from abroad, or "literary intelligence," and the departments. The literary intelligence—which did not consist of gossip and personal remarks, wrote Seldes—was by T. S. Eliot and Ezra Pound, the American poets and critics, in London and Paris respectively; by John Eglinton, the Irish editor and critic, in Dublin; by Raffaello Piccoli, "recently Italian exchange professor in America," in Italy; by Edwin Muir, "(Edward Moore) author of 'We Moderns,'" in Central Europe; and by "writers of equal rank" in the other countries of Europe. In the second category of writing, the departments, Paul Rosenfeld's musical chronicle and Henry McBride's articles on modern art were identified with the names of their authors, but the writer of the monthly review of the theater, Gilbert Seldes, was not

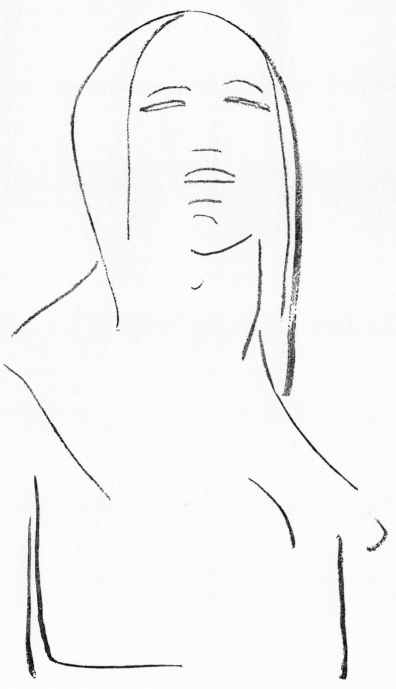

Gaston Lachaise   *Woman's Head*   FEBRUARY 1920

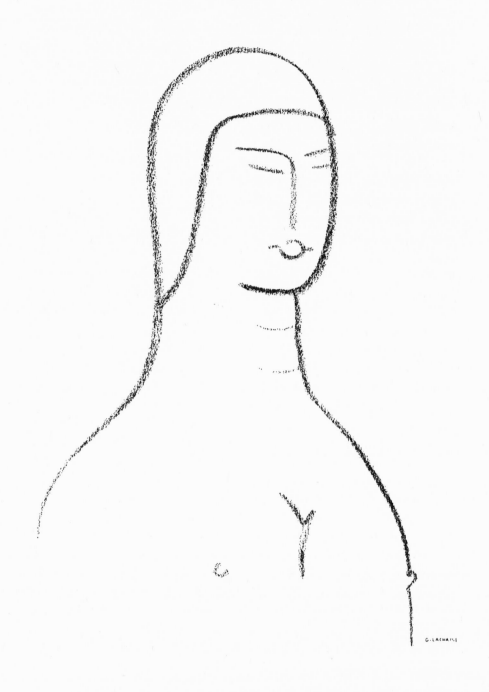

Gaston Lachaise *Head of a Woman* JULY 1921

named, possibly because he himself wrote the copy for the Peacock Folder. *The Dial* justifiably was proud of this publishing record, for it alone among American magazines had been awarded, so the copy asserted, "a rating of 100% for fiction of distinction" published in 1920 by Edward J. O'Brien "in his authoritative review of American magazine short stories, published in the Boston Transcript"; this record meant that *The Dial* "did not publish a single mediocre story during the year."

True, to be sure; yet the Peacock Folder presents at best a partial image of these early years of *The Dial*. Other names and other titles omitted in those four pages would make the record of contributions and contributors even more dazzlingly excellent than the folder alleged. Among the artists whose pictures and sculptures were reproduced in *The Dial* in 1920–21 and who were neither named nor exhibited in the Peacock Folder, are—besides such older masters as Gauguin and Renoir, Van Gogh and Cézanne—George Biddle, Charles Burchfield, Giorgio de Chirico, Arthur B. Davies, Adolf Dehn, Gleb Derujinsky, Arthur Dove, Alfeo Faggi, Robert Edmond Jones, Jacques Lipchitz, Erich Mendelsohn, Kenneth Hayes Miller, Elie Nadelman, Georgia O'Keeffe, Jules Pascin, Carl Sprinchorn, Maurice Vlaminck, Max Weber, Ossip Zadkine, and Marguerite and William Zorach. Three others—Djuna Barnes, E. E. Cummings, and Kahlil Gibran—have become famous primarily for their work in literature. (In contrast, the work of such artists as Richard Boix, Lucy Perkins Ripley, and John Storrs was not cited in the Peacock Folder, nor would it today make *The Dial* famous.)

Obviously the selection of a silhouette by Hunt Diederich for the Peacock Folder rather than, for example, a drawing of Havana by Jules Pascin, or Rockwell Kent's lithograph rather than the one by Arthur B. Davies *The Dial* also published, is ascribable to the taste of the staff of the magazine. Henri Matisse and Pablo Picasso added luster to the renown of *The Dial* through its reproductions of their work, but as Hunt Diederich and Rockwell Kent could not do so, the efforts to publicize their art that the editors made evince a certain partiality. It is to be wondered why, since the review overtly prided itself on having introduced the work of many men and women who had never been published before, *The Dial* did not give, in the Peacock Folder, some publicity to Jules Pascin, Elie Nadelman, and Max Weber—not to speak of E. E. Cummings,

Adolf Dehn, Arthur Dove, and Georgia O'Keeffe, four American artists known to the compilers of the Peacock Folder. Yet these strictures are the only ones reasonably to be made about the taste of *The Dial*, granted its milieu and the bias of Scofield Thayer, who said that he did not like abstractions. At worst the art of *The Dial* is merely, amusingly period–no great evil surely. What are remarkable are the brilliance and sureness of the editorial taste at its best. Perhaps the peaks of *Dial* publication should not appear so high were it not for the obvious valleys as well; the staff as well as the Editor might make an occasional gaffe, but theirs also was the discernment that mingled the witty caricatures of Opffer, Gropper, Robinson, and Dehn with the more serious sculptures of Lachaise and Faggi, the more serious pictures of Picasso and Derain.

The Dial paid for the right to reproduce a picture or object, when it had not been exhibited, at the rate of twenty-five dollars the picture. To save money, therefore, the Editor never accepted unexhibited work except when he ordered or discovered something especially necessary to *The Dial*, as for example in the May 1925 number the portrait of Marianne Moore by Marguerite Zorach, or alternatively pictures that would go on the mat paper of the regular text, which, Thayer pointed out to the staff in his "General Instructions," were "always scarce, and cheaper to reproduce because of [the] saving on paper." That most of the art reproduced in *The Dial* was given to the Editor by dealers and by the artists themselves, is evidenced by the lists of contributors in the Dial papers. For example, in the November 1922 *Dial*, only the reproduction of Delaunay's *St Séverin* was paid for out of all the pictures in the issue, and then the sum was only fifteen dollars, not twenty-five.

As for the writing *The Dial* published and the Peacock Folder praised, it too has suffered its ups and downs. Sherwood Anderson, whom *The Dial* presented with its first annual Award at the close of 1921, occupies a less conspicuous place in American letters than he did in 1920–22, when the magazine was the principal outlet for his work. Julien Benda's much touted *Belphegor*–"the chief work of contemporary criticism"–is forgotten in America, if not in France and elsewhere. And even in 1921, despite the Peacock Folder's official praise for Remy de Gourmont's work, the Editor and at least one of his better known contributors deplored the whole project of publishing Pound's translation of de Gourmont's *Dust for*

Sparrows. At the end of July 1921, D. H. Lawrence concluded a
letter to the Editor by remarking what a cross, irritable paper *The
Dial* was, with its insistence that he be ecstatic about all its writing.
Lawrence was glad Gourmont's sparrow dust had settled, for it
was rubbish. Otherwise he thought *The Dial* fun.

Some writers of older literary generations contributed desultorily to *The Dial* or else sent their later and minor things; Max
Beerbohm, Robert Bridges, Joseph Conrad, Thomas Hardy, Marcel
Proust, Edwin Arlington Robinson, Romain Rolland, and Arthur
Symons belong to this company. Joseph Conrad, for example, can
scarcely be called a contributor in the usual sense, as his three
"Prefaces" to *An Outcast of the Islands, Lord Jim,* and *Nostromo*
came to *The Dial* when his publishers, Doubleday, agreed to give the
magazine the pick of the prefaces to the American edition of Conrad's
collected works. Other older writers on the long list of the better
known contributors had some of their finest work printed by Thayer
and Watson: Johan Bojer, Benedetto Croce, Anatole France, George
Moore, Arthur Schnitzler, and William Butler Yeats. The editors
not only solicited but commissioned work by Bertrand Russell and
James Stephens, and even Santayana agreed, on one memorable
occasion, to review *Civilization in the United States*—though he
insisted his fifteen pages of remarks be called merely "marginal
notes." (And with the rather misleading title of "Marginal Notes on
Civilization in the United States," the review graced the July 1922
Dial.)

To judge by the Peacock Folder, the Editor and his staff considered their most impressive trio of contributors to be Anatole
France, George Santayana (who always appeared here as *G.* Santayana), and William Butler Yeats. Scofield Thayer told Gilbert
Seldes at the end of July 1921 that France's *La Vie en Fleur* was
the most important acquisition, apart from Yeats's *Four Years,* he
had yet made for *The Dial:* "I find the French delicate and subtle
and trust the English will be not less so." Thayer insisted that
the first part of France's memoir occupy "the place of honor in the
October number," which it duly did, and he went on to give detailed
instructions about the serialization of the work and payment to
Calmann-Lévy, the French publishers, for it.

Thayer found at this time that there was no one else in France
besides Pound, whose Paris letter he had already sent along to New

York, and Santayana, whose work it was at the time advantageous for *The Dial* to accept. The Editor added that although Joyce was then occupied with the proofs for *Ulysses*, he had promised Thayer to send anything he wrote to *The Dial*.

Thayer's own extreme fastidiousness is of course intentionally and facetiously exaggerated in this letter; nevertheless, at least with reference to Santayana, he was serious in making his curious remark, for what he wanted was not the well-known essay on Charles Dickens, which was what Santayana gave *The Dial*, but *The Last Puritan*. Thayer directed Seldes to hold "Dickens" over to the November number, so that it might occupy the place of honor in the issue for November 1921; however, George Moore's story, "Peronnik the Fool," pre-empted this favored spot. Seldes knew of course what Thayer was stalking, for a few days previously the Editor had written of his meetings with Santayana:

> Santayana is living his golden days appropriately upon the Boule-vard Poissonière. He takes two cups of camomile tea before retiring. He is sur [. . . .] which as he is not likely to finish for three hundred and forty-five years he is first bringing out his book on England and [. . . .] of the Realism [*sic*] of Being. This novel is to be about a Puritan born in Springfield and who died behind the lines in the great war. Santayana will bring himself into the novel when the young hero at college has the good fortune to listen to him lecture. I imagine the canvas will be very [. . . .] I think it would be an excellent thing for the DIAL to run this novel serially. . . . If I do not nab the novel now we may not get it. The novel is a long one but would not run for more than a year. I am not sure that Santayana will give it to us. However, he says he is not an old fogey, he likes the pictures in the DIAL. . . . , and he doesn't like the pictures in the Luxembourg. He has entertained me at three tables, each time paying the check himself. I do not see why the DIAL should not recoup itself through the generosity of this fine old man. Of course it is not for me to ask to look at the novel before accepting it, but I myself urge that we give Santayana carte blanche, and that if the novel is to be published by us we should pay him at our regular rate of two cents a word. . . . I think that Squire is likely to ask for the novel as soon as he hears about it. Santayana rehearsed the whole plot of the novel to me. Knowing Santayana as well as I do I think that we can safely accept the novel in advance, as we would have Strachey's Queen Victoria if we could have published it in toto and at our regular rates.[1]

The Dial, then did nab the pièce de résistance, as the Editor called it, of Santayana's book on England—the essay on Dickens—but, alas! Thayer never nabbed *The Last Puritan*. Its serialization in *The Dial*, as he realized, would have crowned his publication of Santayana's writing.

One later document that, had it been published, would have been as interesting in its way as *The Last Puritan*, was a long autobiographical sketch from Santayana, undoubtedly the germ of the philosopher's three-volume memoir (*Persons and Places*, *The Middle Span*, and *My Host the World*). Thayer had written to Santayana's nephew George Sturgis, because he had heard "so many diametrically conflicting accounts as to the *Americanità* or *non-Americanità* of your childhood and youth"; and the resultant letter from the philosopher "settled authoritatively and so clearly" this troublesome matter, as Thayer told Santayana (July 23, 1924).

The letter in question, dated May 13, 1924, is ample evidence of the rapport between master and pupil. Santayana outlined the facts pertinent to Thayer's questions about his early life—his being taken to Boston by his father in July 1872; his decade there with his mother, her Sturgis children, and the Sturgises; his return in the summer of 1883 to his father in Avila, after a freshman year at Harvard; and his annual repetition of these visits, even after his father's death during one of them in 1893. As for the degree of his own Americanism, Santayana thought that while others were better judges on that point than himself, his own feeling was that socially he was practically an American, most of his friends being Americans living in Europe or with European affinities, but that sentimentally he had never been an American at all and that although as a philosopher he had tried to be indifferent to such accidents of fortune, he never at any time would have lived in America by preference. Perhaps to soften that particular conclusion, Santayana complimented *The Dial* for its amiability in printing his *Dialogues in Limbo*, caviar to the general as they probably were; indeed, he was glad to have them in *The Dial*, because although there was much in its contributors that he could not take very seriously, he liked the spirit of freedom and of experiment to which Thayer and Watson opened the door.

Indeed, in all their correspondence only a single point of difference between Thayer and Santayana is mentioned: Santayana wrote to Thayer (August 8, 1924) that it was pleasant to know the

Editor welcomed his *Dialogues*, although he suspected Thayer disagreed with the politics of Santayana's Socrates. The reference is to several of Santayana's *Dialogues in Limbo*, published in *The Dial* intermittently from March 1924 through April 1925. The only other twentieth-century philosopher who contributed approximately as often to *The Dial* as did Santayana, was Bertrand Russell; however, much of Russell's material was the merest journalism, and Russell's relationship to Thayer was basically a professional one.

Of the three contributors to *The Dial* of these years who were most greatly admired by Thayer, it was above all Yeats who honored the magazine with some of his work frequently anthologized today, poems and memoirs of his late period. Santayana and Yeats surely remain among the greatest literary men not just of the group who wrote for *The Dial* but of the modern Western world; France, however, has failed to keep the high place he once held. The first installment of *La Vie en Fleur* appeared with Santayana's essay "The Irony of Liberalism" in *The Dial* for October 1921. The monthly clipsheet issued by *The Dial* on September 22, 1921, in its summary of the forthcoming issue, stated that France contributed "the leading feature of the October DIAL" and compared *La Vie en Fleur* with Yeats's *Four Years*, which the magazine had published during the summer of 1921. "The great French master's work is full of delightful passages," specified the clipsheet, "and, in addition to the delicacy and charm always found there, these chapters contain many profound reflections on war, education, morality, and other things." As an example of France's wit and wisdom, the clipsheet contained, besides passages entitled "Anatole France on Education," "A Master's Confession," "Science and Art," and "Wolfish Morality," one entitled "Heresy by Anatole France":

> One day M Dubois asked Mme Nozière to name the most tragic day in history. Mme Nozière did not know.
> "It is," M Dubois told her, "the day of the battle of Poitiers when in 732, the science, the art, and the civilization of Arabia fell back before the barbarism of the Franks."

Thus do tastes change. The evidence of the clipsheets from *The Dial* as well as that furnished by the Peacock Folder and the magazine itself bears out the irony that the editorial perspicacity of *The Dial* sometimes exceeded its editors' awareness of the fact.

Gilbert Seldes in the Peacock Folder termed *The Dial* the leading review in the English language, and it did lead all other reviews not simply because it published the established writers such as Yeats, Santayana, and France but because it also published writers whom it helped establish. Of those the Peacock Folder publicized, such men as Benedetto Croce, T. S. Eliot, D. H. Lawrence, Thomas Mann, Ezra Pound, and Bertrand Russell would now rank as fitting company for Yeats and Santayana. But most of their companions named in the Peacock Folder, distinguished as their accomplishments have been, have for one reason or another never quite achieved the prominence it once seemed they would or, as the case may be, have slipped in critical esteem.

Other contributors of these early years of *The Dial*, ones whom the Peacock Folder did not name, were at that time or have since become considerable if not, in every instance, major figures. Kenneth Burke and Gilbert Seldes may have been omitted because they were members of the editorial staff, yet both Henry McBride and Paul Rosenfeld were editor-critics and were listed among the better known contributors. Marianne Moore, not then on the staff, and E. E. Cummings were among the younger writers whom *The Dial* regularly published, but the Peacock Folder did not list them. The omission of A. E. is questionable, inasmuch as the folder listed other Irish writers such as James Joyce, James Stephens, and William Butler Yeats. Contributors to *The Dial* of Martyn Johnson—Richard Aldington, John Gould Fletcher, Harold Laski, and Padraic Colum—along with members of his staff—Conrad Aiken and John Dewey—also were not named, even though Robert Morss Lovett was listed, along with such other contributors to Johnson's *Dial* as Van Wyck Brooks and George Moore. One cannot fathom the principle of selection that could include Amy Lowell and Carl Sandburg, J. Middleton Murry and May Sinclair among the better known contributors and that at the same time would omit Alfred Kreymborg and Louis Untermeyer, Ford Madox Hueffer and John Drinkwater from this group. In general, the Peacock Folder contented itself with the astute dropping of names and titles and the comprehensive statement that it was generous about bringing out the work of previously unpublished writers.

Certainly *The Dial* lived up to this assertion. Among the writers, both new and established, American and foreign, who contributed to *The Dial* in 1920–21, but whom neither the Peacock Folder nor, in this connection, the present account has thus far listed were J. Donald Adams, Konrad Bercovici, Ernest Boyd, Witter Bynner, Joseph Campbell, Ananda Coomaraswamy, A. E. Coppard, Guy-Charles Cros, S. Foster Damon, Babette Deutsch, John Dos Passos, Waldo Frank, Kahlil Gibran, H. D., Robert Hillyer, Emory Holloway, Richard Hughes, Shane Leslie, Hendrik Willem Van Loon, O. W. de Lubicz-Milosz, John Mosher, Harold Munro, Walter Pach, Ralph Barton Perry, Constance Rourke, Edward Sapir, Evelyn Scott, Osbert Sitwell, André Spire, Ordway Tead, Charles Vildrac, and Cuthbert Wright; Dr. Albert C. Barnes and Deems Taylor also contributed an article apiece.

Of the contributors the Peacock Folder did not name, most were not famous by the end of 1921. Several attained fame through *The Dial*, which presented Kenneth Burke, E. E. Cummings, Marianne Moore, and William Carlos Williams with its Annual Award for 1928, 1925, 1924, and 1926 respectively. Another of these writers, Jean Cocteau, became an Academician of his native country. Still, most of the contributors the Folder omitted were beginning their careers, and not all of them would continue to write for *The Dial;* Edna St. Vincent Millay and Michael Arlen were not to become regular contributors. But Djuna Barnes, Malcolm Cowley, Hart Crane, Thomas Craven, Manuel Komroff, Mina Loy, Paul Morand, Raymond Mortimer, Glenway Wescott, and Edmund Wilson rose to prominence in America with their writing for *The Dial*, published some of their most characteristic work in it, and, at least in the case of Edmund Wilson, were in the late 1950's still culling the issues of *The Dial* for book publication of their contributions.

A writer might not live on his earnings from *The Dial*, but as the Peacock Folder made clear, he would assuredly be given the best possible literary showcase by having his work published in the magazine. D. H. Lawrence exemplifies this working relationship. By the late summer of 1921, Lawrence was, already, one of the more durable glories of the magazine. In a letter commending *Sea and Sardinia* and written on August 17, 1921, soon after the one in which he complained of the worthlessness of *Dust for Sparrows*, Lawrence wrote that even though Thayer probably wouldn't like Sardinia when he saw it, "it was partly at your asking for travel sketches à la Twilight in Italy which made me write [*Sea and*

Sardinia]: half an eye on *The Dial*. So live up to your responsibility.

> '*And then he took a Dial from his poke*
> *And looking on it with lacklustre eye*
> *Said very wisely: "Tis now ten oclock."* '

Lawrence also rubbed up into readable English S. S. Koteliansky's translation of Bunin's *The Gentleman from San Francisco* and sent it to *The Dial* to help his friend the translator. Though Lawrence made nothing by this gesture, he confessed a need of enough dollars to his name so that he could face New York with calm equanimity, and indefatigably he sent *The Dial* his poetry and fiction.

Unlike most little magazines, *The Dial* paid its contributors regular rates; to that extent it attempted to give material recognition of aesthetic worth and to attract the writers it desired, and needed, to publish. The rate for prose in English was two cents a word; this was also the rate for foreign letters and foreign book reviews that the Editor commissioned and that had to be translated into English. Because of the quantity of work in foreign tongues that *The Dial* had to cope with, the Editor drew up some rules, specifying in his "General Instructions" that such work was to be paid for at the rate of two cents a word to the original author if it had not been published before. Otherwise one cent per word went to the author and one cent per word for translating done outside the editorial offices. To save money, therefore, the Editor never accepted matter in a foreign tongue that had not been published in that tongue, except foreign letters and "once in a blue moon," a foreign book review, as for example, Élie Faure's review of the *Dial* folio of pictures and sculpture, *Living Art*, in the issue for October 1924.

The rate for verse was twenty dollars per page or fraction thereof. For every poem, whether it was three lines or thirty-seven lines long, provided that it was intended to appear upon only one page of the magazine, *The Dial* paid twenty dollars. If a poem was accepted with the definite understanding of the Editor or his assistants that it would be run not as the first poem of a group and in a group, then more lines might be got on one page than would otherwise be the case; this arrangement did not affect the rate, however. The editorial staff was never paid for any writing or translating its members did for *The Dial*, but they were paid for their creative work it published.

Unlike any comparably solvent magazine, *The Dial* consistently took chances with unknown writers, whom it published as equals of the better known contributors. The bias of Thayer and Watson was not solely favorable to literary and artistic experimentalism, nor was *The Dial* oriented toward the new aesthetic forms at the expense of the traditional ones despite its hospitality to the new formalism. What *The Dial* demanded of its prospective contributors was simple excellence. Nothing else would do, and that alone was usually sufficient. Of course Thayer and Watson made mistakes occasionally; for example, they rejected Ernest Hemingway's early poems and stories, even though Ezra Pound recommended the young writer to Thayer. On stylistic grounds, *The Dial* objected to Theodore Dreiser's novels. These editorial lapses are minor, however, compared with the positive accomplishment of *The Dial* and its staff and patrons in publishing, in the first two years of the Twenties, the artists and poets and novelists, the critics and scholars and reviewers whom it named as being among its better known contributors, and the host of young men and women whom it did not name in the Peacock Folder but whom it nevertheless published and helped support.

The most widely publicized aid *The Dial* ever gave writers was the annual Award that Scofield Thayer announced in his editorial "Comment" for June 1921. After a year and a half of publication, wrote Thayer, *The Dial* found itself in a position to say a very few words, placed as it then was to do at least one young American writer a good turn every year: "THE DIAL announces that on January the first of each year it will acknowledge the service to letters of some one of those who have, during the twelvemonth, contributed to its pages by the payment to him of two thousand dollars." This payment, specified the Editor, was in no sense a prize, because in the arts the idea and feeling of competition are not required, just as they have no place in worship. But artists—like mendicant friars—must live, even in our community. Whereas in the South Sea islands, in Greece, in the Middle Age, in the Renaissance, and in the eighteenth century ("the last in which men knew to live well"), and even in the disrupted and bankrupt Europe of the twentieth century, other cultures made shift to feed and clothe their artists, America, "sound as a nut and rich as Tophet, feeds 'em air." The sausage-kings do indeed go the whole hog when it is a question of Franz Hals and Raphael Sanzio, but when it is another question—that of supporting the young artists and writers of America—they have no answer. Instead, the rich American collector prides himself on "the distinguished vulgarity of tearing out beautiful objects from that European frame which is their flesh."

Having achieved, in its brief course of publication, considerable recognition in America and Europe, and having cut its annual deficit sufficiently, *The Dial*, asserted "Comment," would try to give public recognition of good work at home, in the hope that future Henry Jameses and Mary Gardens would not have to go abroad for recognition. "Among those who realize THE DIAL to be intellectually sound, there will be some worth to a man in our mere endorsement of his name; and the two thousand dollars will pass current even among those to whom the name of THE DIAL is not yet a household word." The Editor explicitly recognized in this "Comment" that a gift of money would be the least significant of gifts to recipients: "like a bad work of art it requires a descriptive tag." What the Dial Award would signify, however, and what the donor wished to give was leisure, "leisure through which at least one artist may serve God (or go to the Devil) according to his own lights." The recipient might be a live wire who could smuggle himself out to Italy, and there, favored by sunlight and a favorable rate of exchange, his service to God might be proportionately prolonged. On the other hand, the recipient might be a live genius who would blow a whole year in one night.

Thayer's announcement—incidentally, his penciled draft for this "Comment" is in the Dial papers—concluded with one pointed remark and an even more pointed question. The remark discounted current complaints about the American environment and its fabled hostility to artistic production: "The only environment that counts is liberty; the only liberty that counts is leisure; and this all good artists know. They know that leisure is—at least for such as they—quintessentially and intimately the Good Environment: they would rather—in so far as they are worth their salt—be remittance-men in Hell than master-financiers in Heaven. And they are the kind of remittance-men Yankee Land wants." So much for the artists! And as for the master-financiers?—"Why doesn't somebody else (some fine fellow who doesn't know what the word deficit means) come over with two HUNDRED thousand? Why not?"

Why not? But no fine fellows stepped forward. The reception

the announcement of the Dial Award had might fairly be described as mildly sensational, were it not that sensations last for nine days, while the Dial Award each year for eight years steadily became more impressive. Here was unprecedented generosity. Both "Comment" and the Peacock Folder reprinted excerpts from the press praising this "most interesting experiment," as *The Duluth Herald* called the offer of the Dial Award. *The Chicago Post* was quoted by "Comment" in October 1921 as hoping the suggestion that someone do the thing on a larger scale would be taken up and as favoring the Dial Award for its "straight, honest offer" as against "the Pulitzer prizes with their silly reservations about moral influences." The Guild of Free Lance Artists, the graphic arts section of The Authors League of America, passed a resolution commending *The Dial*, and *The Dial* in turn commended and printed the resolution, which with unusual foresight asserted that "although the gift is for 'the artist in literature' our appreciation is none the less hearty – as the growth of one particular art gives strength to the others."

Thayer and Watson were aware that the Dial Award as they made it was deficient in its neglect of the plastic arts. Agreeing with the Guild of Free Lance Artists that the gift was for the artist in literature, the October 1921 "Comment" apologized that "obviously, THE DIAL's award was a beginning and . . . we should like nothing better than to announce a further award for workers in the field of the Guild." Very handsomely the editors did not say they had spent more time in 1921 trying to secure an award for artists than they had spent for the award announced for writers. Scofield Thayer had written on January 29 of that year to a lady whom we shall call Mrs. Smythe, as one whose generosity was widely known, who was a subscriber to *The Dial*, and whose interest in American art and letters might lead her to look favorably upon his proposition that she co-operate with himself and Dr. Watson in offering a series of prizes such as those given by "a magazine called Poetry" and some other magazines and associations that were trying "to help our starveling literature in this unbusinesslike fashion."

As Thayer outlined his plans, which of course also were those of Watson, *The Dial* was anxious to offer an annual prize for the best poem published during the year in the magazine, another for the best story, and a third for the best essay. The trouble was that neither young man was financially in a position that would permit him to offer any prizes he considered commensurate with the dignity of the undertaking, because as the backers of *The Dial* Thayer and Watson were still engaged in putting their business in order.

They had decided that if they were to offer prizes, the sums offered must be not less than one thousand dollars apiece. If, Thayer pointed out, the backers of *The Dial* could find one person who would pledge three thousand a year in the old Medicean fashion, the matter would be settled. If such a person would pledge two thousand dollars, *The Dial* might give two prizes, and the hunt would be on for a third donor. If such a person pledged one thousand dollars, *The Dial* should at any rate be able to give one prize and should try to find one or two other people to give the other two prizes.

In March 1921, Thayer was still writing to Mrs. Smythe for an appointment that she had suggested he make the latter part of the month. But by July 22, Mrs. Smythe had decided nothing. She and her husband read *The Dial* with great interest each month, she averred, and as Mr. Smythe put it, *The Dial* had class. Mr. and Mrs. Smythe were interested more in the plastic arts, but they realized that all art is so intimately associated that the development of one depends on the development of the other. Personally, Mrs. Smythe explained, she was also interested in what she called " '*civic* organization' (as contrasted to *political*)," for therein lay the germs of "a permanent, a 'dynamic' democracy." Mr. and Mrs. Smythe's interest, time, and finances were thus pretty well tied up, but she generously expressed interest in meeting someone in New York and concluded that if there were any way of giving a "scholarship" in painting or sculpture through *The Dial*, she and her husband might be able to help with it.

Thinking he had found an ally, in August Thayer drew up a letter to Mrs. Smythe in which he proposed the announcement, beginning January 1, 1922, of an honorarium of two thousand dollars to some not too old artist, in the narrower sense, who had contributed to *The Dial* in the preceding year; who would be chosen no later than December 1, 1921, by a committee composed of Mr. Smythe, some painter to be appointed by the Smythes, and the Editor of *The Dial;* and who would be the right choice not because of his work for *The Dial*, but because of the total importance to America of his work. In September 1921, Mrs. Smythe told Dr. Watson she desired to do nothing about this matter for a few months; in 1922 Mr. Smythe died; and thereafter Mrs. Smythe kept silent about any aid to *The*

Dial. In January 1924 Thayer again wrote her, asking whether she might be at all interested in his project to establish an annual award in American painting and sculpture similar to the Dial Award in literature. Apparently Mrs. Smythe never replied to his inquiry, and the Dial Award in the fine arts never took form beyond this correspondence.

An opposite reaction to the news of the new Award in literature was that of Paul Rosenfeld, who not only was one of *The Dial*'s three editor-critics as writer of the "Musical Chronicle" but soon would write the eulogistic essay on Sherwood Anderson on the occasion of Anderson's reception of the first Dial Award. Rosenfeld wondered, to Scofield Thayer, whether even the donors themselves, who were offering a large sum for the award, were quite aware of the importance of the matter. He explained that he of course realized Thayer would be aware of the effect on the fortunate recipient rather than on the public watching the performance from afar, but others besides the recipient would benefit a great deal from the prize. The fact that someone believed sufficiently strongly in a man or woman whose total yearly output might be no more than three or four exquisite lyrics to award such a person two thousand dollars would have, Rosenfeld was convinced, a great moral effect on editors, on public, and again, on writers. No American, he thought, was sufficiently strong to stand free entirely of the prejudices of his fellow countrymen, and he feared that with Americans the willingness to find money was always the ultimate test of sincerity. *The Dial* had already done a great deal for the community in behalf of the new writers whom the commercial magazines had outlawed; but its new act of faith—frankly a gift without any bearing upon the physical amount of the recipient's product and entirely independent of the standards by which work was generally judged—would indubitably make sick the guilty and put new confidence into the whole body of those who worked for the fun of working in a community that was not primarily sportsmanly. Written on July 29, 1921, Rosenfeld's enthusiastic letter gave the first honest hint of the way the advocates of and participants in the New Movement in the arts would receive the news of the munificence of Scofield Thayer and Sibley Watson.

As for the Award itself, to whom would it go? Thayer wrote Gilbert Seldes on September 19, 1921, that Edwin Arlington Robinson was his first choice for the honor, that Sherwood Anderson remained his second choice, and that he could consider no one else. Had Mrs. Smythe given the money for an award in fine arts, Thayer's first choice would have been Lachaise, with Marin as second choice. The Editor directed Seldes to have some form of tribute to the recipient published: "for Robinson I suggest [Charles K.] Trueblood, for Anderson [Paul] Rosenfeld, for Lachaise [Thomas] Craven, for Marin Rosenfeld. But in case Robinson is chosen, I think it would be possible, as you suggest, to publish several tributes from different people of note in addition to the Trueblood essay. Amy Lowell should be got to write about him. Of course all this matter should be in the January number and none of it should slop over into February." As an afterthought, Thayer scribbled that the Managing Editor of course must not have Rosenfeld write on both Anderson and Marin "in case they are the two luckies," and that Henry Mc-Bride be got to celebrate John Marin. As things turned out, nobody at the offices of *The Dial* had to worry over getting Craven, Rosenfeld, or McBride to write about Lachaise or Marin. Through letter and cablegram, Thayer and Watson agreed by the middle of October to choose Sherwood Anderson to give the first Dial Award to; one reason was that although Robinson was fifty-two at the time and therefore not much older than Anderson, who was forty-five, the latter was definitely of the younger group of writers.

Seldes replied to Thayer on October 21 that Anderson had very gratefully accepted the Dial Award, following the Editor's cable—"it so happens that he is very poor this year and appreciates it highly." This was true, but Anderson's appreciation of *The Dial* and its Editor showed a change, as great as it was recent, from his condescension toward the magazine and toward Thayer when Thayer and Watson were just setting up their *Dial* in December 1919. Then Anderson had asked Waldo Frank to stand out for a price of two hundred dollars for each short story he submitted to *The Dial*. He himself, Anderson said, had wired Carl Sandburg to charge a minimum of twenty-five dollars a page for poems and intended to get two hundred dollars for each story. After all, all Thayer had was money, and if he did not surrender the money, he would be "N. G. to anyone." Frank should write something of this sort to Van Wyck Brooks. "I feel like a labor leader," apologized the future recipient of the first Dial Award, "but if you have ever been in the presence of Thayer's interior decorator's soul, you'll understand, old

Brother." [2] But the Editor's interior decorator's soul evidently was not as fully attuned to the expressions of old Brother as it was to those of Anderson, for Frank published in *The Dial* only a few things—for example, an experimental mélange of verse and prose called "Under the Dome" in October 1920 and five years later a short story called "The Spaniard."

To Seldes, Anderson expressed fulsomely his gratitude and pleasure at getting the Dial Award: "there is no other source in America from which such an offer could come that would give me a fraction of the satisfaction I shall get from having it come from the *Dial*. . . . The offer has made me very happy. I hope it will not make me too unbearably chesty." Anderson also expatiated, as Seldes indicated to Thayer, on his current poverty, due "to the general business depression." [3]

Meanwhile, once the selection was agreed upon, Thayer saw to it that suitable appreciations would be written in time for the January 1922 *Dial*. On November 5, Rosenfeld was asked by Seldes and Watson to write the chief appreciation, and they also commissioned a "brief piece by Lovett, chiefly apropos of Anderson's new book containing . . . all the material which we have published of his," such as the title story "The Triumph of the Egg," and the novelette *Out of Nowhere into Nothing*. Seldes also gave assurance that he and the Publisher were giving deep thought to the editorial announcement for the January number, though it had not yet been written. On learning that his Managing Editor had notified the recipient in October, Thayer asked why Anderson had been told so early, and Seldes explained that *The Dial* informed Anderson of the Award in advance because it had to co-operate with Anderson's publisher Benjamin Huebsch with regard to publicity as well as because it wanted very much to know that the potential recipient actually would receive the Dial Award and that he would not be receiving any other award that might be published ahead of the one offered by *The Dial*. Huebsch had pointed out how fatal it would be to the publicity of *The Dial* for the magazine to announce the Award in the week of Christmas or even ten days earlier. As a publisher, he could not wait until the rush of Christmas shopping would be over; moreover, as a result of putting the day of the announcement forward and thus securing the co-operation of Huebsch, *The Dial* was "getting 60,000 circulars on the covers of which in bold type Huebsch says 'including all the works of Sherwood Anderson who has just been announced as the recipient of the Dial's Award' etc." Perhaps Thayer might agree, suggested Seldes, that by the next year *The Dial* should make its announcement in the December issue and cling technically to the phrasing of the original statement that it would pay the recipient of the Dial Award on the first of January of each year.

The announcement, continued Seldes, had had a terrifically good press, especially outside New York. Through his machinations *The New York Times* reported the story of the Award in detail; the Associated Press and the United Press sent it out; and "the 300 literary and exchange editors did their bit, especially some 50 of them" with whom Seldes had managed to establish more or less personal communication. Caught up in the optimism of the moment (December 15) Seldes admitted that he could not tell what "this is going to amount to in the way of subscriptions, which is the ultimate test of publicity," but, then, it had "amounted to an enormous increase in good will toward The Dial on the part of editors and on the part of private citizens." Why, this additional good will had even been responsible for the sending out, by the head of the Vassar Endowment Fund, of a letter "(we wrote it but she signed it) urging every Vassar graduate to subscribe to The Dial and to get 10 other subscriptions in addition." By way of reciprocating, *The Dial* would contribute the regular agent's commission to the Vassar Endowment Fund; and the returns in the first few days of these extracurricular activities were promising. A month later the Editor answered that he was glad Seldes was so much on the job in getting the announcement of Anderson's reception of the Dial Award into the press and that he was glad, too, to learn his Managing Editor had discovered at last one *raison d'être* for the higher education of women.

Unaware of all the editorial agonizing he was causing, Sherwood Anderson wrote to Paul Rosenfeld, apparently in reply to Rosenfeld's telling about the eulogy he had been asked to write: "You will know how I feel about the *Dial* matter. They had told me something about it, gave me to understand I would probably be the man, etc. After all, the *Dial* is the one thing we have. They are sincerely trying for something the rest of us are after also. How could I be anything but pleased and flattered? Also the money will be a big help this year." [4] A couple of months later, having read Rosenfeld's appreciation that would shortly appear in *The Dial* for January 1922,

Anderson reached the limits of his compliments: "The article is very beautiful, Paul, and in it I feel a hammering on and a breaking-down of walls between us, too." It actually gave Anderson, he averred, the warmest feeling of living comradeship he had ever had.[5] Rosenfeld's essay in the January 1922 *Dial* (reprinted in his 1924 collection, *Port of New York*) remains today as an early and distinguished tribute to a novelist who, as the eulogist wrote, "looks like a racing tout and a divine poet, like a movie-actor and a young priest, a business-man, a hayseed, a mama's boy, a satyr, and an old sit-by-the-stove." In his bread-and-butter-note acknowledging the essay, Anderson gladly admitted to Rosenfeld the acuteness of the passages recognizing "my immense debt to the man [Van Wyck] Brooks" and other subtle things: "the escape from the dominance of women and children, the eternal begging of the question, the waiting for life to be lived by someone else to come after you."

The second appreciation that appeared in *The Dial* for January 1922 was a long review by Robert Morss Lovett, "The Promise of Sherwood Anderson"—a quite different affair from Rosenfeld's rhapsody, an analytical appraisal rather than a eulogy. The point made here is that although Anderson had produced three novels, two volumes of short stories, and one of poems or chants, he had not completely subdued his material to form, had not thoroughly penetrated it with interpretation: "It remains recalcitrant and opaque." Yet he had shown progress in his work, and if that work is imbued with a crude realism, perhaps one reason for this quality is that we Americans are a crude people. The chief issue between the critiques by Rosenfeld and Lovett is that the former praised Anderson for his literary experimentalism and saw him as a leader in expressing the new feeling in America, this power of feeling truly, of searching for touch with one's fellows, whereas Lovett coolly and academically held that although it is true Anderson had been influenced by the technical experiments of his predecessors, in so far as he yielded to them he had failed.

"Comment" for the same issue, written by Gilbert Seldes, eschewed discussion of Anderson's work and left that labor to Rosenfeld and Lovett. (At the end of December, Seldes told Thayer that "although . . . I tried to write the stuff, it got nowhere in time to do anything with it except send it to the press.") The Managing Editor confined himself to pointing out again the significance with which the magazine invested the giving of the Dial Award. The generous and encouraging remark made by *The Nation* on the occasion was gratefully quoted: "If THE DIAL's award each year finds an artist so promising [as Sherwood Anderson] and helps assure him a period of leisure for further work it can become a priceless element in American literary life." As the first comment to come to the editors after the appearance of their announcement of the award in the press in the first week of December 1921, they received it hopefully, wanting to believe it summed up the attitude of intelligent Americans to the award. Thus "Comment" editorially acknowledged the enthusiasm with which the announcement had been recognized as "news of high significance by both news and literary editors throughout the country." Seldes went on to contrast the untouched reservoirs of indifference and hostility to any manifestation of the artistic spirit in America to the situation of the artist in a civilized community, in which he was certain of his place, assured, before he uttered his first word, of attention and of intelligent criticism and spared the destructive conflict with things which when they are conquered cannot serve him. The Dial Award was created, then, to bring about an attentive and critical environment in America; if this necessity did not exist, the Award would be an impertinence. Fortunately the task was not hopeless; the actual welcome of the Award itself and of its gift to Sherwood Anderson indicated that there was in America a "reasonably large number of individuals who want the artist to develop freely and who are particularly anxious for him not to develop in relation to the commerce and publicity which are close to being the dominating elements of our artistic life." Finally, said "Comment," the encouragement and increase of that community were the condition of the success of *The Dial*. Optimistically—too optimistically, when one thinks of the comparative neglect by American readers of their most brilliant review—Seldes reported publicly, as he was doing privately to his Editor, on the steady growth of the number of those who were so far from indifferent as to support *The Dial* enthusiastically, practically, and morally: "We think it is because we put into action their own principles and, on their behalf, are asking more of American artists than has been asked, and allowing more."

After the Award to Anderson had been made, on January 15, 1922, when the dust was settling, the Editor said he found Seldes'

Henri de Toulouse-Lautrec *The American Singer*

"Comment" to be unobjectionable—except for a titbit making reference to Mary Colum's piece on Anderson in *The Freeman:* "we refer our readers to a review by Mrs Mary M. Colum in The Freeman of November 30th." In addition, so little of "Comment" devoted to the "Prize" made it the more obvious that *The Dial* should have run Rosenfeld on Anderson as a header. That and Lovett's review also given the place of honor would then perhaps even with so slight a "Comment" have given sufficient emphasis to the first Dial Award. Ezra Pound pronounced the selection of Anderson diplomatic and therefore good, though Pound's admirers were angry, as he himself wrote the Editor from Paris—so said Thayer on New Year's Day 1922. The affair had been only a qualified success, as the Editor saw it. The facts that Seldes planned to run Rosenfeld's essay on Anderson as a header and that the essay had turned up too long and too late to handle except as *The Dial* did, by putting it in the middle of an issue; that Mrs. Colum's piece about Anderson in *The Freeman* was mentioned in "Comment" because it was excellent and because Seldes used it to cite an outsider's opinion about the recipient of the Dial Award; and that two of "Comment's" three pages were about the Award: these the Editor took calmly in his stride—"I appreciate your difficulties with Rosenfeld, but I cannot understand how you trusted him to count the words in his article. For the Charm of Naiveté see the Little Flowers of St. Francis. . . . My reference to the incisive Mrs. Colum was jocular." And with that exchange, extending through most of March, the dust finally did settle on this particular battleground.

The annual task of making future Dial Awards would be much easier for Thayer and Watson and for the staff, too, as they established a pattern out of the initial helter-skelter. Establishing the Award had offered little difficulty; the difficulty had to do with the actual process of giving the Award and of making it public in a manner most satisfactory to the people concerned—the writer, his publisher, and the magazine itself. Until the termination of the Award, which was last given to Kenneth Burke in January 1929, for the year 1928, the Dial Awards originated with Thayer and Watson. During Marianne Moore's term as Editor, they might ask Miss Moore's opinion or approval when a decision had been made, but they made their annual choice entirely independent of her.[6] Besides Anderson and Burke, Dial Awards went to T. S. Eliot (1922), Van Wyck

Brooks (1923), Marianne Moore (1924), E. E. Cummings (1925), William Carlos Williams (1926), and Ezra Pound (1927).

Anyone gifted with hindsight may accuse Gilbert Seldes and *The Dial* of too great generosity of spirit, of naïve kindliness and optimism, as well as an altogether pardonable attack of self-gratulation. The American public supported a nine days' wonder; so long as *The Dial* shocked and amused, they bought it and increased its circulation. When, however, the novelty of its contributions wore thin, *The Dial* no longer could depend on a substantial group of readers. The Dial Award increased the prestige and the prosperity of a Sherwood Anderson or an E. E. Cummings, but neither the prestige nor the circulation of *The Dial* itself was permanently, favorably affected. The undoubted paradox is that *The Dial* had prestige without mass circulation, mass attractiveness. It attracted the few who set the tone of the Twenties without being able to attract the general who sought to exploit that tone. Instead of John Held, *The Dial* published the caricatures of E. E. Cummings; instead of Edna St. Vincent Millay, it published the more private *longueurs* of T. S. Eliot; and instead of Scott Fitzgerald, it published Thomas Mann.

The Dial had its own views about the work that would set the tone of the decade, and it publicized these attitudes through what the staff wrote about this work in the Peacock Folder, the clipsheets, and essays, reviews, and "Comment." From being laughed at, it rose to triumph—admired by the very writers who once had sneered at its inception. And far from being unbearably chesty about its triumph—as Sherwood Anderson feared the news of the Dial Award might make him—*The Dial*, and its staff, remained conscious of its responsibility, of its fallibility in bringing out a periodical that often seemed, to the editors' eyes, filled with irritating small errors and lapses of taste and insight. But these weaknesses are quite minor. Within its self-recognized limitations *The Dial* did triumph; it published the best works of many of the outstanding artists and writers of its day, traditionalists as well as experimentalists, conservatives as well as liberals, George Santayana as well as Bertrand Russell, André Derain as well as Pablo Picasso, T. S. Eliot as well as William Carlos Williams.

By its Editor's insistence on excellence, *The Dial* triumphed. And by its triumph it set a tone, a tone that in important ways *was* the essential, the significant cultural tone of its decade. Inevitably that tone was evinced by an editorial predilection for certain writers and artists and their work. The real distinction of the editorial taste is shown by the consistent attraction *The Dial* had for those writers and artists whose work has transcended, at least thus far, the period. Was there a "Dial group"?

FOUR

The Staff

D URING 1922, Scofield Thayer continued to edit *The Dial* from Europe, mostly from Vienna. Gilbert Seldes continued to act as Managing Editor in New York. And Dr. James Sibley Watson continued with his duties as Publisher, both in New York and in Europe, where he traveled with his family for the summer and consulted with his partner.

Thayer's energy was no longer taxed so greatly by the technical problems of producing a review, although to be sure he directed and criticized each issue of the monthly *Dial* in pungent, indeed sometimes acrid, detail. But primarily Scofield Thayer had begun collecting pictures and objects to be reproduced in successive issues of his review and eventually in a great folio of photographic and color reproductions, *Living Art*. He was also continuing to meet writers and artists and to commission their work for *The Dial*. By now the Editor could relax in the rare and solid pleasure of contemplating the triumph he had created, a periodical awaited with as evident impatience in London and Vienna each month as it was in the more impressionable cities of America. Prince Kartono of Java, the Editor told Seldes, "adored" *The Dial*, and the royal imps thereabouts were suckled on it. Such was the international renown of the review and its Editor that the French government without permission appropriated his name as a sponsor of its current Molière Festival. Amy Lowell thought the advertisements in *The Dial* so charming that had she not already been a subscriber she would have instantly become one. And Max Beerbohm—while admitting that as his words were few and chosen with care, he could not afford to dispose of them at the rate of two cents apiece—wrote the Editor that *The Dial* was a review he greatly admired. (Beerbohm's sole contribution, "T. Fenning Dodsworth," appeared in the August 1921 *Dial*.)

On January 9, 1923, Gilbert Seldes followed the Editor's lead and sailed on the *Manchuria* for England. Behind him at the office in New York he left Kenneth Burke to manage *The Dial* for the next several months. If it was a departure that meant leaving behind the fairly regular schedule of work on the review each day from nine to five, it was a departure that also meant leaving a job with, for so young a man, a remarkable amount of independence. Having begun working for Thayer and Watson in 1920, Seldes was not quite thirty when he went abroad in 1923. Although he was not consulted much about the works of art reproduced in the review and never accepted fiction or major essays without submitting them first to Thayer or Watson, he had been pretty much on his own with regard to assigning and accepting book reviews and handling the regular departments and entirely on his own with regard to writing his reviews and "The Theatre." Seldes and his editorial assistant—Sophie Wittenberg or Kenneth Burke, as the case might be—read most of the proof aloud at their facing and contiguous desks, each of them sitting beside a window, with to one side a long table loaded with review copies of books. In her essay, "THE DIAL: A Retrospect," Marianne Moore described "the compacted pleasantness of those days at 152 West Thirteenth Street" in that "three-story brick building with carpeted stairs, fireplace and white-mantelpiece rooms," its business office in the first-story front parlor with "in gold-leaf block letters, THE DIAL, on the windows to the right of the brownstone steps leading to the front door." She recalled the flower-crier in summer "with his slowly moving wagon of pansies, petunias, ageratum," the man "with straw-*ber*-ies for sale," and a "certain fisherman with pushcart-scales, and staccato refrain so unvaryingly imperative, summer or winter, that Kenneth Burke's parenthetic remark comes back to me—'I think if he stopped to sell a fish my heart would skip a beat.' "[1] It was a pleasant environment for an ambitious young writer and editor, even at the unassuming fifty dollars a week that was Gilbert Seldes' pay in those days at *The Dial*.

Soon after the Managing Editor had made his departure, Kenneth Burke wrote him a letter about the situation at the review. He had talked to the doctor about his career and as a result was settled at the magazine until the first of October. Seldes had spoken of coming back by the end of July. Things had not yet gone to pot, and the staff was managing to keep the magazine reasonably efficient (even the sun, Seldes must realize, had fallen down four per cent recently), and there had been no howling messes to date, although Thayer got rather bitter now and then. Such information Burke relayed thinking it of some value in determining Seldes' leave. If he returned, Burke would surely disappear one week a month; if not, Burke intended to try disappearing even so. Fortunately, said Burke, he was through with Bayard Q. Morgan's translation of Hauptmann's *Der Ketzer von Soana* as *The Heretic of Soana*, serialized in *The Dial* in April, May, and June, and was a bit less anguished; but he had been dreadfully aged and sobered by the experience. He should have liked to send the manuscript to Ernest Boyd, one of the more unrelenting critics of *The Dial*, for he was sure there was not a single spot in it where the translator varied from the German by a hair's-breadth.

For the remainder of 1923, Gilbert Seldes helped Scofield Thayer assemble the materials of *Living Art* and wrote his most popular book, *The Seven Lively Arts*. Back in New York the staff followed the less exciting but no less arduous routine of bringing out the monthly numbers in the absence of Editor, Managing Editor, and, occasionally, Publisher. As aids Kenneth Burke had Sophie Wittenberg (then newly married to Lewis Mumford), some secretarial help, and the contributions of the three editor-critics. This situation held until Scofield Thayer's return to New York in July 1923. In September Seldes returned to New York, but although by October Kenneth Burke was asking him to assume some of the editorial burdens, Seldes refused to come back to the review except each day after midday. He resumed his duties as writer of "The Theatre" but not as Managing Editor. Burke too departed— though his departure was to prove temporary—and only Sophie Wittenberg remained as an editorial assistant. Gilbert Seldes remained nominally the Managing Editor through the December issue. He had been Associate Editor, under Stewart Mitchell, from February until December 1920; then he had been "Associate" under Thayer; and, beginning with the issue for April 1921, he had been Managing Editor. Even so, he had not finished his association with the magazine.

For the rest of 1923, *The Dial* lacked a managing editor. Then the incredible happened: Alyse Gregory, just recently married to another *Dial* contributor, the young British writer Llewelyn Powys, allowed herself to be persuaded by the Editor, now returned from abroad, and by Sibley Watson, to assume the task of Managing Editor of *The Dial*. The invitation was a repetition of one that Thayer had made from Vienna in a letter to Alyse Gregory of October 26, 1922.

Thayer repeated the invitation in person when shortly after his return from two years in Europe, he and James Sibley Watson called on Alyse Gregory to try once again to persuade her to take over the management of *The Dial*, at a salary of seventy-five dollars a week. She did not say she would not consent to so flattering an offer as theirs, which was, she later admitted, equivalent to saying she would. No sooner was it known that she was to become the Managing Editor of *The Dial* than the world surrounding her appeared to undergo a singular transformation. Young men whose names she could hardly recall would take off their hats in the street with a wide sweep and a low bow. Invitations to parties were continually arriving. Amy Lowell wrote from her home in Concord asking the new staff member of *The Dial* to dine with her when she visited New York. And Scofield Thayer brought Marianne Moore, a poet very different from Amy Lowell, to have tea in his new Managing Editor's rooms at 4 Patchin Place.[2]

Alyse Gregory's assistants during her term as Managing Editor of *The Dial* were Sophie Wittenberg and the soon-returned Kenneth Burke. After Samuel Craig left his position as Secretary-Treasurer of the Dial Publishing Company, at the end of 1923, Lincoln MacVeagh took the post, with Mrs. H. B. Eveline as a business manager for the review. Prior to Craig there had been two other Secretary-Treasurers, as the business managers were more formally called: W. B. Marsh for the first four months of 1920; and Henry W. Toll until Craig's advent at the end of 1920.

MacVeagh continued to hold his post with the Dial Publishing Company until the end; however, he devoted his energies primarily to the direction of the Dial Press from its inception in January 1924. Although the Dial Press occupied rooms in the same brownstone house with the Dial Publishing Company and shared certain officers and stockholders, the two firms were independent of one another. While some of the contributors to *The Dial*, such as Marianne Moore, E. E. Cummings, and Paul Rosenfeld, were published by Lincoln MacVeagh, and while in 1924 MacVeagh brought out an anthology of *Stories from The Dial*, the policies of *The Dial* did not necessarily coincide with those of the Dial Press. Not everybody took proper notice of these distinctions. In *The Independent*, Ernest Boyd, as Scofield Thayer reported to Alyse Gregory in September 1924, unkindly wrote that "although associated, more or less, with The Dial, this firm evidently has too much sense to do business with the kind of literature that association might suggest."

Various memoirs of the Twenties have described both Scofield Thayer and James Sibley Watson in the middle years of the decade, when it seemed that *The Dial* could do no wrong so long as it shocked the middle class. Few people knew Scofield Thayer as intimately as his new Managing Editor, Alyse Gregory, and both she and her husband, Llewelyn Powys, fortunately have left sketches of the two young men who directed *The Dial*. In *The Day Is Gone*, Alyse Gregory observed that in Thayer the monk and the aesthete joined hands, as one of those men the key to whose nature is so obscurely hidden that they alienate people because they remain outside their understanding. "Slender of build, swift of movement, always strikingly pale, with coal-black hair, black eyes veiled and flashing, and lips that curved like those of Lord Byron"—a trait portrayed by Adolf Dehn in a *Dial* caricature of Thayer entitled *Le Byron de nos jours*—"he seemed to many the embodiment of the aesthete with overrefined tastes and sensibilities. This was far from the case. Art and letters he pursued, but it was with a purpose so elevated and so impassioned that he remained insulated from the ironical comments about him. . . . He had . . . a most gentle heart. He administered his wealth largely as a trust, supporting or helping to support many young writers and artists. He dressed with a considered simplicity, pleased to be seen in a suit of clothes he had worn since his university days. What were taken for affectations were mannerisms indigenous to his character. His irony, though as swift as Randolph's"—an allusion to the mutual friend who introduced Thayer to Miss Gregory, Randolph Bourne—"was seldom as light. He was ice on the surface and molten lava underneath." [3] Thayer himself considered Alyse Gregory as one of his three closest friends, along with Robert von Erdberg and Raymond Mortimer.

Miss Gregory's picture of the second of "these two delightful and distinguished young men" emphasizes his modesty and silence: "I would sometimes catch sidelong glances from the large, expressive eyes of Dr. Watson—the most expressive eyes I have ever encountered. He was tall and strikingly good-looking, with fair hair, a fair mustache, and unusually beautiful hands. But perhaps the most unusual thing about him was the quality of his silence, a silence so charged with perception, so poised on intensity, so subtly and evasively provocative that it was difficult to tell whether it was offered as a lure to oneself or constituted his own sole means of escape." [4] And she contrasted Thayer and Watson as they appeared in the fall of 1923, in her apartment, asking her to come to *The Dial*, seated side by side on her divan, one so dark and erect, the other so fair and withdrawn.

Llewelyn Powys agreed with his wife that to see Sibley Watson and Scofield Thayer together was something to remember. It would have required a Henry James, Powys wrote in his memoir of 1927, *The Verdict of Bridlegoose*, to tabulate and record each interesting tarot card of this astounding association. And yet these two millionaires, in the face of the crass stupidity of the Philistine world, and in the face of the sneering hostility of a score of pseudoliterary cliques, managed to produce in America a review that without doubt was "the most distinguished of its kind to appear in the English language since the publication of the *Yellow Book*." Powys exclaimed over how "quaint" it was to see Thayer and Watson working together for the aesthetic enlightenment of the Western world. "It was like seeing a proud, self-willed, bull-calf bison, fed on nothing but golden oats, yoked to the plough with a dainty, fetlocked, dapple-grey unicorn, who would, an' he could, step delicately over the traces and scamper to the edge of the prairie, where, under the protective colouring of a grove of pale wattle trees, he might be lost to the view of the world." Rather unfairly, perhaps, Powys suggested a certain contrast in the patronage as well as the tastes of Thayer and Watson: "The taste of Scofield Thayer was the austere aristocratic taste of a Roman noble, of a Roman connoisseur, who has filled his marble hall with the work of his Greek slaves; while the Doctor's taste was that of a super-subtle Nicodemus, who had a mania for collecting at night, by proxy, images of unknown gods, put together by indigent artists whose lack of rice was never for long out of the mind of this generous young man." [5]

But Scofield Thayer's "Roman" manner, or what appeared to be his Roman manner to Llewelyn Powys, disguised, as Alyse Gregory well knew, a gentle heart and a generous purse. An anecdote related by Miss Gregory illustrates how easily contributors to *The Dial* received an erroneous impression of the Editor. It has to do with the well-known Dial dinners, which beginning in December 1923 and running into the latter part of April 1924, and held for a similar portion of the season in 1924–25, took place weekday evenings when the Editor was in town. Typically, Scofield Thayer wrote Gilbert Seldes on December 8, 1924, that "We begin the Dial dinners this evening, and are sorry you are not to be with us," as Seldes and his wife were then in Palm Beach. "For your information," the Editor added, "I mentioned that, as the cook at the Dial is no longer identical with my valet, this year, instead of telephoning to my apartment when coming to dinner, one will telephone to the Dial where the telephone girl will have a pad ready to take down the names of those guests who are coming and to inquire whether they are bringing guests or not. And one should telephone to the Dial between the hours of nine and three. After three o'clock it will be too late to arrange for a place at the table, for the cook will leave at that hour to do his buying. Dinner is, as last year, at six-thirty every evening except Saturday and Sunday." The top floor of the house in which *The Dial* had its offices was thus given over to a dining room where the contributors could meet with the Editor for a meal when they pleased and where authors and artists visiting New York were entertained for dinner.

Sibley Watson was apt to be absent on these occasions, and Scofield Thayer would preside at the head of the table, communicating by his air of frozen civility a feeling of constraint. When Alyse Gregory remonstrated with him once, saying she feared he had been bored, "Not bored, in torture," was his reply. Yet Thayer could be the most delightful, and certainly the most brilliant, of companions. He had so high a standard and so imperious a manner that at first sound of his voice everyone would stand at attention, "as if Tiberius himself had set foot on the stair"—though all were fond of him, Miss Gregory added. And she recalled Thayer's satisfaction when the staff at *The Dial* received a cable from Hugo von Hofmannsthal about the placing of a comma. "How we resemble one another!" said the Editor.[6] The imperious, Roman manner was, then, armor to conceal diffidence in casual society rather than boredom.

Marianne Moore, too, expressed something of the inner truth about the two backers of *The Dial:* "Above all, for an inflexible morality against 'the nearly good'; for a non-exploiting helpfulness to art and the artist, for living the doctrine that 'a love of letters knows no frontiers,' Scofield Thayer and Dr. Watson are the indestructible symbol." Miss Moore singled out two aspects of *The Dial* for special praise in this connection—the support by Thayer and Watson of James Joyce when *The Little Review* was censored for publishing *Ulysses,* and their insistence that the Dial Award was not a prize, not something competed for but something given to afford the recipient an opportunity to do what he wished and out of that to enrich and develop his work. Miss Moore testified that never was a gift more complete and without victimizing involvements. With characteristic modesty she felt that "the devisers of the organization" could do better than herself and the other staff members what they were trying to do and that those who had worked for *The Dial* would "ever feel their strength of purpose toward straightness, spontaneity, and usefulness." [7]

Both Scofield Thayer and James Sibley Watson inspired an extraordinary loyalty from the staff of *The Dial* and from most of the contributors to the review; the comment by Miss Moore is typical. But what also was typical was the opposition to *The Dial* that came from ideologically committed groups within the New Movement and from the people outside the New Movement and opposed to it for various reasons. It is true that the staff of *The Dial* were loyal, but it is true, too, that they were few. Their loyalty met the opposition of the small groups that published little magazines such as *Secession* and of the self-styled conservatives who told reporters that *The Dial* was "an intellectual sewer." *The Dial* never was able to establish a *modus vivendi* for itself, so strong was the opposition toward it; and, fortuitously or not, this opposition overwhelmingly combined with a large public indifference not toward the experimentalism that received the lion's share of publicity but rather toward the insistence on formal excellence in the arts that *The Dial* stood for.

Lincoln MacVeagh told Scofield Thayer and Sibley Watson early in 1924 that by the end of the year the deficit of *The Dial* might be reduced to forty thousand dollars a year. This did happen but not because the review benefited from higher revenues growing out of greater circulation and increased advertising, that is to say, from a wider public acceptance. Still, the backers apparently were not immediately concerned about the finances of *The Dial* for most of 1924. Sibley Watson went West for the summer, taking Llewelyn Powys with him on that expedition into the Rocky Mountains described in Powys' *The Verdict of Bridlegoose*.

Out West Powys experienced a hemorrhage from the consumption from which he suffered, and one result of this fearful episode was that Alyse and Llewelyn Powys moved from Greenwich Village to Montoma in Ulster County in upstate New York, near Woodstock, to live in the countryside and there hopefully to procure the fresh milk and eggs he needed. Their only neighbors besides the farm people of the district were the sculptor Alfeo Faggi and his wife. Malcolm Cowley [8] describes that countryside out from New York City, where old farmhouses might be without conveniences but were easy to find and rented for ten dollars a month. In that farming area of New Jersey or upstate New York or Connecticut, the writer or artist could grow his own vegetables, make his own cider, dress cheaply in denim or khaki, and travel the roads on foot or in the oldest Model T that would hold together. Also, he could pick his own jobs, take his time over them, do his best work, and live as it were on a private island—an island the opposite of that where Greenwich Village is. It was from this milieu that Alyse Gregory commuted when she worked as Managing Editor of *The Dial*.

Meanwhile, the Editor himself was as peripatetic as his partner. He spent the summer of 1924 mostly in Edgartown, on Martha's Vineyard. In December Thayer returned to New York; then in a few weeks he was off for Bermuda; then back to New York. Writing from Bermuda on New Year's Day of 1925, Scofield Thayer asked his Managing Editor: "Do you realize that in the January 1925 number we have fewer pages of paid advertising than ever before since we took over The Dial? This even though we now have (at least so a Miss Gregory, late of New York, informed me) a modicum of prestige and several times the number of subscribers we had when we took over The Dial? I cannot understand it. Can you? Despite The American Mercury and the rest of the vulgar monthly drool." He went on to point out that the advertising manager of *The Dial* was then leaving the staff and suggested that Alyse Gregory try to get some impression of the competence of the remaining business staff of the review. Thayer added, "In the old days Johnson never had a special advertising manager. The Business Manager looked after the advertising in his odd moments. And although we were losing advertising constantly as being thought pro-German, nevertheless we had more advertising than we now have." Thayer directed, with his usual generosity toward her, that Alyse Gregory not concern herself with the advertising of *The Dial* until Llewelyn Powys had recovered and that she arrange to be in New York for her monthly sojourn as soon after the Editor's return as fitted with her schedule and that of *The Dial* in general.

Veering to another delicate problem, Thayer admitted that he must give way to Watson now and then, although, "looking over The Dial and considering my years with it, I agree with my friend Cuthbert Wright that the most remarkable thing about it is the fact that, although I am the Editor of it, no one who knew me would guess this fact. This is of course attributable to many things, but chiefly to Watson's constant and subterranean pull to the left. I myself detest all Modern Art. In particular I detest Paul Rosenfeld, who seems to me more and more obviously the Compleat American Asse." Yet in the same letter, disenchanted as he was with Modern Art, the Editor could turn his wit against himself. Noting that a manuscript by D. H. Lawrence had arrived—probably not *The Woman Who Rode Away*, which *The Dial* serialized in July and August 1925, but one the review rejected—and that Miss Parker, his personal secretary, had read it to him, Thayer explained, "I am getting too old to read Lawrence myself."

Meantime the Managing Editor was having difficulties in taking care of her ailing husband and at the same time managing *The Dial*. With both Thayer and Watson away from the review, she could not spare the time needed to direct it suitably. She made the trip from Montoma to Greenwich Village to attend to the business of *The Dial* as seldom as she could, preferably but once a month. Even so the drain on her strength was too great. Relations between Marianne Moore and Alyse Gregory were especially cordial, and on hearing of Miss Gregory's problem, Miss Moore offered assistance to Alyse Gregory as early as August 15, 1924, hoping she could be useful in some way, for at any time, it would be the greatest kindness to be allowed to serve *The Dial*—in any way, the more mundane the better. She announced herself as free on Monday, Tuesday, and Friday mornings and Wednesday, Thursday, and Saturday afternoons and wondered whether there might be something she could do at the Dial office in the morning so that Alyse Gregory need not come to town so early. Gratefully as Miss Moore's suggestion was received at *The Dial*, the crisis had not yet reached its breaking point, and she did not yet come to the review. In this difficulty, Kenneth Burke returned to *The Dial;* he too lived in the country, in New Jersey, but he arranged to stay in the city two or three nights a week in order to look after the affairs of the review, and from this time Burke worked full-time for *The Dial*.

Marianne Moore's offer was not forgotten, however, by Thayer, Watson, and Miss Gregory. Its generosity was much appreciated. The Dial Award for 1924 may have been an expression of their regard. The two donors selected Marianne Moore for the Award, which the Editor directed must be announced to the staff in November 1924, to the poet about the first of December, and to the press just before Christmas, when the January 1925 *Dial* appeared on newsstands and to its subscribers. A month before Christmas the Editor wrote Sophie Wittenberg that the January number, announcing Marianne Moore's selection as recipient for the Dial Award for 1924 was "going to be more a Moore number than any other January number has been an Anderson or an Eliot or a Brooks number. And this is, at last, as it should be. Do not, however, forget, that Miss Moore does not herself know what she is in for."

Being informed that *The Dial* would welcome a poem by her in the event of Glenway Wescott's "review" of *Observations*—actually this was the *éloge* on the occasion of the Dial Award—Marianne Moore unsuspectingly submitted "The Monkey Puzzler" to appear in the January 1925 issue of *The Dial*. When she was sent a copy of the Award number, the poet wrote Thayer on December 13, 1924, that his courage and kindness, and her own amazement in *The Dial*'s selection, as it appeared in the announcement she had just received, robbed her of words. The question was whether she dared permit the Editor to assume such championship. When she thought of others being as amazed as herself, she trembled at the fact of *The Dial*'s martial fearlessness. Thayer's most austere and sensitive manner of writing—a gift indeed!—would in a measure blunt the reader's resentment of the unexpectedness of Miss Moore as the recipient of the Dial Award.

Miss Moore's reception of the Dial Award for 1924 coincided with the sudden need by *The Dial* of a new editorial assistant. Llewelyn Powys told Gertrude Powys (March 10, 1925): "It's disgraceful of me to have persuaded Alyse to give up *The Dial*. But I WANT TO COME HOME." [9] By February 1925 Alyse Gregory had resigned as Managing Editor. Van Wyck Brooks recently has said that in 1925 Thayer offered the editorship of *The Dial* to him. No longer interested in editing a magazine, and at the beginning of a serious nervous breakdown, Brooks refused and agreed to keep silence about Thayer's apparently verbal offer. Watson was not informed,[10] though in March 1923 he had suggested to Thayer that Brooks might be their Strong Man, and the negotiations for a successor to Miss Gregory turned in another direction. Alyse Gregory agreed on February 13 to remain as a sort of "privileged semi-present" Managing Editor, when Marianne Moore would come to *The Dial* in a position technically inferior to that of herself, in order that someone with taste, discretion, and intelligence, not to mention conscientiousness, might be in charge of the office during working hours. This, of course, was far different from doing volunteer chores for *The Dial*, but at the continued insistence of Scofield Thayer and Dr. Watson, on March 9 Miss Moore finally agreed to work for them beginning Monday, April 27, 1925. She would leave her position at the Hudson Park Branch of the New York Public Library to come to work for *The Dial*, having been persuaded by her mother and her brother to take the position with the distinct understanding that, no matter what happened, she would never have to come to the Dial offices in the afternoon and that her work would be over by one o'clock. "Miss Moore," wrote the Editor on February 13 to Alyse Gregory, "legitimately, in my opinion, requires this ruling because she finds that she must lie down for an hour after luncheon, and because she finds that she gets no literary work done unless she has the rest of the day after this nap uninterrupted."

Ellen Thayer, Scofield Thayer's cousin and friend, also agreed about this time to come to *The Dial* to take the place of Sophie Wittenberg. Miss Thayer was briefly at the Dial offices in the last week of March 1925, learning about her new post from Alyse Gregory and Sophie Wittenberg prior to a summer trip to Europe; after this she would return to *The Dial* to work with Marianne Moore. The resignation of Sophie Wittenberg and the appointment of Ellen Thayer the Editor announced in "Notes on Contributors" for May 1925. The major announcement of a triple change, he told Alyse Gregory on March 12, would come with the following issue, that for June: "I intend to announce your resignation and my half-resignation and Miss Moore's appointment as Acting Editor in the June issue, but to have your name as usual and not Miss Moore's on the inside cover of that issue, inasmuch as you and I will have prepared it before the coming of Miss Moore. I much prefer that until the June issue appears no one should know that you are leaving and that I am half-leaving and that Miss Moore is coming. I have told no one but Miss Moore and the one or two other people here, and they are pledged to secrecy. Could you also keep it secret." "Here" referred to New York, but Scofield Thayer remained in the city only a few months before leaving *The Dial* once for all. After a short stay in Edgartown, he returned to New York and suddenly made, on July 22, the final decision to go abroad as soon as possible. He would not return again to the review he had so courageously founded and so munificently supported, with his friend Sibley Watson.

Scofield Thayer left *The Dial* intending to devote his time to his writing. In this course he had received oblique encouragement from those who had admired his "Comment"—Sibley Watson, Gilbert Seldes, Henry McBride, Llewelyn Powys, and others. From Marianne Moore and Alyse Gregory, however, he had received encouragement more direct. Alyse Gregory was sorry that *The Dial* took all the Editor's time. That was most distressing. But the "Comment," she asserted in a letter of November 14, 1924, had lasting value and was not time lost; she was sure that in the year 2024 many a person would enquire for just those especial bound volumes containing those Comments in which Thayer's worried nerves had tattooed such lasting images. Adding to her previous praise of the Editor's most austere and sensitive manner of writing, Marianne Moore in another letter (March 22, 1925) told him that his overwhelmingly dextrous comment in which, as Georg Brandes would say, the imagination of the poet and the logic of the jurist were combined, was amazing. Before she had known of his own poems, she had been on the point of saying, at one time, that his comment was much more nearly poetry than anything of hers upon which he had been commenting. Looking to the future, when she would be at *The Dial* and the Editor would be at his leisure, Miss Moore felt a freedom in his behalf that must be a hundredfold welcome to the Editor, in the prospect of his soon having leisure to write upon themes uniquely his own. Her brother, she concluded, felt Thayer's cumulative comment to be a miracle of dynamic creation.

Miss Moore's praise was evoked by the four consecutive months of "Comment" that Scofield Thayer devoted to a critique of her poetry. The "Announcement" that appeared in the January 1925 number of *The Dial* was of course a more general assessment of the work of Miss Moore as worthy of one who seemed to *The Dial* "so incomparably, since the death of Emily Dickinson, America's most distinguished poetess," yet a poetess hitherto meagerly relished and signally unacclaimed. The "Comment" for February, March, and April kept alight "our beacon for Miss Marianne Moore," analyzing the maneuvers of her intellect and the graces of her style. The three months of "Comment," taken together, served "by way of a back-stoop *éloge* upon the literary activities of the recipient of our Annual Award," as one of those poetesses "who have 'Ransacked the ages' and 'spoiled the climes' " that they may tender their readers the fruits of their learned imaginations.

It was on the wave of this acclaim that Marianne Moore arrived at *The Dial* late in the spring of 1925, to enable Scofield Thayer to write upon the themes that were uniquely his own. Several poems and a "Berlin Letter" appeared in the year or more following the Editor's resignation. The authors of *The Little Magazine* [11] state that Scofield Thayer's "estimable verse" in 1925 was about to be published in book form but unfortunately never appeared; but it is doubtful that this was the case, as of Thayer's twenty-two signed poems in *The Dial*, only six were published in 1925. His first signed poem, "Counsel to a Young Man," appeared in the July 1925 number, after he had announced his resignation, and his last, "Wherefore," appeared in the October 1927 number. There are one or two casual references to an autobiography under way, but no volume of memoirs or of verse ever appeared. The literary remains of Scofield Thayer rest in the pages of his *Dial*.

A more public, and probably a more unexpected, tribute to the accomplishment of *The Dial* and its Editor was paid that spring of 1925 by *The Harvard Advocate* in its annual parody number, which burlesqued *The Dial*. Having served on the *Harvard Monthly* and having written for it, Scofield Thayer must have been entertained all the more by the dreadful jocularity of the *Advocate*. As with most such undergraduate efforts, the idea and the page of contents proved more amusing than the details of the issue: O. O. Goings contributed "Three Poems"; T. S. Tellalot was represented by "Portrait of an Ex-Lady"; and there were the writings of Oneway Waistcoat, and Marianne Most, P. Moron (who wrote the "Paris Letter"), E. Monkey-Stilson, Jr., Henry O'Slide, and Rosy Rusinblume. Possibly the most interesting aspect of this parody of *The Dial* is its evidence that the review had attained the kind of fashionable renown that demands the burlesque of the original; but there was no great amount of philistinism in the *Advocate*'s parody. Indeed, the President of the Board of Editors of that year's *Advocate*, a youthful Mr. W. D. Edmonds, Jr., '26, later appeared in *The Dial* with a more serious contribution, when his regional story "The Swamper" was published in March 1928. This must have been among Walter D. Edmonds's earliest pieces of fiction to receive recognition, as the March 1928 "Notes on Contributors" stated that he had contributed stories to *Scribner's* and to *The Atlantic Monthly*. There is irony in the imitation of *The Dial*, as the chief emblem of the movement of the Twenties, by literary undergraduates of the leading American college at the very time when the two editors of *The Dial*, who had brought the review to such a peak of imitable excellence, were resigning from their duties.

In place of the usual "Comment" for June 1925 appeared the Editor's final editorial, an "Announcement" of his resignation as well as that of Alyse Gregory and of the appointment of an Acting Editor. The "Announcement" also was by way of being an apologia for *The Dial* and its accomplishment. Noting that with the current issue of *The Dial* the eleventh volume of the monthly review was brought to completion, Thayer went on to paraphrase what he had written at the outset of his venture with Sibley Watson and to canvas what he and Dr. Watson had accomplished. Their joint intention had been that of establishing in America a monthly magazine that should be devoted exclusively, and in the most general sense, to art and letters. In starting the monthly *Dial*, the two directors had in mind, said the Editor, no literary or artistic propaganda, no dependence upon an aesthetic system of their own or others' devising to guide them in selecting what should be the contents of their review: "We did not, and do not, deem that it is feasible, in aesthetic matters, to judge by reference to any detailed theoretic code." In taking over *The Dial*, Thayer and Watson set out together from the mere recognition, which they shared, of the absence of any regular publication much interested in bringing out the sort of writing they liked to read and the sort of pictures they liked to see. They believed their tastes to be superior, and their consequent inability to take satisfaction in the periodical provender so abundantly tendered them was not due to any personal shortcomings. So it had seemed worthwhile to set up a journal where they and others of their way of feeling and of thinking could sit at ease and perhaps even encounter moments of delight. Then, too, they knew people whose work was not getting published and whose work they thought the public should at least have a chance at. As obvious corollary, they thought these people entitled to the support *The Dial* could give them.

Thayer admitted that he had previously written all this in different words and in editorial comment as well as in *Dial* advertisements. He had resumed it, he said, in this "Announcement," because a change, though in this instance an inessential change, was to take place in the direction of *The Dial*, beginning with the next issue. The Editor next paid generous tribute to the work of the staff of *The Dial*, especially important because of the kind of periodical it was: "The fact that Dr Watson and I were possessed of no fast aesthetic dogma made the personality of those members of the DIAL staff who were to pass upon manuscript and pictures the decisive factor in the contents and, indeed, in the whole life of the magazine." On the occasion of his withdrawal from the responsibility, shared with Sibley Watson, of examining and of choosing manuscripts and pictures for *The Dial*, Scofield Thayer gave the record of this aspect of its direction. For most of the five and a half years of their joint control, both he and Sibley Watson had alone been responsible for the contents. Stewart Mitchell, when he had been Managing Editor in 1920, had shared this crucial work, and so had Alyse Gregory for the previous year and a half; Gilbert Seldes as Managing Editor had not, however, thus shared "except as good counsellor."

The "Announcement" concluded with the naming of Scofield Thayer's successor and a brief indication of her responsibilities. With the resignation of Alyse Gregory, to accompany her husband to live in England, and with the Editor also leaving America for an indefinite period to seek a little leisure to write for *The Dial*, he and Sibley Watson found it necessary to appoint, for the time of the Editor's absence, what they had decided to call an Acting Editor. The Acting Editor would include among her duties, in addition to those of Managing Editor, many hitherto belonging to the Editor himself. In particular, she would be associated with Dr. Watson in determining the contents of *The Dial*. This Acting Editor was Miss Marianne Moore, and because the Editor felt so much sympathy with the work and with the point of view of Miss Moore, he professed not to regard this change in the direction of *The Dial*, howsoever at the core, as requiring the use of the word *essential*. Thayer announced also that for the rest of 1925 he intended to retain control of the pictures in *The Dial*, with Dr. Watson, but that afterward Miss Moore would take his place. The choice of the colored frontispieces (which he would still be able to supervise from Central Europe, though Thayer did not say so here), the determination of the Dial Award, and any appointment to regular collaboration in *The Dial* (and here Thayer announced Maxim Gorki as the Russian Correspondent), these and many other such less detailed matters would continue to be referred to Sibley Watson and himself.

Behind this dignified leave-taking announced in measured terms was a weariness with *The Dial*. While neither Scofield Thayer nor James Sibley Watson seems to have considered seriously during this period withdrawing the subsidy that made the review possible, both men seem to have desired less active personal participation in the direction of *The Dial*. At times in October 1924, Alyse Gregory was not able to reach Watson because she did not know where he was residing; and, clearly, Scofield Thayer had wanted for almost a year to give over his editorial responsibilities in order that he might find time for his own writing. Both men had done about as much as they could with *The Dial*. *Living Art* had not received the reception that would have encouraged a series of similar folios and that might have resulted in a substantial lessening in the subsidy needed to publish the review. True, out in Michigan the "very nice and genuine" Constance Rourke subscribed to *The Dial* for its pictures even more than for its words. She told Alyse Gregory that she could not really express how much *The Dial* meant to her in Michigan and that while the literature in it meant a great deal, the pictures had meant even more. But the advertisers who might have bailed out *The Dial* did not agree with Miss Rourke. As the Editor reminded Alyse Gregory (September 29, 1924) apropos of paying Alfeo Faggi for some photographs of his sculptures, *The Dial* published reproductions of works of art at great expense to itself. All the people who had considered *The Dial* from a business point of view had advised its backers to omit pictures from the issues. "There is not the slightest doubt," he added, "that by doing so we could double its circulation and double its advertising and so make up half our deficit within a year, and probably do better than that. We are running these pictures at a cost of twenty to forty thousand dollars a year for the sake of such artists as Faggi. It is only fair that the artists should bear some minute percentage of the loss incurred by ourselves in helping them. It would seem absurd to pay them for the privilege of spending twenty to forty thousand dollars a year on them." Under these circumstances, with the directors adamant about the appearance of pictures in their review, circulation decreased. By November 1925, only ten thousand copies of *The Dial* were being printed monthly. As for advertising, the kind *The Dial* concocted seemed to do little good, and Sibley Watson wondered aloud why *The Dial* had to advertise at all.

Scofield Thayer still entertained notions of change for *The Dial* as late as the fall of 1924. He thought it would be amusing to run one month in place of "Comment" a section entitled "Americana," which might bear on the cover, in the column of authors' names, the words *Durchschnitt Americans*, if only for the sake of including Nathan and Mencken where they belonged. "You know of course," he wrote Alyse Gregory (October 8, 1924), "that they run such a pair of pages every month in The American Mercury, quite innocent that they themselves belong in these pages. I am therefore collecting prize asininities from the pens of our countrymen." Such items might be from the press or from books. The Editor asked Alyse and Llewelyn Powys to keep their eyes open for such anfractuosities of the indigenous character as might crop up. He had not yet found the right words from either Nathan or Mencken. "Mum is the word: it is essential that nobody except you and Llewelyn and Miss Parker and myself should know anything about this until the matter is to pass into the printer's hands. Anyhow I may not have my pages appropriately filled for several months." Thayer collected materials toward a department of "Americana," which repose in the Dial papers, but the department itself never eventuated. The fact that "Americana" was not carried through meant that *The Dial* had hardened in its mold. Five years earlier the directors had been willing to risk the experiment of "Modern Forms" and had been equally willing to drop the department after six months.

There was thus a certain weariness with *The Dial*, by the middle of 1925, on the part of its two directors; also they had interests besides *The Dial*, interests increasingly encroaching on the time once given to the review. Not only did Scofield Thayer leave his post because he wanted the leisure for writing for *The Dial;* in 1925 Dr. James Sibley Watson moved permanently to Rochester and there became interested in experimental films in the latter Twenties and eventually in radiology. Dr. Watson retained his position as Publisher of The Dial Publishing Company to the end; but on July 22, 1925, Scofield Thayer told Alyse Gregory that he had determined to go to Europe and to sever his connection with his review:

> The fact that the Benedick and the adjoining buildings have been sold to the New York University, which is going to put up a new large building there, and that I have to begin next week to dismantle my apartment, has made it the easier for me to decide definitely to resign my editorship at The Dial—in the December number of this year. The fact that I am resigning is no longer a secret and will be announced in the December number. I am severing all connections with The Dial. I shall continue merely a stock holder who may occasionally contribute to the paper's financial support. I desire that I may have as few distractions from my writing as possible during the years I now hope for in Europe. . . . Miss Moore recently had me out to luncheon to persuade me to make my home in Edgartown rather than in Europe. She based her argument largely upon the fact that I was not "spiritually an expatriate." By the end of a two hours' conversation she knew me better and said, rather sadly, "I am afraid you are, Mr. Thayer, a spiritual expatriate." That being so, she was willing to relinquish me, although loyally.

Scofield Thayer did not resign his post so completely as he here indicated to Alyse Gregory that he would. Not until June 1926 did *The Dial* print his "Announcement" of resignation: "I am happy to announce my resignation from the editorship of THE DIAL. I am also happy to announce that Miss Marianne Moore has accepted the

invitation of Mr Watson and myself to become the Editor of THE
DIAL." Thereafter Miss Moore acted as full Editor of *The Dial*, with
Scofield Thayer the Adviser.

Alyse Gregory had left *The Dial* after setting it in its final order
by compiling a detailed pamphlet of "General Instructions for Editorial Department," the general tenor of which has been discussed
in an earlier chapter. These the Editor approved, and presumably
the Publisher. On a Friday at the end of April 1925, Alyse Gregory
and Scofield Thayer said their farewells at the offices in the old
brownstone house in Greenwich Village. After the Editor departed,
Alyse Gregory penciled a last note before she left *The Dial*.

Alyse Gregory's leave of *The Dial* and of its Editor was deeply
emotional. Already affected to the point of tears after Thayer left the
office on her last day, when she discovered his generous gift of vaca-
tion money, she found herself at a loss for where to go. Memories
crowded the office where everyone suddenly seemed unreal—of
Thayer's kindness, of long and happy talks, of a unique community
of response and feeling despite her own touchiness and quickness of
temper. Grateful for her friend's goodness and his distinction, she
now wished she might in some way have lightened his burden. Instead, in leaving America, she left Scofield Thayer and *The Dial*,
where she had been happier and more at peace than ever before, and
she could only pray for his peace and happiness.

But the physical leavetaking was not to be Alyse Gregory's
farewell to *The Dial* itself, as she wrote for it more often after her
resignation than she had done before she came to it as Managing
Editor. In the issues for June and August 1926 appeared two chapters, "The Picnic" and "New York Impressions" respectively, of a
novel she was writing, *She Shall Have Music*, and this work, so
footnotes to the two selections specified, would be published by
Harcourt, Brace and Company. In the December 1926 *Dial*,
Charles K. Trueblood's review, "Fiat Harmonia," described the
heroine of Alyse Gregory's novel, Sylvia Brown, "as taking the same
extra-marital freedom in the encounters of sex as a man of fastidiousness corresponding to hers might take," and with nothing "permitted
to cast the slightest question upon her integrity, her aristocracy of
heart." The reviewer, though muted, was frank: "Directly dealing
though the novel is, one must needs listen, amid its shielded har-
monies, amid the fine discriminations, massed but insulated, that

make up the volume of its concert, to detect the muffled clamour of life." In all, she contributed fifteen signed reviews to *The Dial*, three before she became Managing Editor but none during her period as an editor. Despite Thayer's invitation to write for *The Dial* then, she pleaded that she was too busy to do so. After her resignation, Alyse Gregory appeared in *The Dial* as a regular reviewer both of the longer, signed reviews and of the unsigned paragraphs in "Briefer Mention." In 1926, William A. Drake included her review of Van Wyck Brooks' *The Pilgrimage of Henry James* in the compilation *American Criticism, 1926*, which Drake edited and for which he wrote an introduction. Entitled "A Superb Brief," the review had appeared in the September 1925 *Dial;* Drake also selected two essays from *The Dial* for his volume, Logan Pearsall Smith's "Madame de Sevigné in the Country," from the July 1925 issue, and Charles K. Trueblood's "Emily Dickinson," from the April 1926 issue. It was a distinct compliment that Alyse Gregory's review should appear in company with two literary essays from *The Dial* in an anthology that, as the anonymous reviewer in the April 1927 "Briefer Mention" wrote, ranged from the sarcasms of Sinclair Lewis to the reveries of Agnes Repplier, from the scholarly Logan Pearsall Smith to the epithetic—but never apathetic—Mr. Mencken. In 1927 Alyse Gregory also contributed two essays, one on the language of poetry, the other on eighteenth-century women; but except for her consistent and distinguished contribution to the magazine, she seems not to have kept closely in touch with it after Scofield Thayer left.

Marianne Moore as Editor of *The Dial* during its last three years enjoyed a degree of independence unknown to anyone on the staff except her predecessor. She had known both Scofield Thayer and Sibley Watson for some years, she was uniquely hailed as the recipient of a Dial Award, and she came to work for *The Dial* at a time when both its directors had decided to be away from the review most of the time. Also Miss Moore was fortunate in being able to comply with a clearcut set of editorial instructions, the hard-won result of several years of experience in publishing *The Dial*.

As Scofield Thayer pointed out in the announcement of his resignation, no one except Alyse Gregory and Stewart Mitchell had customarily shared with the Editor and the Publisher the responsibility for the contents of *The Dial*. Now Miss Moore was chief and at times sole arbiter of the contents in so far as writing was con-

cerned. She was tireless as well as sympathetic in her advice to
younger writers, and the integrity of her intentions was beyond
question. To be sure, try as she might, she could not invariably
satisfy all the contributors. In her early months as Editor, Miss
Moore put Hart Crane out of temper precisely through her admirable
and well-intentioned care with manuscripts submitted. Crane had
sent *The Dial* his poem "The Wine Menagerie," but, so he wrote
Charlotte and Richard Rychtarik, Miss Moore insisted "on changing
it around and cutting it up until you would not even recognize it.
She even changed the title to 'Again.' What it all means now I can't
make out, and I would never have consented to such an outrageous
joke if I had not so desperately needed the twenty dollars." [12] The
change, of course, was merely suggested by Miss Moore, and the
poem as it appeared in *The Dial* for April 1926 was published as the
poet had revised it, in accordance with Miss Moore's suggestion.
The Dial had no more strictly followed editorial rule than the one
forbidding editors to make changes in an author's manuscript without his permission. Many years later in an interview with Donald
Hall, Marianne Moore said she felt in compassion she should dis-
regard the rule. "Well, if you would modify it a little," she said to
Hart Crane, "we would like it better." He was so *anxious* to have
The Dial take "that thing," and so *delighted;* his gratitude was
ardent and later his repudiation of it commensurate.[13] It may have
been with a contributor such as Hart Crane in mind that Marianne
Moore wrote, in her retrospect of *The Dial*, that to some contributors
—as to some noncontributors—*The Dial*, and herself in particular,
may have seemed quarrelsome, and she added characteristically that
it was "regrettable that manners should be subordinated to matter."
Mishaps and anomalies, however, but served to emphasize for Miss
Moore the untoxic soundness of most writers. She regarded them
with goodhumored and impersonal equanimity: "And today, previous victims of mine have to dread from me, as pre-empting the
privilege of the last word, nothing more than solicitude that all of us
may write better." [14]

Most of the contributors to *The Dial* were less easily outraged
by its Editor's consideration than was Hart Crane. There was George
Dillon, for example, a young poet in Chicago only just beginning to
send his poems out to the various reviews and little magazines. He
aroused the interest of both Scofield Thayer and the new Editor, and

a correspondence ensued, resulting in the publication by *The Dial* of seven of Dillon's poems during the latter Twenties. When *Boy in the Wind*, the young poet's first volume, was published, Robert Morss Lovett, reviewing it for the June 1928 *Dial*, praised the clearness Dillon had achieved "by a reserve so guarded, a simplicity so austere, that one is moved to wonder at the rigour of exclusion or the severity of discipline by which it must have been attained." George Dillon recalled more than thirty years later that *The Dial* had opened up a new world for him. Others, according to Miss Moore, gratefully acknowledged her editorial advice: George Haven Schauffler, for suggesting a verbal change or two in his translation of Thomas Mann's *Disorder and Early Sorrow;* Gilbert Seldes, for proposing excisions in "Jonathan Edwards"; and Mark Van Doren, for the decision to keep in some final lines of one of his poems that previously the Editor had wished he would omit.[15]

Besides the occasional aid given by Scofield Thayer at the beginning of her editorship and given by Sibley Watson until the end, Marianne Moore could depend on the assistance of Kenneth Burke and Ellen Thayer. Nothing supplanted in Miss Moore's recollection what she has termed the undozing linguistics and scholarly resourcefulness of Ellen Thayer as Assistant Editor, "occasional untender accusations from authors, of stupidity or neglect of revisions, being found invariably to be reversible" by Miss Thayer.

Miss Moore admired the humor in the editorial correspondence, the satire, too, and one ostensible formality of *The Dial*, concocted by Kenneth Burke as an answer to an advertising manager who had complained that if books receiving long reviews and unanimous approbation elsewhere were to be damned at *The Dial* by brief notices and faint praise, might they not be damned somewhat more promptly? The complaint had come from an acquaintance of Burke's who had not foreseen that someone he knew might be answering it. Kenneth Burke, in replying, asked, "Why not give *The Dial* credit? As you have said, under our silence the book went through five editions. Now that we have spoken there may never be a sixth. Further, we are happy to learn that whereas we had feared that our 'Briefer Mention' was a week or two late, the continued success of the book has kept our comment green. We are, you might say, reviewing a reprint—a courtesy not all gazettes will afford you. . . . And are you, after all, so sure that a book benefits by having the reviews all let off at once like something gone wrong in the arsenal, followed by an eternity of charred silence!"

Miss Moore also recalled the explicit manual of duties with which the office was provided—the "General Instructions" compiled by Alyse Gregory—and in this connection, the inviolateness to the editors, despite their occasional remonstrance, of the contributing editor-critics, Gilbert Seldes, Henry McBride, Paul Rosenfeld, and Kenneth Burke: "Ever recklessly against the false good, they surely did represent *The Dial* in 'encouraging a tolerance for fresh experiments and opening the way for fresh understanding of them.' "

Of the men and women less officially but no less intimately connected with *The Dial* as friends and contributors, Miss Moore remembered many names. D. H. Lawrence, William Butler Yeats, Paul Valéry, William Carlos Williams, Wallace Stevens, Ezra Pound, T. S. Eliot, H. D., E. E. Cummings, Padraic Colum—though both Cummings and Colum were at different times the writers of "The Theatre" and hence among the contributing editor-critics—L. A. G. Strong, Yvor Winters, George Saintsbury, Charles Sears Baldwin, Llewelyn and John Cowper Powys, and Gordon Craig were among the writers who contributed to *The Dial*, most of them while she was its Editor. Of the artists, Miss Moore recalled Charles Sheeler, photographing Gaston Lachaise's head of Scofield Thayer; and Lachaise himself, with his stubbornness and naturalness that constituted a work of art above even the most important sculpture. She remembered his saying with an almost primitive-tribal moroseness, "But I believe in a large amount of work," and on another occasion, "Cats. I could learn a million things from cats." Of the pictures in *The Dial*, Marianne Moore wrote chiefly of those reproduced, "as intensives on the text," before she became associated officially with the review: "three verdure-tapestry-like woodcuts by Galanis; Rousseau's lion among lotuses; 'The Philosophers' by Stuart Davis; Adolph Dehn's 'Viennese Coffee House'; and Kuniyoshi's curious 'Heifer'—the forehead with a star on it of separate whorled strokes like propeller fins; Ernest Fiene, Charles Sheeler, Arthur Dove, John Marin, Georgia O'Keefe, Max Weber, Carl Sprinchorn, the Zorachs, and Bertram Hartman; Wyndham Lewis, Brancusi, Lachaise, Elie Nadelman, Picasso and Chirico, Cocteau line drawings, and Seurat's 'Circus.' " [16]

Miss Moore's relation to the pictures in *The Dial* continued to be one of appreciation rather than of industrious engagement with their selection. Pictures continued to be bought by Scofield Thayer and Dr. Watson—usually by Scofield Thayer, she wrote on May 3, 1958. Most of them were on hand when she came to the office, but some few were added, as Thayer or Watson felt that recognition was owed someone not already published, or as encouragement was fitting. The color reproductions continued to be furnished by Julius Meier-Graefe through arrangements made by Scofield Thayer when he went to Europe in 1925.

In two other respects, Miss Moore did not exercise an editorial control comparable to Scofield Thayer's when he had actively been directing *The Dial*. She knew nothing about circulation figures or anything pertaining to the business department of *The Dial*, except that the review paid persons published for the first time as much as it paid well-known contributors. In her retrospect, she quoted the rates paid contributors, and these are, of course, the rates as instituted by Thayer and Watson and as specified by Alyse Gregory in the "General Instructions" she compiled. As for the Dial Awards, they originated with Scofield Thayer and Sibley Watson. Thayer and Watson might ask Miss Moore's opinion or approval when a decision had been made, but they made the final choice entirely independent of their Editor.

The departing Editor had not regarded the change in the direction of *The Dial* as requiring the use of the word *essential*, and events proved him right in his prophecy; the change was indeed inessential. One change, however, was, if inessential, regrettable; after she assumed the editorship of *The Dial*, Marianne Moore published no more poems in it. Distinguished though her "Comment" was, it could not replace the poems she might have published in *The Dial*. The review was immeasurably the richer for publishing "Picking and Choosing" and "England," in April 1920, her first appearance; "When I Buy Pictures" and "A Graveyard," in July 1921; "New York" and "The Labours of Hercules," in December 1921; "People's Surroundings," in June 1922; "Novices," in February 1923; "Silence," in October 1924; "Sea Unicorns and Land Unicorns," in November 1924; "An Octopus," in December 1924; and "The Monkey Puzzler," in January 1925, the issue in which Scofield Thayer announced Marianne Moore as recipient of the Dial Award for 1924.

Henri Matisse   *Nude, Face Partly Showing*

After she became Editor, Miss Moore ordinarily wrote the editorial "Comment," but of the nineteen signed reviews she published in *The Dial* all save one were written before she became Editor, and the majority appeared before she was officially associated with the review. Her first review, "Jacopone da Todi," dealt with Evelyn Underhill's biography of the medieval Italian mystic and appeared in the January 1921 *Dial;* her tenth review, "Histrionic Seclusion," canvassed George Moore's *Conversations in Ebury Street* and appeared in *The Dial* for March 1925. Here she put in his proper place one who had caused *The Dial* much grief: "There are depths of colour in these imaginings and there are flaws. As a verbal virtuoso, Mr Moore is sometimes disappointing, presenting the paradox of a naturalness as oral as Bunyan's; and a naturalness so studied as to annihilate itself. There are inharmonious echoes of the Bible and of the English prayer-book, and an intentional impertinence that on occasion becomes insult; one feels the lack of aesthetic tone in Mr Moore's displeasure with Hardy." During her first year at *The Dial*, Miss Moore published eight reviews, the last of these appearing in August 1926: "Natives of Rock," a review of Glenway Wescott's volume of poems bearing the same title. In all probability, Miss Moore wrote this review before her appointment as Editor, and after its publication, she published in *The Dial* only one other review, in the issue for September 1928, "A House-Party," which dealt with Mary Butts' novel *Armed with Madness*.

Miss Moore published little in *The Dial* outside her poems, "Comment," and book reviews. In December 1922 had appeared her essay on Alfeo Faggi, "Is the Real the Actual?," accompanied by photographs of Faggi's sculptures *Ka* and *Mother and Child*. Her essay on "Sir Francis Bacon" appeared in the April 1924 issue, and one on her friend William Carlos Williams, "A Poet of the Quattrocento," appeared in the March 1927 *Dial*. Most of what Marianne Moore published in *The Dial* has remained uncollected. The poems have been gathered, but only four of the dozens of signed and unsigned prose pieces—"Comment," reviews, essays, "Briefer Mention"—are among the author's *Predilections*, her first prose volume of collected writings (1955): "Sir Francis Bacon"; "Besitz und Gemeingut," a review of Georg Brandes' biography of Goethe, published in the June 1925 *Dial;* " 'Literature the Noblest of the Arts,' " also a review, of George Saintsbury's *Collected Essays and Papers*,

Henri Matisse   *Nude Seated in a Wicker Chair*

1875–1920, published in the October 1925 *Dial;* and "THE DIAL Award," a brief appreciation, once forming a part of the "Announcement" that replaced "Comment" in January 1927 on the occasion of William Carlos Williams' reception of the Dial Award for 1926. Both the reviews and the "Comment" are of major importance to any extended study of Marianne Moore's work, but what is of greater concern is the fact of their excellence. That they are in danger of being forgotten is lamentable. From the evidence in the Dial papers, to Miss Moore as author may be ascribed the "Comment" for July, October, and November 1925; June (signed "M. M.") and December 1926; June, July, and August 1927; May, June, July, August, September, and October 1928; and January (the "Announcement" of the Dial Award for 1928 to Kenneth Burke), February, March, April, and June 1929. Who would not resuscitate the brief essay, in the August 1927 issue, on snakes, with its opening sentence: "The usefulness, companionableness, and gentleness of snakes is sometimes alluded to in print by scientists and by amateurs"? or the essay, in the April 1929 issue, on the "respective gains of peace and armament" that contains the gnomic remark: "War is pillage versus resistance"?

A remarkable staff was responsible for *The Dial*. The unusual sympathy of tastes, the dominance of intelligence without pedantry, the suave rich cosmopolitanism, the mysterious and perhaps inexplicable rhythm of the contents in their order: these fused to create an object of art. *The Dial* itself became a work of art, an aesthetic triumph.

That it did so is due to the point of view that dominated the production and the contents of the review itself. In this respect *The Dial* was not a glittering, and occasionally silly, hodgepodge like *The Little Review* but was a disciplined and ordered artifact. Unlike *The Little Review*, *The Dial* believed in more than self-expression; both shared an interest in art and aesthetics, but *The Dial* adhered (though not dogmatically) to an articulated, consistent point of view about art and aesthetics. In "Comment" for August 1922, the editorial writer (probably Gilbert Seldes), pointed up the contrast between the attitudes of *The Little Review* and *The Dial*. The lack of homogeneity in the contents of *The Dial*, which Gorham Munson had alleged in the first number of *Secession* (Spring 1922), was only apparent; what interested *The Dial* was "aesthetic perfection," keeping the eye on the object and letting "economics and interpretation and analyses go hang."

What *The Dial* did not care a hang about, however, was imposing an ideological consistency on its issues, even in the realm of art and aesthetics. Here, of course, *The Dial* and *The Little Review* were in agreement. If at its best *The Dial* was a successful work of art, it succeeded not because of a consistency or a lack of consistency in the ideas presented by various contributors to a given issue; there simply was no such consistency except within very broad, very vaguely defined limits. Moreover, to expect to find an ideology, a system of related ideas in various fields, expressed by *The Dial* is to fail to deal with the review on its own terms. What *The Dial* sought was aesthetic perfection, perfection of form, and it expressly decried a preoccupation with politics and social reform.

Every poem, every work of art reproduced, every essay, every review that appeared in *The Dial* was scrutinized by the editorial staff from this standpoint. Scofield Thayer and his colleagues were concerned with style, structure, texture, technique; except for the problem of censorship, which the tribulations of *The Little Review* exacerbated for Thayer, the content of a story or a poem or a picture was secondary to the art of its execution. Thayer tried sometimes to compromise between art and commerce; he deplored a photograph of Brancusi's *Golden Bird*, not because he disliked the statue but because the photograph was "commercially suicidal" for *The Dial* to print. That stricture nevertheless was a minor qualification, if a surprising one for the Editor to make. In general *The Dial* did not compromise with its ideal of aesthetic perfection; the major exception occurred late in 1922 and early in 1923, when Thayer, Watson, and their Business Manager were hopeful of increasing the circulation of *The Dial* to the number of copies that would make the review self-sustaining.

Also the assertion that at its best *The Dial* fulfilled itself as a work of art on its own terms is to make a judgment that goes beyond the consideration of any single item in the issue as a work of art. For example, such an assertion intentionally goes beyond the attempt to analyze isolatedly and individually Robert Delaunay's *St Séverin* or *The Waste Land*, but rather considers them as parts of the ensemble that was *The Dial* for November 1922. The task of analysis and evaluation of individual works of art others have accomplished:

Delaunay's paintings and Eliot's poems have become recognized as among the most inventive and forward-leading artistic productions of our century. One may take for granted a general acceptance of the worth of most of the individual items themselves composing a given issue of *The Dial*. Instead, what is under discussion here is the review itself: besides the quality of its contents, the care with which the various poems and pictures and essays and stories and reviews are ordered and displayed to advantage, the physical appearance of the cover and inside pages.

Scofield Thayer was in the habit of conducting post mortems regularly after the appearance of each issue, personally or by correspondence as the case necessitated. For Alyse Gregory these fearsome tribunals held each month were like sessions of Parliament after some public scandal. Thayer "would arrive with a long sheet of paper on which he had meticulously noted down every error, and each would be remorselessly tracked to the guilty person." Miss Gregory regarded these post mortem meetings as painful occasions, "redeemed by the presence of Dr. Watson, whose quick and indulgent understanding offered balm to all. The most tangled problem he could unravel, the most ruffled feelings appease." And, Alyse Gregory added feelingly, "there is no more unhappy experience for an editor, or for an author, than to have errors he is responsible for jump up at him out of the page like so many stinging scorpions. There are writers who take no pleasure in seeing their work in print because of some mistake in grammar, some redundancy, pleonasm, cliché, or wretched split infinitive." [17] So relentless was Thayer's search for the impeccable, unassailably error-free *Dial* that once when a small, last-minute alteration in an essay of William Butler Yeats came as the review, already off the press, was about to be sent out to the newsstands, he had the whole issue—could it have been *The Dial* for September 1924 containing Yeats's "The Bounty of Sweden"?—destroyed and a fresh one made.

Thayer's striving to realize the platonic ideal of the perfect issue of *The Dial* is perhaps best illustrated by his editorial assessment of a particular, representative issue. That for November 1922 is especially exemplary, because not only is it the most famous single issue of *The Dial* but it also prompted detailed comment by Scofield Thayer and Gilbert Seldes. The frontispiece is a color reproduction, made in Berlin by Herwarth Walden, of Robert Delaunay's *St*

Séverin, and other pictures reproduced in the issue are by Picasso, Adolf Dehn, and Duncan Grant; Brancusi's own photograph of his sculpture, *Golden Bird*, appears, accompanied by Mina Loy's poem, "Brancusi's Golden Bird." *The Waste Land* leads off the issue, followed by Yeats's *The Player Queen*, the fifth and last instalment of Schnitzler's *Doctor Graesler*, Élie Faure's "Reflections on the Greek Genius," the second instalment of Sherwood Anderson's *Many Marriages*, Ezra Pound's "Paris Letter," Gilbert Seldes' "American Letter" (purportedly written by "Sebastien Cauliflower"), and reviews by Bertrand Russell, Malcolm Cowley, Edward Sapir, Padraic Colum, and Gilbert Seldes. The issue concluded with the regular monthly departments on the arts contributed by Seldes, Paul Rosenfeld, and Henry McBride and the editorial "Comment," probably written by Seldes.

Beginning some time in the latter half of 1922, for a few months *The Dial* sold out each issue. Like its immediate predecessors, the November *Dial* rapidly sold out, and for several months afterward sixteen to eighteen thousand copies per issue were printed. The Secretary-Treasurer, Samuel Craig, and the Editor were hopeful that the magazine might maintain this level of public acceptance and perhaps rise to a printing of twenty thousand copies. Thus Thayer's comments about the November issue must be understood as relating to his struggle to increase circulation as well as in relation to his striving to achieve qualitative and mechanical perfection in each issue.

The Editor thought the November *Dial* about as imperfect as usual; it contained, he wrote his Managing Editor, the usual lot of thorns. "I try always," he explained in a lengthy letter of November 28, from Vienna, "in writing home so far as possible to dwell rather upon the roses, therefore allow me to congratulate you and Mr. Watson upon the delightful Picassos so perfectly reproduced, upon the excellent placing of the Delaunay, upon the excellent reproductions of the Duncan Grants, upon the superb review of Santayana, and upon *your*, dear Gilbert, very lovely Corbett and Fitzsimmons exordium," probably a reference to the pseudonymous "American Letter." He continued:

The following thorns drew blood—

1] Why does Brancusi precede Delaunay contrary to the order arranged for by me for Notes on Contributors?

2] Upon page one of the advertising section I find the word "fantastis" where "fantastic" is presumably wanted. [In the Harcourt Brace advertisement, Sandburg's *Rootabaga Stories* were "Imaginative and fantastis."]

3] Upon page eleven of the advertising section I find the word "he" where obviously "the" is intended. [For Doubleday Page, Edna Ferber was "he leading American short story writer."]

4] The placing of the Yeats (quite apart from the question of type) anywhere other than at the beginning of the number I find quite beyond words.

5] The photograph of "The Golden Bird" should of course never have been accepted. We should only have pictures in The Dial (Mr. Watson agreed with me as to this question in Berlin and assured me he would see to it that such things sh'd not further appear in The Dial) which at once have *aesthetic value* and are *not commercially suicidal*. The picture in question has *no aesthetic value whatever* and is *commercially suicidal*. As to the quality of "The Golden Bird," having only seen this picture I of course have no idea whatever.

6] I find despite my repeated exhortations you are proceeding with the publication of "Many Marriages" (cf. length of Nov. installment) on precisely the scale of the publication of "Doktor Gräsler," thus destroying any aesthetic value which the matter might otherwise have.

7] I had spent considerable time considering the best titles for the Dehn pictures and had had those titles sent to you. Now the pictures appear in this number with both titles changed, thus sacrificing the point in the juxtaposition of those pictures. Please explain precisely why you changed my titles for these pictures. Please publish the two remaining Dehn pictures with the *exact* titles that I gave for them.

That was bad enough! But Thayer expended his intenser ire on the house advertisement that the hapless Managing Editor had made up for the November 1922 *Dial*. This double-page spread for *The Dial* was "the worst advertisement we have yet published," exploded the Editor, and he went on to specify his objections. Like the Peacock Folder, the November spread had surrounded Seldes' prose with photographs of notable contributors to the review: Sherwood Anderson, Hugo von Hofmannsthal, D. H. Lawrence, Ezra Pound, Bertrand Russell, G. Santayana, Arthur Schnitzler, and W. B. Yeats.

The advertisement had announced as contributors to *The Dial* A. E. Coppard, Paul Morand, John Eglinton, and T. S. Eliot, as well as Marie Laurencin and André Derain with "art reproductions." "Of special interest," asserted the spread, "will be the publication, during the fall and winter, of the best work now being produced in the Germanic countries. A great artistic and literary revival is going on in Central Europe, and The Dial will present to the American public the finest products of this renaissance." Among the work from Central Europe that would appear in *The Dial* were promised *"Essays"* by Hermann Bahr, Stefan Zweig, and Hugo von Hofmannsthal; *"Fiction"* by Thomas Mann, Heinrich Mann, and Arthur Schnitzler; and *"Reproductions of Art work"* by Emil Orlik, Oskar Kokoska (*sic*), Willie (*sic*) Geiger, Arnold Roennebeck, Hermann Haller, and Felix Albrecht Harta.

The Editor objected to the photographs, the names of writers and artists announced in the spread, and the tenor of the entire advertisement. To him, the photograph of Ezra Pound looked more like Richard Cobb, the headmaster of Milton Academy, than like Pound. Of course Pound should not have been featured, but if he was to be featured, it was even more essential to have a decent photograph of him than of people whose place in such a gallery was unassailable. The Hofmannsthal photograph was askew. The phrase "art reproductions" was unbelievably vulgar. The reference to "this renaissance" in Central Europe was more ridiculous than, without spending more hours and pages than the Editor had at his command, he could make his unlucky subordinate understand: "It should have been obvious from my letters and was certainly explained to Mr. Watson by myself last summer that I find none of the new work being done in Germany since the war worth while. You talk about 'a great artistic and literary revival' and then go on to quote the names of men all of whom did their best work before the war." The name of Heinrich Mann should not have been included until the New York office of *The Dial* was aware that Scofield Thayer had accepted something from his pen. Apart from the taste of such unwarranted announcements, in this case the fact that Heinrich Mann's brother Thomas was German correspondent for *The Dial* and that he would see the advertisement and that he would doubtless ask his brother about it and that he would then learn that *The Dial* was announcing things by authors who had probably never heard of it would—but the Editor, unable to complete his period, left that task for the Managing Editor.

Thayer went on to object to the phrase "Art work" as going "art reproductions" just one better. The list of artists, too, was the most astonishingly unfortunate one that could have been imagined. Hermann Haller, one of the best-known sculptors in Europe, was Swiss, not German, and his inclusion in the German list would not impress European readers of *The Dial* as to the cultivation of the staff of *The Dial*. Thayer affirmed that he had taken, for his review, work by all the best German and Austrian artists but that for different reasons at different times he had accepted work by secondary artists, usually for the sake of the subject, as with Arnold Roennebeck's bust of Charles Demuth and Willi Geiger's portrait of Heinrich Mann, which were reproduced in *The Dial* in, respectively, September and October 1925. (That detail, incidentally, gives an inkling of the large backlog of art suitable for reproduction in its pages to which *The Dial* possessed publication rights, beyond the pictures and objects Thayer and Watson owned.) The list Gilbert Seldes compiled for the offensive spread included, said his Editor, only one first-rate contemporary Central European artist, Kokoschka, and his name was misspelled. Under the circumstances, Thayer continued, he did not expect Seldes to make up an intelligent list of contemporary German artists, especially as the Editor had not yet turned over to *The Dial* in New York even half of what he had accepted. What Scofield Thayer did expect was that the staff of *The Dial* would refrain from discussing a subject with which they were not acquainted.—At least they might send such an advertisement to Vienna for him to correct; he could have put it in order in five minutes. And now he, the Editor, would be answerable. He did not say as much, but Scofield Thayer probably was thinking of the often voiced complaints to him of such Viennese acquaintances as Frau von Hofmannsthal (she objected to Kokoschka's horrible portrait in *The Dial* of that "nice man" Max Reinhardt) and Dr. Schnitzler (when would he be paid for his stories in *The Dial?*).

For the employees of *The Dial* such lectures were all in the day's work, and Gilbert Seldes, and his successors as well, defended themselves without rancor as valiantly as they could. In his reply of December 14 to Thayer's criticisms, Seldes confessed to their mutual bleeding over the November number and proceeded to make only "a few whimpering comments" about the Editor's questions. The Brancusi note had preceded the Delaunay note in "Notes on Contributors," because it was wrongly placed on the final proofs, and despite Seldes' telephoned instructions the printers still got the placing of "Notes on Contributors" wrong. This, as the Managing Editor implied by the tone of his comment, is trifling; but Seldes' defense of his placing T. S. Eliot's *The Waste Land* at the front of the review in the place of honor is of substantial interest. In its October forecast of the contents of the next number, which probably was written by Seldes as usual, the *"Editors of The Dial"* had taken exceptional pleasure in announcing the publication of two works—*The Waste Land* and *The Player Queen*. "The Waste Land is a long poem, the first by Mr Eliot in several years. Those who have read it are unanimous in believing that it is a work of profound significance and that its publication is an event of capital importance. It is not improbable that the appearance of The Waste Land will rank with that of Ulysses in the degree of interest it will call forth."

In contrast to these prophetic and skilfully tantalizing words about *The Waste Land*, Seldes, though he praised *The Player Queen* as a play of "fantasy, humour, and poetry," emphasized not its intrinsic importance but its connection with Yeats's "preoccupation with the theatre—an interest which has led him before to playwriting, but never in this vein." Seldes' answer to Thayer's strictures was therefore not unnaturally a defense of his position assumed prior to publication of *The Waste Land*, a position that by December 1922 he already felt to be vindicated by the reception of the poem and that the mere passage of time has proven an exceptionally sensible and percipient view of *The Waste Land* in contrast to the Editor's dubiety about it. "Considering that we had published Yeats steadily, that we had never published a poem by Eliot, that we intended to announce the award to Eliot shortly, that in our opinion it was a very fine piece of work—we gave it the place of honor in the November number," wrote Seldes. As to the play by Yeats, which was printed in type of smaller size than was usual, the Managing Editor recognized the point the Editor had made before, that small type, if used at all "(under conditions which are very clear in my mind, I assure you)," should be used for works appearing at the beginning of an issue. Apart from this fault in the November issue, Seldes asserted his and Watson's simple disagreement with Thayer regarding the placing of the two contributions by Eliot and Yeats; he and the Publisher differed editorially with the Editor in this instance, a disagreement that they had always recognized as being possible. And the same was true of the Brancusi *Golden Bird;* Seldes had assumed Thayer's knowledge of the work "since you wrote that you were going to send it, and as the photograph was by Brancusi himself and he considered it perfect, the aesthetic value was to be taken for granted. As for commercially suicidal, the only row which occurred in that connection was over the poem—not the picture." (The "poem" was Mina Loy's "Brancusi's Golden Bird," which accompanied the photograph.)

About the Editor's other strictures, Seldes could say relatively little by way of explanation. The Anderson serial, *Many Marriages*, must run for six months, "which we consider not excessive for the story." He must go through the files to discover the truth of the matter, with regard to the titles for the Dehn pictures—although he thought he had taken them from a letter he had received. As for the Editor's criticisms concerning the spread advertisement, Seldes made "only these two points, plaintively—first that you wrote in a letter that you would send us something by Heinrich Mann—I speak from memory now, of course, but I was certain of it then—second, that Kokoschka's name came to me misspelled on the contributor's note. . . . God knows we all accept your bouquets as we seriously wince not only under your lash, my dear Scofield, but under the scorn of our self-insufficiency." And Seldes signed himself "Faithfully."

One must mediate between the opinions of Scofield Thayer and Gilbert Seldes to arrive at any aesthetic judgment of *The Dial*. There is, first of all, a remarkable area of agreement: both men were concerned with matters of form rather than with ideas, and both were in complete agreement about the format of *The Dial*. These two matters, after all, were settled components of editorial policy. A previous chapter has discussed the format of *The Dial*, which displayed its contents with such telling results. For example, the juxtaposition in the issue of the Delaunay painting and the Eliot poem —both sharing a combined modernity of treatment and religiosity of material—is a triumph of editorial taste, as was, to a lesser extent, the juxtaposition of the Brancusi sculpture to Mina Loy's verses about it. If anything, this careful placing of the contents, the carefully ordered rhythm created by such joining and juxtaposition and separating, succeeded at least momentarily, while a reader perused the issue, in making some of the contributions seem better than they really were. *The Dial* gave everything it printed a glossy sheen, if not a patina, an appearance of having arrived.

To be sure, there is point in Scofield Thayer's criticisms of the November 1922 issue, though only three of them are substantial, while two others are a matter of taste, in one of which time has supported him and in the other of which time has gone against him. The Editor obviously was right to object that it is not pleasing to have to read *The Player Queen* in small type, placed as it is in the body of the number. The temporary arrangement, adhered to from October 1922 through May 1923, that placed "Comment" first among the regular editorial departments and the "Musical Chronicle" last was not a happy one, for it left the review without that final fillip almost invariably given it by the witty, tart *Dial* editorials. Finally, one must agree with Scofield Thayer, that the November advertising spread is a most uneven affair, valuable as most well-intentioned advertising is—the names and pictures of the various contributors surely must have stimulated some interest and respect among potential advertisers and the readers of *The Dial*—but as inaccurate as the Editor alleged. Still the spread was accurate to the extent that it publicized the interest of *The Dial* in Central European writing and art. As to the disagreement about the placing of *The Waste Land* and *The Player Queen*, thus far in history Gilbert Seldes has been proven right and Scofield Thayer wrong. How serious a matter was this condescension by the Editor toward his old schoolmate Eliot? Writing on October 22, 1922, Thayer told Alyse Gregory, whom he was currently trying to persuade to come to *The Dial* as his Managing Editor, "as to the literary contents too I feel forced to refrain in the future from publishing such matter as the silly cantos of Ezra Pound and as the very disappointing 'Waste Land' and I should like to secure for The Dial the work of such recognised American authors as Edith Wharton." But although *The Dial* cast an amazingly wide net, it did not catch Mrs. Wharton—if, actually, it ever tried to land her. Perhaps this instance of Thayer's expressed preferences should not be taken seriously. As for Sherwood Anderson's *Many Marriages*, the Editor surely was right in believing it to have little aesthetic worth and therefore to be a distinct detriment to *The Dial* when run for six months as a serial.

All these, however, are minor errors; some of them are minute. Viewed in perspective, the achievement of *The Dial* effaces the small blemishes on the November 1922 issue. The brilliance of the individual contributions and of the array of names who created them: these stand out, first of all. They together constitute the supreme excellence of an age. Alyse Gregory has said that *The Dial*, in publishing the work of distinguished Europeans, sought to widen and to instruct the taste of American readers, while encouraging native writers and poets with original talent to contribute to its pages. Not many reviews could, or would, have published T. S. Eliot and Sherwood Anderson in the same number, and no other review could have brought off the feat with comparable taste, gaiety, and aplomb. The second excellence *The Dial* evinced was its consistency of taste, under which lay the editorial demand for formal excellence.

A third distinctive excellence of *The Dial* proceeds from the other two, the free play of opposing views advanced by the various contributors and even the owners and editors themselves. Perhaps in this aspect of the achievement of the review lay the puzzle to some of its contemporaries—its pluralism that occasionally seemed to amount to indifference to the values of opposing ideas. Again Alyse Gregory witnesses that on the one hand *The Dial* "was criticized for being too orthodox, and on the other, for being too experimental." [18] E. E. Cummings, in his 1952 Norton Lectures, noted the same enmity toward *The Dial:* "Never have I seen courage and courtesy, taste and intelligence, prodigious patience and incredible generosity, quite so jealously mistrusted or so basely misprized or so savagely detested as by The Dial's detractors." [19] Under its circumstances the bias of *The Dial* was liberal; Scofield Thayer and Sibley Watson nevertheless permitted a free play of the opposing views that participated in the Western tradition. Bertrand Russell might attack George Santayana, but then George Santayana might with equal freedom attack, in another issue, liberalism. *The Dial* constituted, to use a favorite cliché of its decade, a marketplace of ideas; and for a later generation this attitude toward ideology may appear overly optimistic, even naïve. Such a liberalism properly belonged to the wealthy middle class, monarchs of whatever they surveyed in the Twenties; the liberalism of *The Dial* was the liberalism of secure and well-educated people, who could afford to tolerate oppositions. Only toward the late Twenties do there appear portents of the end of this regime, as in Ezra Pound's critique of William Carlos Williams in the November 1928 issue, and in Albert Halper's essay about whites writing up the blacks in the January 1929 issue. The sweaty, poverty-stricken, quarrelsome Thirties are opposite in spirit to the Twenties as met in *The Dial* for November 1922 and for most of its life. Its liberalism was an adventure not a compulsion. This is not to assert that *The Dial* ignored the famous neuroses of the Twenties. *The Dial* witnessed the American Earthquake; after all, it did publish *The Waste Land*. People on its staff were psychoanalyzed or had unhappy love affairs, committed suicide or went insane and were given to deep thinking about the Ziegfeld Follies and Dada as well as about Dr. Freud and Bertrand Russell and *Ulysses*. All these were among the vicissitudes of the great adventure, of being feck-lessly emancipated, of leading the New Movement in the arts. The interest in liberalism makes *The Dial* typical of its age and milieu, however, rather than unique.

What makes it unique was the search for aesthetic perfection, conducted by the owners and staff, in which certain qualities—intel-ligence, courage, good taste, learning, curiosity—came into play. Of these qualities the review is the concrete resolution. The publication of *The Waste Land*, *Death in Venice*, and various Cantos, the re-production of *Nasturtiums and the "Dance,"* the *Golden Bird*, and various Picasso *Harlequins*, and the consistent appearance of the best of a decade's art and letters and learning in such a generously provided and beautiful form, a review distributed over the Western world month after month at a cost far exceeding the dollars and cents so lavishly expended—all this uniquely *The Dial* realized. In its way, it was a work of art as distinguished as any it made available to the readers and viewers of the Twenties.

FIVE

Editor-Contributors and "Comment"

THE BACK PAGES of *The Dial* were consistently among the best-written and most significant contributions. They included the three monthly chronicles of the arts contributed by the three editor-contributors (or, as they were also termed, editor-critics) — Gilbert Seldes, Henry McBride, and Paul Rosenfeld — and the editorial pages of "Comment." The privilege of writing the monthly "Comment" seems to have been allowed to Scofield Thayer, Marianne Moore, Sibley Watson, Gilbert Seldes, and, in all probability, Kenneth Burke. The regular appearance of the three monthly chronicles of the arts was guaranteed by the conscientiousness of the editor-critics, but from time to time as circumstances necessitated, their work was pieced out or was replaced by the contributions of others either on the regular staff or on the staff while the assignment lasted. In the cases of Gilbert Seldes and Kenneth Burke, the regular staff acted as editor-critics; usually an editor-critic had no duties except to contribute his chronicle eight or nine times a year. In the summer doldrums the chronicles of the arts were in abeyance. It was here, in these four regular departments, that *The Dial* spoke its policy, such as that was, commented on the aesthetic Twenties, and engaged in controversy.

By no means were all the readers of *The Dial* sympathetic — not just the journalists who could or would not understand E. E. Cummings' "misspelling" of the first person singular and who, with some cause, termed *The Waste Land* a "strange poem," but writers and artists as well. There was, for example, the portrait painter, John Christen Johansen, who, brought to the Editor's native city to limn for posterity the features of Clark University's president, informed *The Worcester Telegram* that *The Dial* was an intellectual sewer—a remark that while causing Scofield Thayer exquisite outrage also caused him to compose one of his more sardonic "Comments" in the May 1925 issue.

Even some members of the vanguard attacked *The Dial*. In the first number of *Secession* (Spring 1922), Gorham Munson admitted, for purposes of strategy, that *The Dial* was, he supposed, generally considered to be America's leading magazine of literary expression: "One critic has even called it the recognized organ of the young generation!" But to Munson a copy of *The Dial* gave the impression of splitting apart in his hand, because its chief effect was one of diffuseness. Moreover, it featured a wallowing ox of a stylist who retailed each month acres of vague impressionistic excrement on music, painting, and books; and the Dial Award to Sherwood Anderson had been made not to a young writer but to an established one, forty-five years old and with six books to his credit. *The Dial* condescended to the inclusion of certain young writers, some of whom were both very promising and desperately impecunious, but it also insulated them by the cooling remains of prewar literature and assigned its Award to a man with an influential public. Munson pled with *The Dial* to go one way or the other: "Stay on dry land like the *Atlantic Monthly* or leap headfirst into the contemporary stream. *If you wish a good swim, take off your life-belt!*" The existence of this *Yale-Review*-in-a-Harvard-blazer was one of the bitter necessities calling for *Secession*. Munson also objected to Scofield Thayer's chief editorial mission of these years—the importation of art from central Europe. *The Dial*, as official importer, landed too many dead fish: "Portrait of Richard Strauss by Max Liebermann (geboren 1847, now President of the Berlin Academy of Arts), Richard Specht on Schnitzler, Stefan Zweig on Dickens." Over a year later, in *Secession* for July 1923, Munson recommended as a counter-irritant Ludwig Kassák's Hungarian activist review, which excelled in experimental typographical composition, reproduced the latest work of Moholy-Nagy, Mondrian, Man Ray, and the Russian constructivists, and published translations from the avant-garde writers in Germany,

France, Russia, and America, "the last being represented so far by Malcolm Cowley, Gorham B. Munson, and William Carlos Williams." *The Dial*, on the occasion of Munson's first onslaught, formulated a strategy to answer his attack; the editors chose to let Jane Heap of *The Little Review* make their defense for them and then "to give publicity to her renunciation," because, as she had said, *The Dial* had a larger audience than did *The Little Review*. Jane Heap also saved the editors from the necessity of replying to Munson's "ill-mannered reference" to Sherwood Anderson's years. "Why make the physical age of the creative artist a measurement?" asked *The Little Review*. To which "Comment" for August 1922 added: "Good."

But, then, *The Dial* would applaud the attitude of Margaret Anderson and Jane Heap without emulating the policy of their review. For *The Little Review* quite obviously was a hodge-podge, without plan or regular periodicity. People took for granted that since its editors had no money, there would be no talk of remuneration. As a result (for the worse as well as for the better), practically everything *The Little Review* published during its first years was material that would have been accepted by no other magazine in the world at the moment. Later, as Margaret Anderson remarked, all the art magazines wanted to print her contributors and, besides, pay them. She added that the contributors took the same stand as Sherwood Anderson: if they had something *The Little Review* especially wanted, they gave the work to Miss Anderson before *The Dial* was permitted to see it—and pay. The "best" European writers and painters did the same.

At least one of the owners of *The Dial* financially as well as verbally encouraged the absolute anarchy of Margaret Anderson and Jane Heap. At tea time one Christmas Day—an especially impoverished Christmastide for the proprietors of *The Little Review* in their bookshop-apartment in the Village—a tall blond man arrived, introduced himself as J. S. Watson of *The Dial*, and said he wanted to buy a copy of Eliot's *Prufrock and Other Poems*. Inasmuch as the two ladies had published some of Eliot's poetry, they took a pardonable pride in stocking his book, which sold for seventy-five cents. Watson gave Margaret Anderson what she thought was a dollar bill and refused his change; as she put the bill away, she noticed it was for a hundred dollars. She ran after Watson and told him he had made a mistake, but he assured her that he had brought the money for *The Little Review* and that it was good. The couple returned to the apartment and talked; they became friends and so remained during all the attacks *The Little Review* made on *The Dial* as "a de-alcoholized version of the *Little Review*." Watson, moreover, came several times with his salutary hundred-dollar bill that kept the magazine alive when otherwise it would have succumbed. As Jane Heap said, he knew a good magazine when he saw one.[1]

Wasn't *The Dial* a good magazine? It certainly attempted a unity of a kind alcoholically ignored by *The Little Review*. Was it really, as *Secession* saw the case, a diffuse hodge-podge in monthly danger of splitting at the seams? Or did it express a valid taste, an eclectic yet reasonably self-consistent attitude? In an interview with Donald Hall, Marianne Moore asserted that "We certainly didn't have a policy, except I remember hearing the word 'intensity' very often. A thing must have 'intensity." That seemed to be the criterion."[2] When Eliot founded his *Criterion*, it would be—as Gorham Munson had demanded that the best review be—exclusive, not satisfied to be a fortuitous concourse of compositions of fiction, verse, and belles lettres. Each contributor to *The Criterion* would be a contributor to the formation of a design and the execution of a purpose; its advertising for October 1923 asserted that it aimed at the affirmation and development of tradition, the assertion of order and discipline, and the maintenance of order and discipline in literary taste. In contrast, the contents of *The Dial* may seem mutually conflicting rather than eclectic. The clipsheet issued by the editors for June 1922 quotes from reviews and essays by George Santayana, Hermann Hesse (one of Thayer's discoveries that he handed on to Eliot and *The Criterion*), Yeats, Paul Rosenfeld, and Julius von Ludassy and reprints Hart Crane's poem "Praise for an Urn." The clipsheet for the July 1922 *Dial* actually proclaimed this diversity as a virtue: "An exceptionally diverse and interesting list of contents is to be found in THE DIAL for July." It is as though *The Dial* actually prided itself on its Whitmanesque ability to realize itself most fully through containing opposites: "The issue begins with the first installment of a novel by Arthur Schnitzler and the other fiction in the number is from Russia (Ivan Bunin) and from England (D. H. Lawrence). The poetry is entirely the work of Americans: Wallace Stevens, Mina Loy, and the late Adelaide Crapsey are rep-

resented. A brilliant and devastating analysis of modern art is contributed by George Santayana, many of whose essays now appear in
THE DIAL, and there is another essay on the methods as teacher and
painter of Henri Matisse, written by his pupil Hans Purrmann. Hugo
von Hofmannsthal, the celebrated Viennese poet, contributes a number of epigrams, Elizabeth Shepley Sergeant two prose sketches, one
of a notable, but unnamed poet. Remarkable among the pictures are
four drawings by the Russian painter Marc Chagall."

A brilliant but motley group! And the clipsheet has left out of
account the variety added by T. S. Eliot's "London Letter" and reviews
by John Dos Passos, Thomas Craven, Gilbert Seldes, and Malcolm
Cowley. The only poem the clipsheet quotes is "Frogs Eat Butter-
flies, Snakes Eat Frogs, Hogs Eat Snakes, Men Eat Hogs," one of
six poems by Wallace Stevens collected under the comprehensive
title of *Revue*. (The best known of these are "The Emperor of Ice
Cream" and "Bantams in Pine-Woods," respectively the last and first
of the poems in *Revue*.) Elizabeth Shepley Sergeant's Imagist sitting
"in pink kimono by a ninth floor hotel window smoking a cigar" and
staring "at the black open-work of a skyscraper in the making" was
of course Amy Lowell. And George Santayana was concerned to
point out that the very painters and poets whose work was being
reproduced in this issue of *The Dial*—a Joseph's coat of many colors
—were revolutionaries leading us all back to a kind of childish art,
with a difference: "little children who instead of blowing a tin trum-
pet blow by chance through a whole orchestra, but with the same
emotion as the child; or who, instead of daubing a geometrical
skeleton with a piece of chalk, can daub a cross-eyed cross-section of
the entire spectrum or a compound fracture of a nightmare. Such is
Cubism: by no means an inexpert or meaningless thing." And what
about all the heady, garish racket made by clanging so many opposites together? Presented with this almost perverse delight in irrec-
oncilables, this pleasure in looking at the pictures of Chagall and
Matisse—the Shchukin version of his *Nasturtiums and the "Dance"*
was the frontispiece to the July issue as *Les Capucines*—in company
with a denunciation of the tendencies of modern art, surely it is easy
to agree with those readers of *The Dial* who decried its diffuseness,
its being a fortuitous concourse of fiction and verse and belletristic
writing?

By no means. "Comment," in the same July *Dial* ably apologizes for the policy of *The Dial* as neither diffuse nor dependent on luck. The occasion for this month's "Comment" was Professor Joel Spingarn's "The Younger Generation: A New Manifesto," which had appeared in *The Freeman* for June 7, 1922. Although Spingarn did not mention *The Dial* in his manifesto, according to "Comment," *The New York Times* suggested that *The Dial* was the target. "Comment" stated that it did not believe "The Younger Generation" was a recantation of Spingarn's earlier stand as the prophet of the "New Criticism" and that he knew that he had never called upon young men for rebellion for the sake of rebellion; rather, the whole essay in *The Freeman* asserted again "the dignity and the excellence of the creative life against the gross and trivial things of the acquisitive life which make the creative life so harsh and difficult." Spingarn attacked not the younger generation of writers and artists but those who think that the "fragile and ephemeral moment of physical youth is . . . the sole test of excellence," and he attacked not modernity but the habit of mind that holds the test of ideas to be "not truth or the test of art, excellence, but the only test of both" to be modernity. He attacked not new forms but "the disease of the intellectualist who strives to make up for his artistic emptiness by the purely intellectual creation of 'new forms.'" As for the stand of *The Dial*, the July "Comment" could only agree with Spingarn and proceed to affirm its previously announced stand, in much the same words it had used before. That is to say, the life of the spirit found the terms "modern" and "traditional" irrelevant. *The Dial* believed that to publish the best work available in both the accepted and the unconventional forms of expression was closer to the ideal of a journal of arts and letters than to publish work, however undistinguished, because the author was young or old or American or European or a member of the old school or of the new. As a result, *The Dial* published work in forms not yet familiar and had been held to be a defender "not of the specific works, but of the idea of 'new forms.'" But it was simply not interested in the silly hubbub about the age of this second-rate poet or the youth of that insignificant novelist. The only tolerable criterion was neither one of youth nor of age but of works of art. It was "the younger generation itself which has repudiated the chatter of the middle-aged concerning youth. It is they who have been seeking and, when it was appropriate to them, finding an 'ancient wisdom and austere control.'"

Thus, shortly after the founding of *Secession* and even as *The Criterion* was being conceived, *The Dial* was making its stand clear. Now what *Secession* stood for was not simple modernity, although in its first issue Gorham Munson phrased his "Exposé" in terms that seemed to be a call for modernity against the traditionalism overtly espoused by Eliot's *Criterion*. Actually both Munson in *Secession* and Eliot in *The Criterion* were calling for a different kind of review from the kind *The Dial* represented. They wanted the kind of review that was ideologically self-consistent, and Thayer and Watson specifically had reprehended all "isms" when they founded their *Dial*. Both Munson and Eliot strove for excellence, to be sure, but their two divergent and fundamentally opposing excellences existed within respective frameworks of extra-aesthetic values. In contrast, while *The Dial* owned to a clear notion of excellence, this excellence existed within a framework of aesthetic value. *The Dial* was not concerned, save inside the actual pragmatic limits of the American milieu, with any ideology.

Ideologically *The Dial* was rather a hodge-podge; aesthetically, it was coherent and self-consistent. *The Dial* ideologically speaking mirrored the increasing pluralism of American society—of Western society as a whole in the decade between the end of the Great War and the beginning of the Great Depression. It accepted the liberal foundations of American culture, even insisted on the functional necessity of certain American constitutional guarantees it found desirable in order to continue publication with freedom. *The Dial*, for example, was concerned with freedom of the press. Thayer and Watson did not attempt to publish parts of *Ulysses*, but they were concerned about the censorship that confiscated the book, both when it was serialized and when it was imported into the United States. At the same time, in their January 1921 issue they gave space to John S. Sumner's essay on "The Truth about 'Literary Lynching,' " in which the head of the New York Society for the Suppression of Vice defended the prosecution it undertook against *The Little Review*—and the essay immediately preceded three drawings, by Gaston Lachaise, of female nudes. Such freedom of expression seemed quixotic, but granted the frame of reference of *The Dial*, its hospitality to various, even conflicting, opinions was essential. The only recognized limitation was the personal taste of the Editor, the Publisher, and to a lesser degree, the staff. *The Dial* even deemed

Jules Pascin   *Maltese Family*   OCTOBER 1922

it infeasible, "in aesthetic matters, to judge by reference to any detailed theoretic code," and the fact that neither Thayer nor Watson
was possessed of any "fast aesthetic dogma made the personality of
those members of the DIAL staff who were to pass upon manuscript
and pictures the decisive factor in the contents and, indeed, in the
whole life of the magazine," as Thayer noted in the "Announcement"
of his resignation in June 1925. The extreme personalism of such an
editorial policy and the exclusively aesthetic interests of Thayer and
Watson as well as the quality of their tastes constituted both the
strength and the weakness of *The Dial*. That Thayer and Watson
eschewed ideology probably was a main reason why Gorham Munson and T. S. Eliot condescended to *The Dial* and even disliked what
it printed; but *The Dial* in doing what it did as it did was mirroring
the pluralist quality of American life. Also, in doing what it did as it
did with such success, *The Dial* was, in a way, propagandizing—
was showing the viability of American pluralism, was encouraging
a new formalism in American life and one that, for all its aestheticism, would have applications far more immediately practical than
they would have been in Europe. Surely George Santayana was right,
in July 1922, in writing about the art of Cubism as a use of the whole
orchestra, the entire spectrum. *The Dial*, like Cubism, was neither
inexpert nor meaningless. It was a unified artistic entity, constructed
with care and by making use of the whole orchestra and all the colors
of art.

In this orchestration, "Comment" played the part of a conductor,
and the three chronicles of the arts played as it were the leaders of the
various sections of the symphony. Most months "Comment" concluded the issues of *The Dial*, but exceptionally, as in the issues from
November 1922 to June 1923, the Managing Editor changed the
customary order of contents. It was hoped that by printing "Comment" ahead of the three monthly articles on the arts and by placing
Rosenfeld's contribution last, just before the advertisements in the
rear, *The Dial* would gain an entering wedge with "those large corporations which control national advertising." It was not to be expected, the Managing Editor told Scofield Thayer, "that musical
advertising was to appear in large quantities, but we now have some
connection with N. W. Ayer and Company, the advertising agents,
and I believe we are going to carry more of these national com-
modities." There was, too, a double importance in the fact, Seldes

held in this letter of November 16, 1922, because the book publishers on whom *The Dial* had been depending so much theretofore respected advertising pages only when they were cluttered with other things.

But the large national corporations that controlled national advertising would not despoil *The Dial*. Not enough people were interested in its advocacy of the aesthetic best to make worth while the cluttering up of its pages with advertising-*cum*-art, to create an imitation of *Vanity Fair*. *The Dial* was not *Vanity Fair; Vanity Fair*, commercial and comparatively watered down as it was, could not attain the dignity and unity of appearance *The Dial* displayed. And in June 1923 *The Dial* returned to its usual order of contents, with only minor future variations.

The regular departments of "The Theatre," "Modern Art," and "Musical Chronicle" were personal contributions and as such did not reflect the "official" attitude of *The Dial*. It was, by intention, reserved for the monthly "Comment" concluding each issue to be the editorial conscience of the magazine. Scofield Thayer had a clear notion of this aspect of the position of *The Dial* and of its importance. He was, also, amusedly sensitive to the irony involved in the moral stand taken by his review, which alarmed and repelled so many simpleminded *bienpensants*. All at once, *The Dial* must propagandize for certain ideas and institutions, must never compromise but must also bow to the dictates of the law in order to escape the censor, and must entertain as well as edify; it must use a strategy as complicated as the personality of its Editor. The Editor thought Gilbert Seldes too sentimental, too much of a piece, to write satisfactorily the important editorial pronouncements in "Comment." Remarking on the "Comment" written by his Managing Editor, Thayer wrote Alyse Gregory (October 22, 1922) that he felt "this Comment should be in character more like the 'literary intelligence' of such departments [as those] of the London Mercury only let us hope less porous and seedy. But it should be informative and if possible creative in the sense of furthering other movements in line with The Dial such as for example the abolition of duties on the importation of books and pictures into America." But such matters as duties on books and works of art possessed an importance in the Twenties that today has vanished, the battle having moved to other fields, and, too, this particular legal question was but a part of the major battle *The Dial* fought, to make acceptable to America the New Movement in art and literature. "Comment" thus had an essential place in *The Dial*.

After she became Editor, Miss Moore ordinarily wrote the editorial "Comment." Accordingly "Comment" became less combative, in the sense that it usually eschewed the literary controversies of the later Twenties. Its tone, content, and form evolved away from the timely or hortatory editorial and toward the traditional periodical essay of belles lettres. "Comment" gradually was given over to little essays on fashions in literature and the ideal of excellence, as in the April 1926 issue; on the form of the letter, with animadversions on changes in the mode of address, the sale of famous letters, and the like, as in April 1927; on treatises dealing with medicinal herbs, especially Sir E. A. Wallis Budge's *Divine Origin of the Craft of the Herbalist*, as in August 1928; and on bravura as one of the attributes of the seventeenth century, as in June 1929. There was, of course, topical "Comment," too: Blake's centenary was noted in June 1927; Paul Rosenfeld's presentation of new music by Copland, Still, Sessions, and others was commended in July 1927; in February 1928 appeared an obituary on Thomas Hardy, one of a series that Scofield Thayer had instituted and that included similar obituaries on Joseph Conrad and Anatole France in, respectively, the issues for October and November 1924; the next month, "Comment" noted the visit of AE to America; and in May 1929, it spoke favorably about the exhibition of Soviet Russian art and handicraft then appearing at the Grand Central Palace. All in all, "Comment" during the latter Twenties is reminiscent of the methods and attitudes of the eighteenth-century British essay journal, an impression reinforced by the additional knowledge of Miss Moore's abiding interest in all matters Augustan and rococo.

Valuable historically and entertaining intermittently as the monthly chronicles of the theater, music, and modern art are, they also are uneven in quality. First of all, these three chronicles of the arts were, undisguisedly, journalism—hack work on the very highest level, but nonetheless journalism that reported month by month the goings on in the Twenties. Whatever the critical equipment of reviewers as formidable as Edmund Wilson, who for a while supplanted Gilbert Seldes as the reviewer for "The Theatre," and Kenneth Burke, who in December 1927 replaced Paul Rosenfeld as writer of the "Musical Chronicle," their duties as reviewers and chroniclers for *The Dial* were bound to muffle their other abilities. Second, these chronicles of the arts lack the reflective qualities of good history, and all the vivid immediacy of the reporter who was on the scene cannot counterbalance the comprehensive and more calmly analytical virtues of the historian. Edmund Wilson has published much of his theatrical reviewing for *The Dial* in his collection of writing done during the Twenties, *The American Earthquake;* but these brief pieces lack the solidity of his much earlier *Axel's Castle* or even of *Classics and Commercials*, the first of Wilson's collections of old reviews. In short, the contributions of the various editor-critics tend—in considerably varying degrees, admittedly—to be impressionistic and fragmentary rather than analytical and comprehensive.

Perhaps the least valuable aesthetically, if the most entertaining, of the regular chronicles of the arts in *The Dial* is "The Theatre." It lacked the continuity of authorship the other two chronicles fortunately possessed during the critically formative years of *The Dial*, and not until the closing months of publications did "The Theatre" acquire, in Padraic Colum, a reviewer to rank with Kenneth Burke, Henry McBride, and Paul Rosenfeld. From March 1920 through January 1929 Gilbert Seldes regularly wrote "The Theatre," contributing a total of seventy-three reviews. From November 1920 through June 1921 he shared its pages with Watson and Thayer, each reviewer being identified by the proper initials; once, in June 1921, the Publisher helped write the department along with the Editor and Seldes; the other months the Editor shared with Seldes or wrote "The Theatre" entirely. For eight consecutive issues, from March through November 1923, Edmund Wilson wrote "The Theatre"; E. E. Cummings wrote it for two issues, April and May 1926; and for five months, February through June 1929, Padraic Colum assumed temporarily, it was then supposed, Seldes' chores while Seldes was in Bermuda for the winter.

Of the reviewers who wrote "The Theatre," none except Gilbert Seldes and Padraic Colum seem seriously to have concerned themselves with the art of dramatic criticism. Watson, Thayer, and Edmund Wilson consciously tried to amuse their public, and undoubtedly they succeeded. E. E. Cummings's two contributions to "The Theatre" do not offer an opportunity for adequate understanding of his possibilities as a drama critic; in them he exhorted rather than analyzed. Yet, in drawing attention to their own cleverness at the expense of the theater they reviewed, these men denied to *The Dial* the very critical excellence that they were, elsewhere in its pages, asserting as basic to the New Movement in the arts. Edmund Wilson's review of the Ziegfeld Follies, reprinted in *The American Earthquake*, is facetious and anthropological but hardly serious as criticism—though how could it be? Of course, *The Dial* explicitly termed its chronicle "The Theatre." What it gave its readers was a sightseer's impression of theatrical evenings.

Nor did Gilbert Seldes report more profoundly than Wilson, only more comprehensively. His "Theatre" for November 1922, for example, opens with some "serious thoughts about the future of our stage" forced on him by "the exceptionally beautiful and successful GREENWICH VILLAGE FOLLIES of this year," but the serious thoughts are never set down in any detail. Perhaps Seldes never intended anything else than dealing with mention of the "magnificent" Bert Savoy, the Krazy Kat Ballet, which he noted had been excised from the revue, and the singing of the exquisite Yvonne George. He devoted one paragraph of his chronicle to *R. U. R.*:

> *R. U. R.* is far from being a great play; but it is an intensely interesting one, and like *Liliom* it shows how ideas can be dramatized and can keep audiences steadily interested and thrilled. To me it seemed that the Guild gave the play an almost perfect production — in *décor*, in acting, and in the inner harmony which has no name. I say almost because the cutting of the peroration flattened the ending terribly and because in the moment when the automaton Helena first experiences the shock of emotion the director permitted her to assume an attitude good in itself, but fatally reminiscent of musical comedy tenderness. The exact shade of the uncanny, the exciting, and the terrifying was given to the Robots; the relations of human beings to Robots and to each other were skilfully differentiated; the sculptural effect slightly corrupted by machinery was visible in the movements of the separate Robots and in their massing. Mr Simonson's sets were beautiful, but more than that, they were wise, an improvement over his work in *He*.

This is, however brief and casual, criticism of the object seen. In general Seldes rarely tried his hand at more detailed consideration of a theatrical piece; he was fascinated with spectacle and its mechanisms. Because of his liking for the machinery of theater, customarily he treated an intimate revue with the consideration he gave to a drama of ideas. The possibilities latent in the casual and transient brightness of vaudeville, musical comedy, and the revue appealed to Seldes. In an essay entitled "Our Beggar's Opera," published in the March 1921 issue, Seldes wrote that in justice to the American theater "be it said that if we let The Beggar's Opera fail, we did not, at any rate, defile a New York theatre with a run of two thousand consecutive performances of Chu Chin Chow." He added that "Three men of our time were fit by their experience and by their intentions to learn every last line of the lesson conveyed by The Beggar's Opera: Mr Florenz Ziegfeld, Mr George M. Cohan, and Mr Irving Berlin." Seldes was prophetic in his criticism. *The Beggar's Opera* was exactly the sort of thing the New York musical comedy stage had not ventured to produce in the early Twenties, and when it did turn to raffish social satire in the Thirties, it drew on precisely those sources that in his January 1928 review Seldes considered "our most uncorrupted theatre": burlesque, vaudeville, and the revue. To agree with Seldes on this point is by no means tantamount to agreeing with him in his evaluation of the popular or "lively" arts and in his questionable opposition of the "lively" and the "high" in art; but that is a different story from the story of *The Dial*.

Scofield Thayer apparently felt he had been a formative influence on Seldes as reviewer. In a letter of October 22, 1922, the Editor confided to Alyse Gregory that Seldes' theatrical comment was no worse than other Americans would write and perhaps no better than the American theater deserved. Thayer owned he could not be persuaded that Gilbert Seldes was "A real master of criticism and of prose," even though Sibley Watson and E. E. Cummings had succumbed to admiration of his work. Thayer, to the contrary, found Seldes' writing not worse than the average of "our present contributors" but also found that what he wrote "almost always tires me and his theatrical criticism and his Comment I find comically influenced by my own contributions to those sections and not for the better. . . . The Dial seems to me hopelessly Seldes and I should far rather have it hopelessly Watson."

"The Theatre" continued to be hopelessly Seldes until Gilbert Seldes finally resigned in January 1929. Then Padraic Colum wrote the theatrical reviews of the last six months of publication. For the first time *The Dial* possessed a reviewer for "The Theatre" who seriously devoted his time to more than trifles. Colum, for example, would devote two pages to Eugene O'Neill's *Dynamo*, with further instructive comparison and contrast between *Dynamo* and Martinez Sierra's *The Kingdom of God;* moreover, he treated both plays as he saw them performed, even while he tried to inform his readers of their qualities as drama. And in his chronicle for April 1929, Colum disposed of *Fioretta*, "something which is described as a Romantic Venetian Comedy," in a paragraph, without attempting to construct an entire aesthetic on the japeries of Fanny Brice and Leon Errol, or an entire theory of American womanhood out of the appearance in *Fioretta* of Earl Carroll's chorus girls. To be sure, the girls in *Fioretta* were lovely, "and if loveliness can be made more lovely by its own excess *Fioretta* as a beauty-shop must outshine everything that has been or that can be put on," but, the reviewer feared, "even in this line there is a law of diminishing returns, and . . . making mobs and then more mobs of lovely girls doesn't add much to the original appeal." Colum also feared he did not like the humorous turns as well as he should have liked them (the neat modesty of that dismissal!): "Fanny Brice and Leon Erroll [*sic*] are amusing —Leon Erroll has invention that helps out his funny turns. But neither of them has any drollery. And without drollery clowns are not to be remembered."

In opposition to Colum, Seldes conscientiously held that the "lively" arts could bear the same continuous criticism given to the "major" arts, "and if the criticism itself isn't bogus there is no reason why these arts should become self-conscious in any pejorative sense." [3] It was an attitude that permitted Seldes to write at length in "The Theatre" for April 1928 on Eugene O'Neill's *Strange Interlude* to the point that it "is a play of exceptional merits almost entirely spoiled by technical infelicities." The review of over three pages is taken up with objections to O'Neill's experiment with the aside and the soliloquy and devotes a single paragraph to the dramatist's "philosophy which is almost meaningless to me." The plot and architectonics of the play went unnoted, and an entire page was given over to praise of the director, Philip Moeller, who by his inventiveness "helped O'Neill enormously." This kind of writing exemplifies Seldes' fascination with theatrics, with the externals of performance, with spectacle, rather than with thought and action.

He could and did discuss the techniques of Al Jolson and the Green-wich Village Follies with greater enthusiasm than he had for *Strange Interlude* and *R. U. R.* It was an attitude that displeased the Editor of *The Dial*, despite the tribute implied by imitation; yet the rather different reviews of the Twenties written by Stark Young were no more pleasing to Scofield Thayer. Stark Young's criticism, he said to Alyse Gregory (June 11, 1923), bored him to death; but he liked at least some of Edmund Wilson's writing. Probably the editorial displeasure lay in the fact that the pages in *The Dial* devoted to the theater of the Twenties in New York shared with the "Musical Chronicle" a lack of primary, deep concern on the part of the princi-pal backers with the progress of the arts chronicled in these two departments.

Except for theater, music, and the plastic arts, the arts of the decade received little attention in the magazine. For example, save desultorily in "The Theatre," *The Dial* had no regular chronicle of the movies even though Sibley Watson was intensely interested in cinematic experiment both artistic and technological. As "Vivian Shaw," Gilbert Seldes contributed a department of "Moving Pic-tures" to a single issue, in January 1923; it appeared after he had left for Europe to write *The Seven Lively Arts* and to act as courier for *The Dial*. Seldes and Padraic Colum very occasionally reported on new movies in "The Theatre"; Alexander Bakshy contributed to the January 1928 issue a brief note on Charlie Chaplin and *The Circus*, and in April 1929 Alfred Richman wrote on Serge Eisen-stein. "Comment" also devoted space very occasionally to the art of the movies; in the latter years of the decade a brief flurry of dissent came and went, when "Comment" for February 1927 took issue with Thomas Craven's essay in the December 1926 issue "withering the movies root and branch" and praised Ralph Block's essay in the January 1927 issue defending them as "Not Theatre, Not Literature, Not Painting." Otherwise *The Dial* pretty well left the movies alone. The dance and architecture received similar neglect. The only con-temporary architect to appear in *The Dial* was the German Erich Mendelsohn who contributed four drawings of an aerodrome, a box-ing and packing establishment, a factory for optical instruments, and something called *The House of Friendship* for an accompanying essay by Herman George Scheffauer, "Dynamic Architecture: New Forms of the Future," to *The Dial* for March 1921. The dance received occasional notice in the monthly theatrical chronicle or even in Paul Rosenfeld's "Musical Chronicle."

Assiduously as *The Dial* reported the theater, nevertheless by virtue of what it was and by virtue of its backers' interests the chronicle that gained pre-eminence was Henry McBride's "Modern Art." Thayer was not interested in the theater save as an ironical observer; on one occasion he refused to back a play proposed for production in New York, with the excuse that he was putting all his money in *The Dial*.

The entire connection of *The Dial* and the theater is ambiguous. Under Scofield Thayer *The Dial* published eleven plays and dialogues, under Marianne Moore it published four; consistently it published such works without regard for their qualities as practicable pieces for the theater. The only two dramatic pieces *The Dial* printed and later reviewed when they were produced were Leonid Andreyev's *He, the One Who Gets Slapped*, in Gregory Zilboorg's translation, published in March 1921 (and later issued by *The Dial* as a pamphlet), and E. E. Cummings' *Him*, published in part in August 1927. Gilbert Seldes reviewed performances of both plays. Of *He Who Gets Slapped*—as the Theater Guild called its production—Seldes noted in his March 1922 chronicle that "exactly a year ago" *The Dial* had printed it, "so that nothing need be said of it," and accordingly he confined his remarks to the production itself, which he found to be excellent but wrongheaded: "Briefly, these gentlemen have given to a play which is a dramatization of chaos a setting which is almost the last word in organization, coherence, integration." In "The Theatre" for July 1928, *Him* Seldes defended against all the critics who assaulted the play, the poet, and the Provincetown Playhouse for producing it in 1928. Seldes quoted Aristotle to prove his point that the critics—George Jean Nathan alone was singled out by name, but he was "typical"—had abused the play as "mad and sophomoric and dirty; they put adjectives to it—not nouns or verbs; they quoted an inept programme note, and talked about Mr Cummings' typography, his poetry, his prose. But they gave no clue to the perfectly apparent character and nature of the play itself." In telling the majority of their readers that they would not like *Him*, the critics were right; "they would have failed in their duty if they had sent the whole patronage of the FOLLIES and THE GREEN HAT and STRANGE INTERLUDE to see HIM. But they failed utterly to inform the minority what HIM was." Yet in producing *Him*, Seldes contended, the Provincetown Playhouse completely fulfilled its function, which was to hold the critical respect of nobody except those interested in experimentation in the theater.

Here perhaps is the crux of the problem: *The Dial* was interested in the experiments in the theater of the New Movement—though a later generation imagines the New Movement as having largely consolidated itself by 1928—and it was interested in experimentation regardless of its immediate dramatic viability. The dream fantasy of *Him* and its expressionist satire are aspects of the play that a third of a century later the theatrical audience takes for granted. Playwrights such as Arthur Laurents and Tennessee Williams have incorporated these techniques successfully into the main tradition of the American theater, have separated the dramatically viable from the awkward or merely mystifying, and have, to an extent, justified Cummings' early experiment. By its attitude toward *Him*, *The Dial* foreshadowed a wider public for a different theater, though its sponsoring what was not, in the Twenties, the practical side of the theater exemplifies the wilful unpopularity of the magazine. Alternatively it was interested in spectacle—vaudeville, musical comedy, and revue—what the Editor once described as "The Show," and what Gilbert Seldes popularized as being among the Seven Lively Arts.

Whatever excellent things one may say of E. E. Cummings' dramatic experiments in the Twenties, most of his readers will also agree that his most distinguished achievement was made as a poet and that the foremost dramatist of the decade was Eugene O'Neill. "The Theatre" reviewed O'Neill, but its reviews were usually antipathetic; moreover, *The Dial* never printed any original work of O'Neill's, and when it dealt with the book publication of his work, the review was likely to consist of a single paragraph stuffed away in a corner of "Briefer Mention," as happened in August 1926 with *The Great God Brown, The Moon of the Caribbees, and Six Other Plays of the Sea:*

> Mr O'Neill's Pegasus might be likened, in these days, to a second-hand Ford that does go up the hill and down again but with an immense deal of squeaking and puffing. There is some art in the driving but not a trace of the art that conceals art. This writer aims to be a complete pessimist but does not do it beautifully, like

'B. V.' Thompson, nor bitingly, like Strindberg. He torments himself to no conclusion about God and revels in ugly curses. "The best good is not be be born," is his constantly reiterated philosophy. . . . Well, the discontented young undoubtedly accept him as their spokesman, but it is difficult to imagine a fairly successful person of over forty who could look with anything except amused tolerance on the petulant rebellion against life that streaks through The Great God Brown.

But, then, *The Dial* was not perfect; it was merely the best that was possible in its decade. Its condescension toward Eugene O'Neill and its heated defense of E. E. Cummings exemplify the consistently held editorial attitude toward the theater of the Twenties.

Both Scofield Thayer and Sibley Watson were collectors of works of art and patrons of artists even before the Editor's long European stay. When they changed *The Dial* from a fortnightly to a monthly review, they announced their policy as emphasizing art and literature; they would, moreover, publish some "drawings." From the beginning Thayer and Watson made good their promise to publish reproductions of pictures, but not until the first issue of their second semi-annual volume, July 1920, did Watson succeed in persuading the rest of the staff of *The Dial* to experiment with the section given over to experimental verse and prose and reproductions, critical comment, and reporting entitled "Modern Forms," the subtitle of which warned readers that "*This department of The Dial is devoted to exposition and consideration of the less traditional types of art.*" For *The Dial* of July 1920, Henry McBride wrote the "Foreword," which constituted the critical essay in the first "Modern Forms"; after six months, "Modern Forms" was abandoned; and thenceforward McBride was the editor-critic who published in *The Dial* most months, except the summer ones, the department of "Modern Art." The last of his seventy-three pieces as contributor to "Modern Forms" and as writer of "Modern Art" was printed in June 1929, the penultimate issue of *The Dial*. Neither "Comment" nor the other two chronicles are by a single author, and even considered in itself and without reference to other departments of *The Dial*, "Modern Art" remains an extensive as well as a distinguished achievement.

Like Thayer and Watson, McBride sought to create an understanding, receptive public for the work of "the new poets and the

newest artists." This objective he announced on his first appearance
as editor-critic, in the "Foreword" to the short-lived "Modern Forms."
McBride adapted the strategy of Addison and Steele to his own
needs; he wittily sought to amuse people into "improving" their
tastes and manners. His integrity, suavity, and wit at the service of
profound ideals of aesthetic excellence are suggested in Marianne
Moore's recollection of "His punctuality and his punctuation, each
comma placed with unaccidental permanence, and the comfortable
equability of his pitiless ultimatums. One does not lose that sense of
'creeping up on the French,' of music, of poetry, of fiction, of society
sparkle, that came with his visits to the office. He did not 'specialize
in frights,' nor in defamation, nor nurse grudges; and too reverent to
speak in religious accents often, could not trust himself to dwell on
personal losses, sentiment with him was so intense." [4] Such respect
as Miss Moore's was shared by Scofield Thayer himself, who told
his editor-critic on at least one occasion—in a note dated November 18, 1924, written after reading McBride's essay dealing with
current publication about art in *The Dial* for November 1924—that
"Modern Art" was always delightful. In conversation McBride made
little of his intimacy with the staff of *The Dial*, but one accepted this
modesty as temperamental.

From the beginning of his official association, Henry McBride
was clear in his attitude and in his approach to his duties. His
"Foreword" to "Modern Forms" exemplifies his overt propagandizing and his tactics of smiling, witty persuasion. Here McBride used
as his example of the most advanced collection of the then most
advanced art the collection of Mr. and Mrs. Walter Arensberg consisting of, notably, the "shiny brass 'Portrait' of the Princesse
Buonaparte by Brancusi that almost got rejected from this year's
Salon des Indépendants in Paris upon the grounds of immorality,"
and of "Things by Gris, Braque, and Metzinger in vivid colours,"
which so pulled "the eye of him who enters the door that the big,
and still uncompleted, chef-d'oeuvre in glass by Marcel Duchamp
that is posed near the entrance is sobriety itself by contrast" and
assumed all the reticence of a piece of furniture or of a Rembrandt
in the Metropolitan Museum of Art.

McBride contrasted the reaction of an aesthetically conservative friend to his own reaction to the Arensbergs' collection. Citing
Marcel Duchamp's "latest" creation—a glass bulb with a curious tail

to it, containing air from Paris hermetically sealed at a particular
street corner in that city—McBride pointed out that he and Mr.
Arensberg laughed at the notion of this droll joke, but that perhaps
the joke did not apply to himself so much as it did to his educated
friend. This good bourgeois was annoyed, but at the wrong thing;
the "only drawback to *épaté*-ing the bourgeois is that half the time
they don't know when they are *épaté*-ed." What, then, ought one to
do to get people to accept modern art? McBride refused, he said, to
drag in a plea for it; instead he pointed out that the Arensbergs and
their friends were "having a mediaevally good time with it." Moreover, there were distinct social possibilities in the new things that
the Horace Walpoles of the Twenties ought to look into. Collecting
and looking at the old masters would not assist; one might just
as well be—in fact, would be—a dealer in second-hand goods. Instead, people with money to spend must consent to mount Parnassus
hand-in-hand with new geniuses, and McBride recommended to
those in doubt upon this point that they should know a "modern"
artist. To "drop into plain English, cubists are not so bad. Some of
them are cubists for moral reasons. Was it Trelawney or one of the
Gisbornes who met a young man at the house of a friend in Italy
who seemed to be all goodness and purity but who bore the dreaded
name of Percy Bysshe Shelley, and who left the house demanding
inwardly, 'Can this innocent creature really be the monster that is
horrifying all Europe?'" The little parable might well stand as
significant for the entire endeavor of *The Dial*, in all the realm of
the arts of the decade, to persuade its readers that familiarity with
the new art would soon rob it of terror.

Who were these monsters McBride introduced to the public of
The Dial? He began by writing of Gauguin and Van Gogh, but also
he wrote of Elie Nadelman, Jules Pascin, Gaston Lachaise (a personal friend), Charles Burchfield, and Stuart Davis at the same
time, in the summer and fall of 1920. In 1921 Henry McBride was
writing about American artists then in New York, because he saw a
movement of independence away from Paris and, concomitantly, a
distinct American gain "since the grand dispersal in Paris, 1914."
By January 1921 "we" had "An Independent Society of Art, a
Montmartre in the shape of Greenwich Village, the New Society of
Artists, the Société Anonyme, and last but not least, THE DIAL";
all that remained to be wished for was a public that should be capable

of thinking for itself. Among the artists McBride commented on in the first six issues for 1921 were Marsden Hartley, Charles Demuth, the *douanier* Rousseau, and John Marin ("We are beating the world in water-colours, just now. . . . Mr Marin carries the art to a new high level"). Defending and publicizing what he admired, McBride opposed in "Modern Art" for April 1921 the meretricious aspects of the new "art" of photography exploited by Alfred Stieglitz: "He's a dear, delightful duck, and I verily believe that if he were to assemble into an exhibition an hundred pairs of old shoes all his followers would find lively qualities in them and the dealers in new shoes would suddenly discover that they had acute pains in the side like the photogaphers." The trouble with photographic art was that it gave the knock-out punch to "individualism," and once this was understood, Henry McBride doubted very much whether even "democratic Alfred Stieglitz would lend his skill to the anonymous duplicatory system that we seem to be drifting into."

As the years of the decade went by, the critic grew more hospitable to the School of Paris. Like the backers of *The Dial*, McBride admired Picasso and commented on Picasso's growing success, as was only proper in the review that couragously published Picasso's work more often than it published the work of any other artist. Alyse Gregory recalled in her memoir, *The Day Is Gone*, that the magazine's drawings were thought fantastic, particularly its Picassos.[5] Picasso undoubtedly would have attained his American success eventually without the aid of *The Dial*, but in fact it was *The Dial*, more than any other periodical outside the group of magazines professionally devoted to the arts, that launched Picasso in the Twenties by constantly reproducing his work. McBride also wrote on the work of Max Beckmann, but he seems otherwise to have paid little attention to the work of the German Expressionists, to whom *The Dial*, because of Scofield Thayer's special interest, was hospitable three decades before a wider public in America became interested in their work. He wrote, toward the end of the Twenties, with enthusiasm about Brancusi and Matisse, Epstein and de Chirico, Picabia and Despiau, Jean Lurçat and, again, the *douanier* Rousseau. "Modern Art" for December 1928 described a visit, the preceding summer, to Paul Guillaume's gallery in Paris, and Modigliani's portrait of the great dealer illustrated McBride's account.

McBride's interest in these European painters and sculptors

did not pre-empt his interest in American artists, and his advocacy of the Americans, if anything, gains further validity from his widely ranging, cosmopolitan observations on the increasingly cosmopolitan New York of the later Twenties. Perhaps, as he had prophesied early in the decade, America had really consolidated its gains made as a result of the grand dispersal in the Paris of 1914. It was in this light that side by side with comment on the Europeans continued the comment on American artists and sculptors, native and naturalized: Oscar Bluemner, Georgia O'Keeffe, Elie Nadelman, Max Weber, Gaston Lachaise (an illuminating essay in the March 1928 issue, dealing with McBride's experiences sitting for his portrait head by Lachaise and illustrated by a photograph of the work), Joseph Stella, Charles Burchfield (in July 1928 McBride observed the "financial successes" of two of the artists frequently mentioned in *The Dial*, Burchfield and Georgia O'Keeffe), John Marin, Peter Arno (dubbed in February 1929, "the Constantin Guys of New York"), and Robert W. Chanler. McBride advised American art students in "Modern Art" for April 1929 to study at home rather than in Europe, satirized in May 1927 American patronage of the arts (in the person of "this Mr Marland who made all the money for himself and the others so quickly," and who gave the statue of the "hitherto unhonoured Pioneer Woman of the Plains" to be set up in Ponca City, Oklahoma), twice (January and December 1927) complained about the Carnegie Institute's International Exhibition in Pittsburgh ("There is something humorous in this year's distribution of prizes at the Pittsburgh International Exhibition and it is impossible not to suspect that a joker stumbled into the jury-room and put a finger in the pie"), and in June 1929 compared the sales of the John Quinn and Arthur Davies collections (the sale of the late Arthur Davies' private collection in the spring of 1929 "had the charm of novelty. There had not been such an event since the famous John Quinn sale," described in "Modern Art" in April 1927; but the Quinn sale did not bring the high prices the Davies Collection brought, for example, $4,000 for a Seurat drawing, though to be sure this was "the best," "a real masterpiece").

For nine years Henry McBride thus performed his duties as the editor-critic of "Modern Art" in *The Dial*. The pages he wrote, if read consecutively, do not, of course, constitute "history." They do form an index to the consolidation of a certain kind of taste, the

Pablo Picasso   *Two Nude Women by the Sea*   FEBRUARY 19

Pablo Picasso   *Three Nude Women by the Sea*   JUNE 1924

THE DIAL COLLECTION

taste often thought of as typical of the Twenties at their best: the spreading popularity of the work of the New Movement, the productions of the generation of Paris in 1914 and of the similar American generation of artists. As viewed in and by *The Dial*, that taste did not boggle at expressive distortion, and it was biased toward art that amused and even shocked; but it dismissed the nonfigurative and the conscious expression of the pathological. Kandinsky's pictures were never reproduced in *The Dial*, nor did Henry McBride publicize them, and the same holds true for Paul Klee. On the other hand, the naïf primitivism of the *douanier* Rousseau and the sophisticated simplifications of Brancusi greatly attracted *The Dial* and its art critic; the abstraction of Brancusi's *Golden Bird* in the November 1922 issue was the extreme to which *The Dial* and Henry McBride, in "Modern Art," went with the advanced artists.

The criticism of "Modern Art" was topical, informal, even conversational in tone. Yet its focus was usually on the work and the process of the artist in creating his works. The pages devoted to exhibitions and private collections do not obviate that generality; in order to advance his cause, the critic must report its vicissitudes and triumphs. Like most people associated with *The Dial*, Henry McBride was interested in problems of aesthetic form. Whether *The Dial* and its art critic were formalist by strict doctrine is doubtful. Certainly their interest led them toward a formalist aesthetic. Formalism evolved during the Twenties, and *The Dial*, through its staff and contributors, played an important part in that evolution. Still, the prevailing attitude among these people, to gauge from their correspondence and their work in *The Dial*, emphasized personal reaction to the work of art, even though what the picture or object was about took second place, all things being equal, to the way it was executed, i.e., to form and process. The authors of *The Little Magazine* have described "Modern Art" as "a discriminating monthly art commentary," but surely it deserves less restrained praise. If, as these authors have admitted, *The Dial* "certainly served modern art well, with more knowledge and taste than any other little magazine of its day," that service was rendered by Henry McBride only second to Scofield Thayer and Sibley Watson themselves.[6] In *The Dial*, as he was elsewhere, McBride was "a consistent defender of the new art, the most ardent opponent of the conservatives and the sharpest critic of academicism."[7]

The other art critic of the Twenties who appeared most often in *The Dial*–a man who rose to prominence largely through his many essays and reviews in *The Dial*–was Thomas Craven. The Editor, however, never displayed the unqualified confidence in Craven that he did in McBride, even when Dr. Albert C. Barnes offered to give an annual award of $2,000 in the field of art provided the first such award went to Thomas Craven. Thayer and Watson refused Barnes's offer, though *The Dial* remained unstintingly hospitable to Craven's work. Scofield Thayer wrote to Kenneth Burke (April 14, 1923), when Burke was managing *The Dial* during Gilbert Seldes' absence abroad: "I also regret extremely that you are allowing so much of Thomas Craven's work to go into the New Republic. I feel that I discovered him and I know that he is the only writer upon the theory of painting in America today whom one cares to read. We ought to have something from his pen in every number of *The Dial* as from that of Miss Gregory. The nucleus of a group." But a few days later, Thayer wrote to Alyse Gregory (April 21, 1923), "After praising you unreasonably, I did the same for Craven. . . . Of course I agree with you that Craven has very little aesthetic perception and therefore cannot do any artistic work of interest. Which does not prevent him having a clear hard head and in his critical work upon painting usually getting the stick by the right end. And I don't know anybody else in America who writes readably on aesthetics. When one compares him with Roger Fry one realises how much better he might write on aesthetics were he able to see what he is talking about."

Editorially *The Dial* evinced no such passionate interest in the musical milieu of the Twenties, though it did have a percipient reviewer in Paul Rosenfeld and had the good luck to serialize in 1928–29 what then must have been a definitive series of articles by Boris de Schloezer on Igor Stravinsky. Scofield Thayer liked to attend musical concerts and operas whenever he could, but he seems never to have displayed the direct interest in musical affairs he showed in modern art and literature. Indeed, the noise normal in the daily life of musicians and composers occasioned in Thayer the most morbid horror. In Vienna he lived in an apartment atop a six-story office building simply to escape the noise of musicians; though he expressed this sentiment facetiously to his friends, he meant it, and they knew he meant it, quite seriously.

Despite the editorial ambivalence, the "Musical Chronicle" by Paul Rosenfeld established standards as high and as forward-looking as McBride's "Modern Art." Rosenfeld had been an occasional contributor to *The Dial* in the years when Martyn Johnson was directing it, knew the *Dial* group personally, and as a contemporary, was in accord with their aims. He was a leader among them not only by virtue of friendships but also because he had been among the earliest champions of the new writers and artists and composers. *The Dial* furnished Rosenfeld appropriate and powerful means for furthering the aesthetic causes he advocated.

On September 12, 1921, Alyse Gregory wrote Scofield Thayer, then in Vienna, that she had had dinner with Paul Rosenfeld, who, unlike his Editor, had not been comfortable in Europe; he seemed rather saddened by his European trip and felt that his place was in America and that Europe though beautiful could give him nothing. Rosenfeld recounted one charming picture of Sherwood Anderson— a writer admired by neither Alyse Gregory nor Scofield Thayer— standing silent in the Place Vendôme with the tears pouring down his cheeks because it was so "beautiful." On October 15, the Editor answered to these anecdotes that it was sad to think of Paul saddened, but nice to think of him bravely and plumply dog-paddling up cold mountain streams. "His first autumn appearance in the 'Dial' was certainly a delight"; this was a reference to Rosenfeld's longish essay, in the October 1922 "Musical Chronicle," in which he described his reactions to the Bach Festival at Bethlehem, Pennsylvania, beginning: "All summer long the Bach Festival at Bethlehem has had me under its broad pinion." "I had heard," continued Thayer, "the Sherwood Anderson story as being set between the wings of the Louvre, but the Place Vendôme does as well. I had also had him pictured as on the run. But to stand when one weeps is more caesarean."

Derive superior amusement as he would from the spectacle of Paul Rosenfeld's love affair with America, Scofield Thayer nevertheless appreciated the cachet his editor-contributor gave *The Dial*. When Alyse Gregory, as Managing Editor, assumed day-to-day control of *The Dial*, Paul Rosenfeld and Henry McBride were the only two writers Thayer specified as necessary to the magazine. What Thayer did object to was Rosenfeld's emotional Americanism *à la* Stieglitz: "Speaking of Paul Rosenfeld," he wrote on January 8,

1922, to Alyse Gregory, "Might you not convey to him my congratulations upon his imposing essay upon American painting. Twixt you and me I felt he went wrong when his course came under his bad star Stieglitz. Pound wrote me about the essay expressing the wish that we should find some one who could do as well by American literature." On December 23, 1921, Pound had indeed written a typically rambunctious letter to Thayer—whom he asked to pardon his vehemence as he had had no time to tone the letter down into careful expression, what with his atelier and a wife in hospital and no hours at all in the day. Contrasting Rosenfeld and McBride, Pound thought Rosenfeld's article excellent. Possibly it was oriental splendor, but it was the kind of thing that should be done, because Rosenfeld was trying to put something on the map, to make art possible in America. If he exaggerated and rolled about in his verbal expression, what of it? Everything got greyed down by contact with the American reader's mind.

Why the hell, wondered the Paris correspondent of *The Dial*, couldn't there be a similar article on American literature. Had Rosenfeld literary sense enough to do it? As for McBride's note on the Rotonde, it was *merde*, the old fool never had seen Greenwich Village, didn't like it, and always told it Paris was better. The Village emigrated, and he toddled over and tried to lick something off the gate post—the Rotonde being the most exterior posterior part of Paris. Still, it was excellent to have him in contrast with Rosenfeld, as McBride was the complete provincial, rubbernecking at the edge of some foreign town. Pound asked the Editor whether he couldn't see that it was better to have Cocteau than to have old McBride sniffing about and learning that Cocteau was "going to be the broth of a boy." Pound opined that the Editor could—and also that most of his letter was useless.

The Editor of course did not agree with Pound's estimates of Rosenfeld and McBride; in his reply dictated on New Year's 1922, he too admitted liking Rosenfeld's "oriental splendour," but he deplored the essay's deprecation of Charles Demuth as wholly unjustifiable: "The two best painters in America remain John Marin and Charles Demuth." Nor did Scofield Thayer "feel like risking an article by Rosenfeld upon contemporary American Letters," even while he appreciated what he blandly termed the moral earnestness of Pound's insistence upon the necessity of such an account taking.

The matter would be taken under advisement when he returned to America; he really should have done something about it in the spring of 1921 and therewith apologized to Pound for his delinquency. As for McBride, "I do not like you feel moral and physical repugnance to Henry McBride's chat and was glad to get a line on Picasso prices." Besides, McBride, like Santayana and Croce, was helpful to *The Dial* in more ways than one; his position in the United States was "much bigger than that of your distinguished Cocteau."

What had aroused Pound's ire was Henry McBride's statement in "Modern Art" for December 1921—despite its hyperbole, almost wholly accurate in retrospect—that "Apparently Greenwich Village had emigrated *en masse* to the Latin Quarter and like a flock of birds in process of migration was agitatedly fluttering about the Café de la Rotonde." The gossip and description of the rest of the piece were obviously written for an American rather than a European public. Perhaps what annoyed Pound was McBride's amusement as well as his accuracy; gossipy descriptions of the Rotonde held for Pound none of the exotic charm of Rosenfeld's essay on American painting, biased though it was in the interests of the Stieglitz group at "291."

As one of the leaders of the Dial group, Rosenfeld nevertheless did appreciate the movement *The Dial* fostered; his admiration for Thayer and Watson was at once intense and large. Writing of the same dinner at which Rosenfeld told her of his discouragement about Europe, Alyse Gregory told Scofield Thayer that Paul Rosenfeld had spoken almost in tearful gratitude of what *The Dial* had done for him. He said he had many times wanted to thank "those boys" but that when he saw them, somehow the words never got further than his throat; he felt that Thayer and Watson had given him prestige and had been very "good" to him, and he wished he knew how he could manage to make Thayer understand his gratitude.

In Alyse Gregory's brief sketch of Paul Rosenfeld, "*Dial* Days," contributed to the 1948 memorial symposium *Paul Rosenfeld: Voyager in the Arts*, she has given a more public portrait of him as editor-critic.[8] He was, she says, excessively sensitive about his own writing. As Scofield Thayer and Alyse Gregory, too, when in 1924–25 she was Managing Editor, held to an established policy of never making unauthorized corrections or alterations in accepted work, they called all questionable passages and problems to the attention of the author to secure his advice. To approach Rosenfeld on such nervous subjects "required the utmost diplomacy and was apt to create a momentary strain"; yet it was always a particular pleasure to greet him when he arrived at *The Dial* with the "Musical Chronicle," "usually just in time for it to be sent to press." And there is a pleasant visual image of Rosenfeld paying his visits to 152 West Thirteenth Street: "He brought gaiety in with him. Though not tall and far from slim, he moved with a deftness that amounted almost to a kind of grace. His step was light and the glance from his expressive eyes that I remember as chestnut in color—but how erroneous our memories are apt to be!—was light, and he could catch, in the matter of glances, everything there was to catch and a great deal more besides."

Generally, the "Musical Chronicle" was similar to "Modern Art." Like Henry McBride, Paul Rosenfeld consistently fought to get a hearing for the artists and writers and composers active in the New Movement. Thus, like McBride, as a critic Rosenfeld appealed to the public and the patron of the arts at the same time that he publicized works of art and their creators. A third similarity is that just as if read consecutively the pages of "Modern Art" do not constitute history, neither do the pages of "Musical Chronicle." Both chronicles form an index to the consolidation of a certain kind of taste.

Paul Rosenfeld began the "Musical Chronicle" with a piece subtitled "Introit" in *The Dial* for November 1920; and he published his fifty-fourth and final "Musical Chronicle" in *The Dial* for June 1927. From its inception, the "Musical Chronicle" usually dealt with current performances of new or at any rate fairly recently composed music, much of which had not yet found a widely sympathetic audience. "Introit" complained of the lugubrious, musty presence of the American concert hall, and of "the misused passion of the audiences that has gone to bloat the stifling presence." Two months later, Rosenfeld praised the masterliness of Ernest Bloch's new viola suite, and paired against this praise is a diatribe against Walter Damrosch as a conductor. The next month Rosenfeld deplored the hostility of American audiences to the new music, here specifically Stravinsky's *Concertino* as played by the Flonzaley

Quartet. In March 1921 he wrote on the young Italian symphonists: Zandonai, Respighi, de Sabata, Ildebrando Pizzetti, Malipiero ("Of the members of the group it is Malipiero . . . who has been most favoured" in New York), and Casella.

To most such observation and encouragement Scofield Thayer gave a hospitable reception, but just as he drew the line in art at outright abstraction, so in music he drew the line at the experiments of Arnold Schönberg. Twice in the first six months of 1923 Rosenfeld reviewed performances given in New York of Schönberg's music. The "Musical Chronicle" in February 1923 devoted three pages to Schönberg's orchestral transcriptions of Bach's choral preludes *Schmücke dich, O liebe Seele* and *Komm, Gott, Schöpfer, Heiliger Geist* as music that had been refelt with sympathy and preserved with delicate simplicity: "The two transcriptions restore to us again a sense of the naïveté, the tenuosity, the seraphic lightness of Bach's manner of feeling." Meeting Schönberg in Vienna a few days after publication of Rosenfeld's praise, Thayer saw the composer as an objectionable little person mooing about Bach, Beethoven, and himself, and a man not of the first order of imaginative sensibility.

Two months later Paul Rosenfeld devoted one of his longer "Musical Chronicles" to Schönberg's *Pierrot Lunaire* (Opus 21), *Quartet* (Opus 7), and *Five Pieces for Orchestra* (Opus 16). Schönberg's music, as Rosenfeld heard it, was as concentrated as something squeezed with relentless might in a fist. It moved with spiritual rapidity, jumped so many intermediary processes as it went that at first encounter it seemed almost grotesque. The refined burning sensuousness of Wagner, of Debussy, and of Scriabine seemed lodged in the Austrian composer. The fourth of the *Five Pieces* brings "more of the silent and atrocious music that goes on in the body during bad quarter hours. Savage tearing *arpeggios* of the brass and woodwind in contrary motion. In the interstices of the grinding storm, the muted horns sing voiceless, broken song; a flight of clarinets; and the world topples in." Moreover, "The ecstatically heaving violin-music of the few measures of Heimweh in Pierrot which set the words

> 'Durch den bleichen Feuerschein des Mondes,
> Durch des Lichtmeers Fluten—schweift die Sehnsucht
> Kühn hinauf, empor zum Heimathimmel—'

are like an oceanic Tristan-climax concentrated in tabloid form."

"Our dear Paul plunges for Schönberg," Thayer noted to Alyse Gregory on April 21, 1923, "not wholly, I daresay, without reason. I recently reread Rosenfeld on Strauss and sadly constatated that he has not since that time improved his literary composition. One has said a great deal about Paul when one says that in his use of the phrase 'in tabloid form' he does not realize that there is a slightly unpleasant overtone." In her reply of May 17–20, Alyse Gregory agreed; she had reread Rosenfeld's essay on Sherwood Anderson and had not realized how really funny it was before. Thayer had not been the first to cry out against "in tabloid form"; and she asked the Editor whether he didn't think that Van Wyck Brooks really wrote far better than Rosenfeld.

On the other hand, Rosenfeld attracted the Editor of *The Dial* because he was consciously a critic whose point of view toward his material approximated that of the poet or the novelist rather than that of the technician of aesthetics. *The Dial* and its editors were nothing if not aesthetic, as Van Wyck Brooks has said, and this aestheticism began as a temperamental posture rather than as an intellectually discriminated, consciously adopted mode of judgment. The rapport between Rosenfeld and *The Dial* did not mean that his weaknesses and those of other aesthetically oriented critics were to be glossed over, or that the critics of Van Wyck Brooks' persuasion lacked ability. Scofield Thayer agreed with Alyse Gregory in a letter of June 11, 1923, that up to a certain point Brooks wrote better than Rosenfeld, that in fact he chiefly did, that his level was distinctly higher, that he never made a fool of himself as Rosenfeld nearly always did. On the other hand, Rosenfeld now and then got off a paragraph of imagination and aesthetic value. This Thayer never found in Brooks, who seemed to him the critic in the narrow and limited sense of the word. Rosenfeld with all his maladies and affectations was an artist to the Editor of *The Dial*, who called as witness his editor-critic's remarks after the death of Saint-Saëns in the "Musical Chronicle" for February 1922, especially the phrase "imperfect clubman," in the statement that such a man of the world as Saint-Saëns would have perceived in Paul Elmer More the imperfect clubman. To Thayer, the excellence of the critic lay not primarily in the lucidity of his style or his adherence to an austerely elevated choice of subject and level of perception but rather in the regard of the critic for his vocation as that of an artist practicing a certain method and in the conception of the best life as the life of the imagination, a life that itself was conceived as an object of art. Here is something other than aesthetic formalism; it is formalism without dogma and molded instead by all the arts of living. Perhaps few persons are so fortunately placed as to be able to practice such a kind of criticism. And inevitably, therefore, the aestheticism of *The Dial* was adulterated so that what it transmitted effectively to the next decade was not a way of life so much as the formalist attitude toward aesthetics.

Whether his Editor approved or disapproved of the music and the composers and the attitudes that the "Musical Chronicle" espoused, Rosenfeld maintained his advocacy of them: in February 1926, Aaron Copland (who "seems destined to promise"); in March, Ernest Bloch's *Concerto Grosso* (within its bounds, "the Concerto grandly satisfies"); in April, Stravinsky's *Les Noces* (which "strikes the middle way of feeling in our time"; none of the composer's pieces, "not even the Symphonies for Wind Instruments, is as classical and objective, or as radically placed outside the artist and alive in its own right"); in June, Edgar Varèse and Angna Enters (Varèse's *Amériques* "affords a delicate glimpse of American life," while because of "its independence of the significancy of music, the dancing of Angna Enters compels mention among musical events"); in January 1927, a recital by Richard Buhling ("the artist, oriented by the deepest heart of the hour," played works by Berg, Bloch, and Bartók); in March, de Falla's concerto for harpsichord; and in May, Paul Hindemith ("Never a poet endowed, say, in Strawinsky's degree with the instinctive capacity for the harmonization of expression and actuality, Hindemith seasonably showed himself responsive to the pace and rhythm of contemporary life").

The last piece Paul Rosenfeld wrote for the "Musical Chronicle" appeared in the issue for June 1927. A review of Stokowski's performance of Edgar Varèse's *Arcanes*, it shows off all the familiar Rosenfeldian approaches and mannerisms:

> More directly even than from the instinct of control, the composition seems to proceed from the feeling of the unity in present things; and to move toward a form for the entire man of the times. The genuine, large, satisfying, smoky, and metallic sonorities, completely free from the iachism of Debussy and his period; the

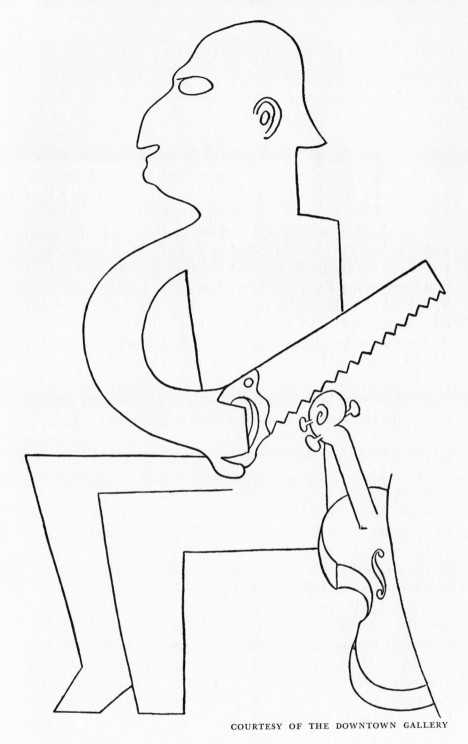

Stuart Davis *Stravinsky* AUGUST 1922

gorgeous explosive violence, its brutal quality mixed so considerably with the feeling of thought, of the cerebral processes; the dry nervous vibration of the Chinese blocks; the high erotic tension converted into the impulse to 'find out,' gathered different emotional strands together and showed them single.

It is an approach diametrically opposed to that of the other writer of the "Musical Chronicle," Kenneth Burke. Where Paul Rosenfeld strove, usually with success, to endow his music criticism with an air of immediacy and excitement, Kenneth Burke strove just as valiantly to give an effect of authority in all its impersonality and stasis. Where Paul Rosenfeld consciously evangelized for the new music of the Twenties and tried to attract a public to listen to it, and did so by hiding his technique as a critic and by using the more general and widely known musical and critical terms, Kenneth Burke wrote to a smaller public that he could take for granted and that he knew would read his writing despite his difficulties of expression.

The contrast in the two critical attitudes is of course attributable to differing temperaments; also it constitutes a kind of highway sign signaling the direction to be taken by some artists and their critics and public, in the latter Twenties. Perhaps a reading of this particular highway sign is significant for a study of *The Dial* as it was both a factor in and a reflection of the growth of the arts in America. Paul Rosenfeld was not much older than Kenneth Burke, no more than seven years or so; nevertheless the older man belonged to the artistic generation that traveled over Europe before 1914 and that wrote for the early *Poetry* and for *The Seven Arts*, that reacted at first hand to the Armory Show in 1913, that struggled with their consciences in the radical years of the Great War and after. These were the men and women who founded *The Dial* and first made it famous. It is revealing that Scofield Thayer, in writing to Alyse Gregory on October 22, 1922, about Kenneth Burke as one of Dr. Watson's protégés, ironically referred to Burke as one of Watson's "masterful young geniuses." That may have been true in 1922, but by 1924 Burke had become friendly with Thayer, too, and spent some time with the Editor at his summer cottage in Edgartown. Burke, despite the few years that separated him in age from Rosenfeld and Thayer and Watson, did belong to the group of Americans that was molded by *The Dial* and the Twenties. The encouragement by Thayer and Watson of a certain critical attitude toward the arts not only substantially influenced the younger men during the Twenties but also, and not altogether unwittingly, discouraged the kind of criticism epitomized by the "Musical Chronicle" and the other essays and reviews Paul Rosenfeld wrote for *The Dial*, which for all their attractiveness are "period" and out of fashion. Both Rosenfeld and Burke knew their metier; both wrote quite differently; and the fact that they both wrote for *The Dial* as music critics at successive times during the Twenties is one of the signs warning that the American artistic and intellectual milieu was changing, greatly and even fundamentally. It was the change that, on a more diluted level than Kenneth Burke's, Gilbert Seldes announced in reviewing Cummings' *Him* and at the same time rebuking the critics of the daily papers in New York. As Seldes said, he himself—unlike the reviewers of the New York dailies—had "the Aristotelian practice of keeping one's eye on the object, of criticizing the thing criticized and not the grandfather of the artist nor his taste in haberdashery nor his private opinions nor his previous efforts."

The Dial had arranged for Lawrence Gilman, then music critic for *The New York Herald-Tribune* since 1923, to assume Paul Rosenfeld's duties as editor-contributor. The plan did not materialize. Kenneth Burke wrote as an "inadequate apology" that, "Mr Rosenfeld having called for a sabbatical year and Mr Gilman having at the last found it impossible to take his place, we enter by a *non-sequitur*, though never for a moment forgetting our office as makeshift," in the "Musical Chronicle" for December 1927. "Notes on Contributors" for November 1927 made no announcement of the resumption of the "Musical Chronicle," but undoubtedly the Gilman of Kenneth Burke's apology was Lawrence Gilman.

The Dial was the most important medium in which Kenneth Burke showed his talents, in the Twenties. The Dial Award was the first recognition on a major scale he received. Much of his early writing was done for *The Dial;* Burke told this writer (November 3, 1958): "I date my beginnings, decidedly, from the time when The Dial took my story, 'Mrs. Maecenas,'" in 1920. Through the decade he consistently appeared in *The Dial:* there are three short stories in 1920; in 1928 and 1929, a series of six "Declamations," experimental prose fiction—indecisively described by the *Dial* clipsheet for November 1928 as "excursions into philosophic fiction" and as a "novel" by the clipsheet for January 1929—with much autobiographical reverie and aesthetics in them; three essays on Remy de Gourmont, Flaubert, and W. C. Williams; an important early essay on "Psychology and Form," in 1925; in February 1929 a group of poems—the *Dial* clipsheet for January 1929 called the work a "poem," however—under the title "From Outside"; sixteen reviews and review-essays on a variety of books ranging from Paul Radin's *Primitive Man as Philosopher* to Virginia Woolf's *Night and Day;* reviews in the department of "Briefer Mention"; and translations, among them versions of Hugo von Hofmannsthal's "Vienna Letters" and Thomas Mann's "German Letters" and *Death in Venice* all written as part of his duties on *The Dial.* This list is grievously incomplete, as many of the translations from the German, e.g., the "Vienna Letter" of von Hofmannsthal, were regularly printed in *The Dial* without a credit line to the translator. Kenneth Burke wrote to this writer (October 17, 1958): "I did much translating that was not explicitly recorded. I did the translating of both the 'Vienna Letter' and Thomas Mann's letters." This constitutes an impressive body of work, but when *The Dial* gave its Award to Kenneth Burke in January 1929, he had not produced any of the books that have brought him fame, his *Counter-Statement,* the first of these, not being published until 1931. He would in future years recall his service on *The Dial.* As lately as 1957, the paperbound abridgement of Burke's *Philosophy of Literary Form* would testify to his memories of *The Dial;* the dedication is to J. S. Watson, Jr., "Out of these several years since the days of *The Dial* amicably indeed." As a writer for *The Dial* and a member of its staff, Kenneth Burke constituted the link between the younger formalist critics and the critics of *The Dial;* his work in *The Dial* adumbrates the typical criticism of the little magazines and the university quarterlies that have been important features of American letters and arts in the past three decades: *Hound and Horn, The Southern Review, Partisan Review, Kenyon Review, Accent* and their many imitations.

The significance of Kenneth Burke, as a force in the development of the arts of America, *The Dial* recognized. An "Announcement" written by Marianne Moore took the place of the usual "Comment" in January 1929 and made public the proffering of the Dial Award for 1928 to Burke for his service to literature, and beyond this for his aesthetics ("Nor in his studies has one art starved another, for music enjoyably and scientifically–enjoyably perhaps because scientifically–is present in his aesthetics"), his translations, and his "creatively investigating interest" in psychology. The Editor perhaps assumed a public awareness that Kenneth Burke had been, for well-nigh a decade, an exceptionally able and loyal *Dial* employee, who had largely run the office in much of 1923 while Gilbert Seldes and Scofield Thayer both were in Europe.

The first of Kenneth Burke's fifteen contributions appeared in the "Musical Chronicle" for December 1927 and is like only one other piece beginning a critical sequence that *The Dial* of the Twenties printed; like Paul Rosenfeld's initial piece for the "Musical Chronicle," it is a manifesto, a full-scale one of fifteen pages. At the end of 1919 and the start of 1920 Scofield Thayer and Sibley Watson frankly had eschewed a manifesto; not until March 1920 did the first editorial "Comment" appear, and even then only the first two paragraphs discussed, in the most tentative and reticent manner, the aims of *The Dial*. Gilbert Seldes' first contribution to "The Theatre" also appeared in the same number, and without ado or fanfare set about reviewing plays currently on Broadway. Henry McBride's first piece as editor-contributor was the "Foreword" to the short-lived department of "Modern Forms," but except for the introductory suggestion offered by this title, the "Foreword" reads like rather intimate avuncular advice about how to look at the art of the New Movement and what attitude to adopt toward its practitioners, especially those of one's own family. There is no manifesto here, either. Paul Rosenfeld's first essay for the "Musical Chronicle," in November 1920, was, perhaps in imitation of McBride's "Foreword," entitled "Introit," and it alone among the regular departments on the arts, as well as "Comment," makes a declaration of belief at its inception. Instead of closing the concert hall entirely, Rosenfeld would enable the creative power of art to war successfully upon the machine, so that the artist, together with his ally the social reformer, might destroy the machine and create life anew: "It is this dream that justifies the criticism of music, and emboldens the critic to his task." In calling out thanks–i.e., in writing his reviews–to the men who are fighting for the integrity of their art, held Rosenfeld, the critic is battling for the life of the republic itself.

Kenneth Burke, then, followed his predecessor's convention if not his point of view. Refusing to discuss music as a "substitute for religion, a secular mysticism, belief without theology," and to analyze a work technically ("Note how the theme of the first movement reappears with a difference in the third!"), Burke chose what was left and turned "to the music itself for the sterling experiencing of those moments wherein the medium of tones is most skilfully and magnanimously exemplified." He categorically refused to be depressed by the fact that he would fail to revive in another medium the equivalent of those wholly musical events. Still criticism would be useful "at those wayward and unpredictable times when a composer's eloquence is happening outside of us rather than within us," for much could still be "made arresting to the prying eye," and we auditors might be rescued from sloth "by substituting investigation for sympathy."

Further analysis by the critic would show that instead of the "classical-modern dichotomy" all of Western music should be interpreted as a continuum, "all of it exemplifying, with varying degrees of observance and violation (the violation being an involute form of observance) the same aesthetic principles." Music is a vocabulary, and all vocabulary is subject to disruption into dialect; thus music erroneously is thought of as "universal," by an error of codification and not as the result of an aesthetic property. It is the indeterminateness of music from the standpoint of the literal and the ideological that has made the question of misunderstanding "a matter of less moment." Burke cautioned his readers against concluding that, when they did not follow a certain musical idiom, they "had no ear for music." He saw the situation as complicated in the late Twenties by the fact that the creation of musical idiom was "in itself a primary pursuit with musicians." They were apparently attaching more importance to the creation of the idiom than to its subsequent exploitation for emotive purposes—not that one should condemn this pursuit in the absolute. Still, the vogue of the age for which they were producing gave these mere exemplifiers a certain temporary importance. Lastly, Burke questioned the concept of "pure" music: "In all music lurks the opera (as Roger Fry says of abstract painting, that it merely utilizes a less obvious set of literal representations.)" The ambition to write pure music might result in pieces that recommended themselves as embodied treatises on musical method or those in which the operatic aspect is a little less obvious than it was heretofore, "the original representative (or realistic; or impressionistic!) element being present, but subjected to a purely musical destiny." Burke's essay, obviously, is not so much concerned with response to a work of art as it is with the preliminaries of terminological analysis. The analysis is conceived of as necessary to later musical criticism; the criticism itself would take priority over any chronicling of musical evenings. Such an attitude adumbrates much American criticism of later decades, especially in the quarterlies.

Because of its historical and aesthetic implications, Burke's manifesto serves to summarize the critical attitude of *The Dial* in its final years and the editorial trend as encouraged toward expression in the three chronicles of the arts and in "Comment." The point of view that *The Dial* admitted was its two directors' shared attitude. Sibley Watson as well as Scofield Thayer encouraged the staff and the contributors to develop such an attitude throughout the decade, ranging in expression from the seldom-stated tenets of Seldes' "Theatre" to the detailed distinctions of Kenneth Burke's first "Musical Chronicle." By 1928 *The Dial* had evolved its critical position, and like a living creature, in realizing its function, which was the creation of an American aesthetic, *The Dial* fulfilled itself and soon would die.

SIX

Some Other Contributors

The Dial WAS THE DEMESNE of its Editor and Publisher; they did not publish it, primarily, to earn profits. Consequently, their personal response to a piece of writing and, to a lesser degree, their personal attitude toward a writer determined acceptance of his work and its exploitation. Such factors as one's relative eminence, closeness to the Dial group, promise for the future, or even shock value determined whether his contribution would begin an issue or would lurk in the middle pages, whether it should be serialized, or whether, after book publication, the work would be reviewed summarily in "Briefer Mention" or in detail among the full-scale book reviews. Relations with contributors ranged from the extreme of formality, as with Yeats, to the opposite extreme of intimacy, when as with Pound or Cummings a contributor might move on or off the staff without official announcement.

Always at the top of the first page of text in *The Dial*, the masthead appeared, consisting of the title of the magazine and its emblem —a picture of a wall sundial placed between the two words of the title, with the date of the issue centered just below in smaller print. Directly beneath began the text; here was the place of honor, variously awarded to a play, a story, a critical essay—or, most famously, a poem. This particular poem was *The Waste Land* by T. S. Eliot, which in the issue for November 1922 occupied thirteen pages of *The Dial*'s rather large print, twelve font on fourteen font in Old Style face. From the initial, outrageous statement that April is the cruellest month to the final invocation of peace, something of the shock the poem first imparted even now communicates itself from those pages. Reading what looks like a group of poems connected by a forbidding title, one is lost in a mélange of tongues, nor does the promise that an edition of *The Waste Land* with annotations by Mr. Eliot would presently be issued by Boni and Liveright, printed at the bottom of the first page of text, solve the immediate problem of understanding.

Significantly, the next contribution in the issue is William Butler Yeats's one-act drama, *The Player Queen*. As an expression of editorial taste, as an encouragement for the artists of the Movement, and as intelligent editing, the placement of *The Waste Land* and *The Player Queen* is still exciting. The contrast of the chef d'oeuvre of the chief poet of the younger generation to the comparatively minor work by the chief poet of the older generation gives an especially piquant juxtaposition.

Yeats published much of his most important later poetry in *The Dial*, beginning in November 1920. In this issue under the collective title of "Ten Poems," appeared "Michael Robartes and the Dancer," "Easter 1916," "Under Saturn," "Sixteen Dead Men," "The Rose Tree," "On a Political Prisoner," "Towards Break of Day," "Demon and Beast," "A Meditation in Time of War," and "The Second Coming." In September 1921 *The Dial* published Yeats's "Thoughts upon the State of the World," here regarded by the poet as a group of six poems, according to his appended note, but later entitled "The Tower." In January 1923 appeared another group of related poems under the heading of "Meditations in Time of Civil War": "Ancestral Houses," "My House," "My Table," "My Descendants," "The Road at My Door," "The Jay's Nest by My Window," and "I See Phantoms of Hatred and of the Heart's Fulness and of the Coming Emptiness." The next year *The Dial* published a group of "Four Poems" in its June issue, with a note preceding the poems and dealing with the first two: "Leda and the Swan," "The Gift of Harun-al-Rashid," "The Lover Speaks," and "The Heart Replies." After a lapse of more than three years, Yeats published in *The Dial* for August 1927 his next to final contribution and one of his greatest poems, "Among Schoolchildren."

Fittingly this was immediately followed by John Eglinton's review-essay, "Mr. Yeats's Autobiographies," which dealt with the famous memoirs the major portion of which Yeats had had serialized in *The Dial* in the early Twenties. As the editors of the review realized, these fragments of autobiography were among the most distinguished contributions they received and were also among the most popular writing they published. The first part of his memoirs that Yeats gave to *The Dial* ran for three numbers, June–July–August 1921, under the title "Four Years," the same title it has as Book I of "The Trembling of the Veil" in the *Autobiographies* (1927). A second portion–to judge by its title, contributed largely because of the success of the first memoirs of the preceding year–was published in six monthly installments from May through October of 1922 as "More Memories." This long segment became Books I–V–"Ireland after Parnell," "Hodos Chameliontos," "The Tragic Generation," and "The Stirring of the Bones"–in the *Autobiographies*, with minor additions to the chapters *The Dial* printed. Yeats contributed to seven issues of *The Dial* in 1922, and by the importance and worth of those contributions as well as by the luster of his name, he enhanced *The Dial*. His attractiveness as a contributor became all the greater the next year, when he received the Nobel Prize in literature.

The number of Yeats's contributions, if not their intrinsic value, decreased after he became a Nobel Laureate. The memoirs trickled in: "An Autobiographical Fragment" in *The Dial* for July 1923; and in September 1924, "The Bounty of Sweden: A Meditation."

According to the clipsheet for the September 1924 issue, in "The Bounty of Sweden," "William Butler Yeats recounts at some length his experiences in Sweden on his recent trip there where he was accorded the Nobel Prize for Literature. Mr. Yeats gives vignettes of the Swedish Royal Family and also tells of how the different representatives from other nations responded to the honours bestowed on them." About half the entire clipsheet, which Alyse Gregory probably compiled, was given over to excerpts, lengthy and brief, from the memoir. *The Dial*, or at any rate its Managing Editor, then Alyse Gregory, did indeed stand in awe of the Nobel Laureate. Writing to Yeats about costs of the changes he had made in the proofs of his memoir, and imagining how he might in a way resent being told the exact sum, she felt her heart rather failed her. To Scofield Thayer she recalled (July 28, 1924) the letters to Yeats from another staff member of *The Dial*, letters that were full of obsequies, which she found sickening; but Yeats addressed her as "Dear Madame"–and was the only one of all the distinguished contributors who seemed to stand on his dignity.

Then in November 1926 *The Dial* published "Estrangement: Being Some Fifty Thoughts from a Diary Kept by William Butler Yeats in the Year Nineteen Hundred and Nine," but actually divided into fifty-five sections and in tone and content reminiscent of Amiel's *Journal Intime*. The poet's final appearance in *The Dial* was made with another autobiographical fragment, "The Death of Synge, and Other Pages from an Old Diary," in April 1928. Besides *The Player Queen*, *The Dial* published another play by Yeats, *The Cat and the Moon: A Play for Dancers*, which appeared in the issue of July 1924. "The Need for Audacity of Thought," an essay on Irish ignorance and censorship that reflects Yeats's preoccupations with the problems of the newly instituted Irish republic, appeared in *The Dial* for February 1926.

Much of the importance of *The Dial* to its decade and to American culture of the Twenties in particular resulted directly from its hospitality to older and ideologically more conservative writers, and chiefly among them to Yeats and Santayana. Both older men lent their prestige to the review and thereby helped make it something more enduring than a journal of experimentalism in the arts. With publication of such writing, it was clear that *The Dial* paid tribute to no isms but stood for excellence alone, regardless of the age of the writer or artist and the genre of his work.

To *The Dial* Yeats was if not an elder at least a middle-aged statesman of letters; it was not a young poet of the Celtic twilight who received the Nobel Prize for literature for 1923. Eliot, in contrast, was a poet and critic of the post-1914 generation that was still avant-garde, and one measure of *The Dial's* editorial courage and percipience was the placing, done by Gilbert Seldes on his own initiative, of *The Waste Land* first in the November 1922 *Dial* rather than the quantitatively more substantial play by Yeats. The editors in this respect were courageous and percipient, but it was enlightened self-interest that prompted Thayer and Watson to print *The Waste Land* after almost losing it as the result of a long argument about rates of payment.

As early as March 1920, Thayer had asked Lincoln MacVeagh, then in London, to drop in on Eliot, whom the Editor of *The Dial* had known since their preparatory-school years at Milton Academy; though as Eliot later recalled (to this writer on July 3, 1958), Thayer had been in a lower form than himself. MacVeagh and Eliot would talk about rates and name some people, "first among them of course yourself," Thayer told Eliot early in March 1920, whose work *The Dial* would be interested in seeing. Because of the mood of the American Post Office, then in one of its recurrent attempts to cleanse the Augean stables of art, Thayer explained, *The Dial* could not undertake to publish anything until he and Watson had seen it. The tribulations of *The Little Review* furnished exemplary warning of what could happen to a reckless or unwary editor, for when *The Little Review* failed to edit an installment of *Ulysses* sufficiently, the Post Office finished the job by not delivering copies of the unsatisfactory issue. Thayer nevertheless expressed himself in so friendly and persuasive a manner that Eliot began sending contributions to *The Dial*, the first of which, "The Possibility of a Poetic Drama," appeared as the leading essay in the issue of November 1920.

The next month appeared Eliot's essay, "The Second-Order Mind," and in April 1921 *The Dial* published the first of Eliot's "London Letters," which appeared about every other month until publication of *The Waste Land*. Then Eliot ceased writing as *The Dial*'s London correspondent, work that he obviously regarded as mere finger exercises but that also brought forty or fifty dollars five or six times a year.

Eliot's "London Letter" was not substantial enough to occupy him for long, and by July 1921 he was planning with Thayer to try to interest Lady Rothermere, whom he had met at the Schiffs' one Sunday, in helping back *The Dial*. At one time these plans had to do with establishing a new international review, with *The Dial* as the American edition and with Eliot as editor of a London edition. On July 20, Mrs. Eliot was of the opinion there was nothing in the "business" with Lady Rothermere, an educated guess that proved correct by the first of August, when Lady Rothermere's secretary, Dorothy Ireland, informed Thayer that she wanted to explain why Lady Rothermere had decided to start if possible a little English review instead of supporting *The Dial*. In the first place she discovered that she could not possibly afford to spend 1,200 pounds a year on a paper—and that decision made it impossible to help *The Dial*, had she decided that she would have liked to do so. In the second place, everyone concerned with the venture seemed to think it would be preferable and more satisfactory in every way to produce even the smallest review, in London entirely. This, concluded Dorothy Ireland, was what Lady Rothermere intended to do, and she would complete arrangements with Eliot the following week for his own review, which eventuated as *The Criterion*. But between trying to work in his bank and to lead a life as a litterateur, Eliot became exhausted and suffered rather a serious breakdown, with the consequence, so Vivien Eliot told Thayer on October 13, that Tom had had to stop all work and go away for three months.

In that space, Eliot wrote the first draft of *The Waste Land*. By January 20, 1922, he was able to offer it to Thayer for publication with the assurance of shortly having ready a poem of about 450 lines, in four parts; and he asked whether *The Dial* wished to print it (it would *not* appear in any periodical on his side of the water) and if so, approximately what *The Dial* would offer. He asked to know quickly as he would postpone all arrangements for publication until Thayer replied. The poem could easily divide to go into four issues, but not more. When *The Dial* received it, it would have been three times through the sieve by Pound as well as the author, so that it should be in final form. By February 18, Pound was enthusiastically recommending the as yet untitled work. Eliot's poem was very important, almost enough to make everyone else shut up shop. But Pound hadn't done so and had sent an "Eighth Canto" to Watson. He added that the Eliot poem, as he assumed the Editor had probably decided, was a whole and oughtn't to be divided. Even before receiving Pound's recommendations, Thayer agreed to accept the poem sight unseen, and on January 29 discussed rates with Eliot in detail, offering to pay $150, a round sum, for a poem of 450 lines or about eleven pages. What must have been the Editor's amazement to receive from Eliot a wire stating that he could not accept under 856 pounds! But Thayer treated the demand urbanely, presuming epistolarily that there was some error on the part of the telegraph service; nevertheless, in the meantime he told Eliot that he had had to notify *The Dial* "that we are apparently not to receive the poem."

Of course there had been no mistake. Garrulous old George Moore had been boasting about how much *The Dial* had paid him for a short story—a hundred pounds—and, with the contempt they felt for Moore's work, Eliot and Pound agreed that $150 for a poem that had taken the poet a year to write and that he called his biggest work was a sum to be declined. Moroever, added Eliot in his reply to Thayer on March 16, to have it first published in a journal was not in any case the way he should choose for bringing it out; and certainly if he were to be offered only thirty to thirty-five pounds for such a publication, it was out of the question. He recalled that Thayer had asked several times that Eliot give him the first refusal of any new work, and so he had given *The Dial* the first refusal of his new poem. Eliot's letter was marginally scribbled in Thayer's scratchy hand, to rebut points made by Eliot, e.g., by Eliot's phrase "first refusal of this poem," is written "not submitted." Still, with Eliot, Thayer preserved a frigid silence; his wrath spent itself on Pound, who, explain as he would, could not escape Thayer's personal and editorial ire.

Meanwhile, Pound had written Watson and Seldes in New York that Eliot had composed an important sequence of poems, and they implored the Editor to try to get it for the magazine. Thayer cabled on March 9 the distressing news that Eliot had refused. At that point, Aldous Huxley, in a London Letter to *Vanity Fair*, announced that Eliot's poem or poems would appear in *The Dial* and gave the impression that this event impended. Fortunately Thayer's cable arrived soon enough for Seldes to be able to scotch Huxley's rumor before it saw print; John Peale Bishop of *Vanity Fair*, who had been good enough to tip Seldes off about Huxley's statement in advance, agreed to change the text of the London Letter so that the thing would be problematical but probable. And at that point, too, Thayer wrote his staff on March 27 that all he could do was still correspond with Eliot on the matter, but that thanks to publication by *The Dial* of John Middleton Murry's essay on Flaubert, which had appeared in the issue of December 1921, and also thanks to Seldes' rejection of a foreign letter by Eliot's friend St. John Hutchinson, the poet was hostile to *The Dial* if not to the Editor. It was a mood Thayer reciprocated: "If Eliot's long poem was anything like Pound's Cantos, perhaps we are unwillingly blessed."

Matters apparently came to a head when on April 30, Thayer informed Pound, "I am too tired to discuss the matter further. What I have previously said to yourself and written to Eliot in regard to The Dial rates [the problem of which had started the argument] is the truth. But I do not propose when conducting a journal for the benefit of contemporary writers at great expense to myself in time as well as in money to waste further time answering letters such as that from Eliot in which he quite definitely implies that in my previous letter I had lied to him."

When Sibley Watson and his family traveled to Europe in the summer of 1922, he and Pound managed to smooth things over. By the middle of August a manuscript of *The Waste Land* was with Dr. Watson in Paris, and on August 16 he sent a copy he had had typed on Hôtel Meurice stationery to Thayer in Vienna. Eliot would receive what was still the regular rate for poetry of ten dollars a page for his poem, a total of only $130, but he was promised the Dial Award at the end of 1922, so that he would receive an additional two thousand dollars. The result was that Editor and contributor were mutually mollified and that simultaneously with its appearance in the first number of Eliot's *Criterion*, *The Waste Land* was published in *The Dial*. It was published, however, without its notes. Seldes informed Watson that *The Dial* would pay Liveright, Eliot's American publisher, nothing, "and we publish the poem without the notes in our November issue. They bring out the book after our date of publication and we send them an order for 350 copies at our usual discount. . . . We take the entire lot of 350 by January 1st and make financial settlement by that time. (The idea, of course, is that we will push the book mightily in connection with our subscriptions. The book sells for $2 so that if it remains a total loss on our hands we will be paying about $350.) I have suggested that they number all the copies of the first edition, giving a bibliographical value to it, and they have promised to use no publicity mentioning the award until we release it. . . . We must assume that Eliot O.K.'s publication in *The Dial* without the notes . . . which are exceedingly interesting and add much to the poem, but don't become interested in them because we simply cannot have them." [1] With this achievement, Eliot might well write Thayer that he profoundly appreciated the honor *The Dial* bestowed on him. T. S. Eliot, in 1958 (to this writer on July 3), recalled that he was certainly indebted to Scofield Thayer for the Dial Award, and for his conversations with Viscountess Rothermere when she was in New York which led to the foundation of *The Criterion*. As he remembered the issues of *The Dial* during its great period and his acceptance of its award, the award was not given for *The Waste Land*—was not given for any particular piece of work but for the general achievement of the author, but the publication of a new poem was considered desirable on the occasion of the award.

The Dial did handsomely by Eliot in the issue of December 1922, announcing his receiving the second Dial Award. "Comment" admitted its editorial pleasure over the Award to Mr. T. S. Eliot. Edmund Wilson contributed an essay, "The Poetry of Drouth," which remains over a third of a century later one of the landmarks in the critical appreciation of Eliot and in modern American literary criticism. And the recipient himself appeared in this *Dial* with a wryly moving "London Letter" about the funeral of Marie Lloyd, with a tribute to the Cockney art of this most distinguished of music-hall comediennes. "Comment" extolled Eliot as man of letters and critic: "poet with true invention, whom lassitude has not led to repeat himself, critic again with invention, and with enough metaphysics to draw the line at the metaphysical, his legend has increased. We do not fancy that we are putting a last touch to this climax." Here also *The Dial* gave certain "hardily gleaned facts" of Eliot's biography and *en passant* welcomed the new *Criterion*. Edmund Wilson treated Eliot, as poet of "our whole world of strained nerves and shattered institutions," from the attitude that is now the famous Wilsonian one of seeing the Twenties as a time of final breakdown for Western culture. Eliot thus was speaking "not only for a personal distress, but for the starvation of a whole civilization." In Eliot, Wilson concluded, the race of poets, grown rarer, was not quite dead: "there is one who, as Mr Pound says, had brought a new personal rhythm into the language and who has lent even to the words of his great predecessors a new music and a new meaning."

Offered as it was in such flattering terms by the editors, the Dial Award to Eliot floated if not precisely on an ocean at least on a small inland sea of publicity. Of all the Dial Awards it proved to be the most widely popular one and the longest remembered. It cinched Eliot's reputation, and quite rightly, for as Ezra Pound told his former teacher, Felix Schelling, "Eliot's *Waste Land* is I think the justification of the 'movement,' of our modern experiment, since 1900." [2]

The contretemps over publishing *The Waste Land* had, all the same, unfortunate consequences. Perhaps the most annoying was the fact that *The Criterion* in its first issue of October 1922 published the poem while *The Dial* apparently published it a month later. Had Thayer not differed with Eliot initially, Eliot's original offer of *The Waste Land* to *The Dial* alone would have obviated such explanations as the reply the Editor had to make to Lewis Galantière

THE
DIAL

NOVEMBER 1922

VOLUME LXXIII   NUMBER 5

50 cents a copy

THE DIAL

SCOFIELD THAYER
Editor

GILBERT SELDES
Managing Editor

NOTES ON CONTRIBUTORS

CONSTANTIN BRANCUSI is a sculptor, born in Rumania and now living in Paris. He first became known in this country through the Armory Exhibition in 1913, and was recently the subject of a special number of The Little Review. He has worked in virtually every material amenable to sculpture.

ROBERT DELAUNAY was born in Paris in 1886. Influenced by the works of Henri Rousseau he turned to the new painting. He is the creator of the absolutely pure abstract painting. His influence on the present generation of French painters is everywhere obvious.

ELIE FAURE is the author of The History of Art which was reviewed by Thomas Craven in the February (1922) issue of THE DIAL. M Faure writes us that the essay we print this month seemed to him a necessary reply to Mr Craven's exceptionally keen criticism of his work.

DUNCAN GRANT was born in 1885 in the Scottish Highlands. He studied in London and Paris; the first painter to exercise an important influence upon him was M Simon Bussy. He has been exhibiting during the last ten years in London, chiefly at the shows of the London Group, of which he is a leading member, and at the Galeries Vildrac in Paris. In Since Cézanne, Mr Clive Bell has written much of Mr Grant.

Since his last appearance in our pages ADOLPH DEHN has been living in Germany and Austria. The sketches we reproduce were made in the latter country.

Like Charles-Augustin de Sainte-Beuve, SEBASTIEN CAULIFLOWER was born on a Monday. Unlike the author of the Monday Chats, however, he does not, according to the account he sends us, spend the better part of a week preparing his critical articles. His aspersions on his native town we publish without endorsement, and only as the "reaction," as he calls it, of a good American.

VOL. LXXIII. No. 5 November 1922

THE DIAL (founded in 1880 by Francis F. Browne) is published monthly at Greenwich, Connecticut by The Dial Publishing Company, Inc.—J. S. Watson, Jr., President— Samuel W. Craig, Secretary-Treasurer. Entered as second class matter at the Post Office at Greenwich, Conn. Publication Office, Greenwich, Connecticut. Editorial and Business Offices at 152 West 13th Street, New York, N. Y. Copyright, 1922, by The Dial Publishing Company, Inc.

$5 a year   Foreign Postage 60 cents   50 cents a copy

(March 9, 1925): "You are wrong in thinking we used 'The Waste Land' after it had appeared in The Criterion. It appeared in The Dial for November 1922; it appeared in The Criterion for October 1922, which number of The Criterion came out the middle of October, while The Dial for November appears the middle of October. Simultaneous publication."

Also Eliot resigned as London correspondent for *The Dial*, resigned in fact sometime in September 1922; he said that he desired more time for the composition of more important work. The "London Letter" in the December 1922 issue is, then, the last fruit of this period of Eliot's career. Instead, as he informed Thayer on November 27, he hoped to be able to present *The Dial* with specimens of the heavy sort of work in which, as he put it, he was less incompetent.

Meanwhile, copies of *The Dial* were difficult to get in London, and even after the middle of December 1922 the recipient of the Dial Award had not been able to procure a copy of the number that announced the giving of the Award to him. To the Editor, on December 18, Eliot expressed his profound appreciation of the honor *The Dial* had bestowed upon him and said he hoped to be able to do his little bit in helping the future success of *The Dial* by always giving it a refusal of whatever he considered to be his best work.

Eliot's termination of his official relation with *The Dial* was not the result of his passing pique with its Editor, of course. The substantial cause for this turn of events was his assuming the editorship of his own review. Even after *The Criterion* had begun publication and was providing Eliot with his own outlet, he made overtures to *The Dial*, suggesting to Thayer the possibility of co-operation between the two reviews. After consulting with Dr. Watson, the Editor of *The Dial* refused the offer; in his reply to Eliot on May 25, 1923, he alleged the enormous deficit *The Dial* annually incurred and the feeling of its backers that such co-operation would not be to their pecuniary advantage. Thayer's comments to Gilbert Seldes had been less inhibited, on March 31. He saw no *raison d'être* for *The Criterion*. All the people whom he had talked with, "including representatives of the extreme left," found *The Criterion* "an immense failure"; and for *The Dial* the going was hard enough anyhow "without hitching up at this crisis with a horse already dead." Finally, Thayer asserted he did not care a hang about English prestige and

further doubted whether an arrangement to share expenses and contributors and translating services with *The Criterion* would be of
help in that direction. But the specter of Eliot's dead horse haunted
Scofield Thayer: "I had prematurely subscribed to the Adelphi of
which you and [Raymond] Mortimer had written," he said ac-
cusingly to Gilbert Seldes on June 16. "The sum is fortunately not
mortal. We must learn to see the good in everything and the good in
the Adelphi is that it makes one less impatient with the Criterion."
All the same, *The Criterion* refused to gasp its last until 1939, ten
years after the cessation of *The Dial*.

Despite their mutual coolness Thayer was politely useful to
Eliot, even helping *The Criterion* secure Hugo von Hofmannsthal
as a contributor; and Eliot corresponded amiably when occasion
demanded. He contributed reviews and essays to *The Dial* until the
last months of its publication; his final appearance, in the September
1928 issue, was as the reviewer of an edition of the Adlington translation of Apuleius' *The Golden Ass*. The only other poem he contributed to *The Dial* consisted of three portions of *The Hollow Men*
(I, II, IV) in the March 1925 issue, followed by reproductions of
Peggy Bacon's line caricatures of *Prufrock* and "The Hippopotamus"
titled *While the True Church Can Never Fail* and *Among the
Saints He Shall Be Seen*. These sections of *The Hollow Men*, however, had previously appeared in, respectively, *Commerce* and *The
Criterion;* and Eliot would send even these "poems," as both he and
Thayer oddly referred to the parts of the "series" in their correspondence in January–February 1925, at the Editor's express urging. The
grim fact was that Eliot did no writing whatever in 1923–24 except
the scrappy contributions and editorials that appeared in his *Criterion;* and the scraps themselves, he said, had been drops of blood
out of an exhausted stone. Pound it was with his translations and his
H. S. Mauberly and portions of the *Cantos* who contributed his
poems much more frequently to *The Dial* throughout the Twenties.

Since 1920, *The Dial* had been paying Pound $750 a year to act
as an agent in finding suitable work; in a letter to Pound dated
March 8, 1920, Thayer made the offer in explicit detail. He first met
Ezra Pound in Paris in July 1921. The Editor's relation of the encounter, to Alyse Gregory (July 30, 1921), expresses his customary
ambiguity about Pound:

> Ezra Pound, of whom I have been seeing more rather than less, is a
> queer duck. One has observed him so awkward as unintentionally to

knock over a waiter and then so self-conscious as to be unable to say he is sorry. But like most other people he means well and unlike most other people he has a finer imagination. At close quarters he is much more fair in his judgments than his correspondence and his books would warrant one to believe. For example he acknowledges that D. H. Lawrence is one of the two or three most important young men writing English today, and he confesses very sweetly to being so opposite in temperament and interest as to be unable to read the Veil. He wears a pointed yellow beard and elliptical pince-nez and an open Byronic collar and an omelette-yellow bath-robe. When one arrives at his hotel on the street of the Holy Fathers, one usually learns from the young lady that Mr. Pound is *au bain*. But the young lady consents to going upstairs to see Mr. Pound and to inquire if Mr. Pound will see guests. Mr. Pound receives beaming and incisive. When in the street Mr. Pound wears what a young lady . . . , having seen us dining vis-à-vis Chez Voisin, calls "Mr. Pound's artistic uniform."

The outcome of the meeting, Scofield Thayer told Alyse Gregory in the same letter, was that Ezra Pound "Now is the regular Dial correspondent from Paris and a letter from him is on its jerky way to America." But by that time Pound had been employed by *The Dial* for well over a year, and he had been writing a literary letter from Paris as early as *The Dial* for October 1920. It is difficult to understand the reason for Thayer's bothering to make a remark that could hardly have been news to this particular correspondent.

About this time occurred the famous and disastrous meeting with Gertrude Stein that she described in *The Autobiography of Alice B. Toklas*. Ezra Pound, according to Gertrude Stein, came calling on her and Alice Toklas and brought with him the Editor of *The Dial*. This time the visit was even more violent than had been Pound's first call, when he had not amused the authoress of *Tender Buttons* with his talk about Japanese prints. In his surprise at the violence, Pound fell out of Gertrude Stein's favorite little armchair, and she was furious. Finally the two gentlemen callers left, "nobody too well pleased." [3] Gertrude Stein did not want to see Pound again, even though, according to her, he did not quite see why. Of this encounter, Scofield Thayer remarked to Alyse Gregory (July 30, 1921) that "Gertrude Stein is five feet high and two feet wide and has a dark brown face and small, wise old Jewess' eyes. She curls up in the corner of a divan and falls over like a doll in trying to receive editors. She possesses the homely finish of a brown buckram bean bag. In conversation she put it all over Ezra, who got back by saying all sorts of things on the way home."

Sibley Watson also became involved in the quarrel a year later, though as an innocent bystander. He tried to seek out a Picasso that Scofield Thayer told him Gertrude Stein owned and paid a visit to Miss Stein—as things turned out, an unpleasant part of his job. Gertrude, Watson wrote, had no painting answering to the description Thayer had given. Also, she allowed that she would not have let Thayer have it, if she had had it. She hated him extraordinarily, so she said, because *The Dial* refused her poems and because he had come to see her introduced not by her "dear friend" Henry McBride but with an "almost total stranger" (a description of himself that Pound was put out at). Watson told her he wished she had made her hatred plainer to Thayer and less so to himself. True, none of Miss Stein's verse ever appeared in *The Dial*, and not until Thayer had resigned as Editor did any of her prose appear. Then in October 1926 *The Dial* printed "Composition as Explanation"—the history of the writing of which is related in *The Autobiography of Alice B. Toklas*—and in September 1927 an essay in the art of autobiography, "A Long Gay Book." (These three contributions had been preceded, in the January 1925 issue, by Frances Cranmer Greenman's charming oil portrait of *Gertrude and Her Flowers*.)

During all the months of Thayer's peregrinations in Europe Pound had been writing the "Paris Letter" and acting as agent for the magazine. Two decades later he told Kitue Kitasono that no editor in America, save Margaret Anderson of *The Little Review*, ever felt the need of, or responsibility for, getting the best writers concentrated, brought together in an American periodical. "*The Dial* might fool the casual observer; but its policy was not to get the best work or best writers. It got some. But Thayer aimed at names, wanted European celebrities and spent vast sums getting their leftovers." [4] Pound's sentiments, however, in the winter of 1920–21 were far different; he was then (December 22, 1921) advising the Editor that he thought the Conrad stuff dull, though it was perfectly right to use. It was good to have "names" *that* year; after another six months he believed they would not be necessary, at least he hoped not.

Presumably it was in his dual role as *Dial* agent and as Eliot's friend that in March 1922 Pound had written Thayer about Eliot's poem—as good in its way as *Ulysses* in its way—which was nevertheless published only after much acrimonious pushing and shoving in a five-sided correspondence between Thayer, Watson, Seldes, Pound, and the author himself. Eliot had had a crisis of some sort, described by his wife to Thayer as rather a serious breakdown, and, Pound protested to the Editor (March 9–10, 1922), this illness would respond to rest: Eliot should have had the December Dial Award, which had gone to Sherwood Anderson; perhaps it would be preferable to chuck *The Dial* and pension him off, to get him out of his bank. Even so, a loan might not cover the case. The outcome of Pound's urging and cogitating was his formulation of the Bel Esprit, which as the Paris correspondent of *The Dial*, he described in his "Paris Letter" in *The Dial* for November 1922.

In essentials Pound's description of Bel Esprit in *The Dial* corresponds to the proposal in typescript he had sent to his friend William Carlos Williams in March 1922, as well as to the proposal of the circular printed by John Rodker for Bel Esprit later the same month.[5] Bel Esprit, said Pound, contained a definitely radical idea as to the modus of freeing the very limited number of talents most capable of producing better writing. This modus was to be a "simple annual subscription of fifty dollars yearly; the society has no running expenses (at least none chargeable to members) and the aim is to free, one at a time, as many writers and artists as possible; this by giving them the deficit difference between a reasonable cost of living and the amount they can make by the sale of their *best* work and nothing but their best work under current conditions." The beneficiaries of this scheme would not be expected to interrupt serious work by doing the vendible trivial; and, moreover, they would not be penalized for destroying their trivial stuff. Each applicant would be treated according to his requirements, as seen first-hand by a certain number of the *beaux esprits* subscribing for the particular artist or writer. The main difference between this proposal and the closely similar ones that Pound circularized to his acquaintances is that the proposal in the "Paris Letter" never mentions Eliot or any other deserving writer; here it is kept to a carefully general level, but elsewhere Pound presented Bel Esprit frankly as an attempt to get Eliot out of his bank and into his study. In his "Paris Letter," Pound blithely went on to add insult to injury by asserting that such an organization as Bel Esprit was called for, as "The individual patron is nearly extinct."

All this in *The Dial!* which, as Thayer had told Pound two

years earlier (September 26, 1920), cost its patrons an annual
amount of $84,000, and which was already awarding meritorious
writers two thousand dollars a year not because they happened to
have had published a widely noticed work but precisely because
they had been doing serious work and needed the money to enable
them to continue. The Dial Award indeed came before Bel Esprit;
yet Pound's scheme for aiding the members of his own clique bore
fruit. The backers of *The Dial* were well aware that the Bel Esprit
award would go to Eliot only when he left his bank and engaged in
writing exclusively. Inasmuch as Bel Esprit had not yet been able to
collect enough money to free Eliot from his financial servitude, the
backers of *The Dial* were mutually agreed that they might as well,
in Watson's words to Thayer in August 1922, "be doing something
moderately popular" in giving T. S. Eliot the Dial Award. The
happy result is known; by receiving the Dial Award, Eliot was
given a sum equal to the one Pound suggested be given by Bel
Esprit, and with no strings attached.

But Ezra Pound made a gaffe by proposing the Bel Esprit
scheme in, of all places, *The Dial*. As the Editor was annoyed with
him anyway, for what he considered his employee's duplicity in the
affair of *The Waste Land*, Pound did not last much longer as Paris
correspondent. Thayer sacked Pound in April 1923 and referred to
the situation as accomplished in a letter to Pound on April 23, 1923.
By May Pound was informing his correspondent Kate Buss:
"*The Dial* has sacked me." [6] And in a letter to Thayer on June 6,
Pound referred to what was obviously something of a humiliation.
The same day (after receiving Pound's letter?), Thayer told Gilbert
Seldes he had never liked the *Cantos* and hoped *The Dial* would
reject the new *Cantos* submitted in May.

Pound continued to be published by *The Dial*, however, largely
through Sibley Watson's consistent enthusiasm for the *Cantos* and
Pound's translations of new and significant European criticism. Besides Remy de Gourmont's *Dust for Sparrows*, Pound contributed a
translation of Boris de Schloezer's long critique of Igor Stravinsky,
which was sporadically serialized under several titles from October
1928 until the end of *The Dial* in July 1929. Pound here exemplified
his theories concerning translation. These theories he bore out by
further writing in *The Dial*, the notable work on Guido Cavalcanti
he published in his critical edition of Cavalcanti's work: "Medi-

Wyndham Lewis *Ezra Pound* SEPTEMBER 1920

aevalism and Mediaevalism (Guido Cavalcanti)," "Donna Mi Prega by Guido Cavalcanti with Traduction and Commentary by Ezra Pound: Followed by Notes and A Consideration of the Sonnet," and in the final issue of *The Dial*, "Guido's Relations."

In the early and late Twenties the *Cantos* appeared in *The Dial*, from "The Fourth Canto" in the issue for June 1920 through "Canto XXII" in the issue for February 1928. A hiatus in publication of the *Cantos* was caused by Thayer's differences with Pound, and then occurred a rapprochement: "Three Cantos" (V, VI, and VII) appeared in the issue for August 1921, the "Eighth Canto" in that for May 1922, and "Part of Canto XXVII" in that for January 1928–the passage beginning

> Sed et universus quoque ecclesie populus,
> *All rushed out and built the duomo,*

and ending

> *Hung there flowered acanthus,*
> *Can you tell the down from the up?*

The passage is followed by T. S. Eliot's "Isolated Superiority," the famous review-essay on Pound's volume of poems, *Personae:* "Pound has had, and has an immense influence but no disciples. . . . It is an interesting anomaly, but perhaps not curious. What is curious is his complete and isolated superiority as a master of verse form."

A more indirect tribute to Pound in the January 1928 *Dial* was its publication of two pen-and-ink drawings by his friend Wyndham Lewis, *The Flute Player* and a *Portrait*. The climax of the entire issue was Dr. Watson's "Announcement" of the Dial Award for 1927 to Ezra Pound, wherein appeared Pound's letter of acceptance reprinted and misprinted in part. *The Dial* published only the first and last sentences of Pound's letter, and it committed a howler by misprinting one word in the last sentence: "It wd. be stupid to make the award on prose-basis as my prose is mostly stopgap; attempts to deal with transient states of murky imbecility or ignorance." But Pound's letter to Watson in *The Letters of Ezra Pound* reads not "murky" but "Murkn"! [7] He had begun his letter by telling Watson that it was impossible for him to accept an award except for his *Cantos* or on his verse as a whole. Also, he thought it would be foolish for him to send in, for the occasion, a prose criticism "of some Whifflepink like friend Morand"–rather a change since the days in early 1923 when he had recommended Paul Morand for the post of Paris correspondent for *The Dial*. As for verse to be published, *The Dial*, he noted, had not definitely requested any, but in any case only parts of the *Cantos* would be available, a stand that may be an oblique reference to Scofield Thayer's dislike of the *Cantos* as unbelievable rot. Pound offered as the "available detachable sections" all of "Canto 22 and the part of 27." These were duly printed, in February and January 1928 respectively; the reversal of order is accounted for by Pound's suggestion to Watson to "use the XXVII by itself; it will take less room and probably cause less friction. . . . As the immediate appearance in the *Dial* is largely a formality perhaps the XXVII will serve."

The Dial announced it had agreed to Pound's proviso without hesitation and went on briefly to draw attention to another service of his to letters, his encouragement to new writers. In this, asserted Watson, he never had made a mistake, and furthermore his encouragement was worth something, in contrast to many encomiums that were "no more valuable than the hair oil applied after a hair cut, the aroma of which had been known to repel people." *The Dial* concluded that prescinding from Pound's deprecation of his prose and apart entirely from the influence of his verse—a reference no doubt to Eliot's estimate—"Mr Pound is one of the most valuable forces in contemporary letters. This is not to say that he sees his ideas taking effect, his theories carried to any conclusion; it is rather a question of life blood." It was a noble healing of the split of previous years between the poet and his benefactors and colleagues. Certainly in justice *The Dial* should have paid tribute to the man who had brought to the review not only much of his most characteristic original work— *H. S. Mauberly*, parts of the *Cantos*, and his Cavalcanti translations and criticism—but also had brought to it such writers of widely varying talents as W. B. Yeats and Paul Morand.

SEVEN

And Still Others

JAMES SIBLEY WATSON WROTE, on the last page of the final *Dial*, that "although a magazine can get along somehow without readers it cannot exist without contributors." Considering the hundreds of letters and postcards that constitute the bulk of the *Dial* Papers, one is above all impressed with the wisdom of Watson's assertion. True, letters from readers acknowledge by their very existence the tie that bound *The Dial* to its audience fit though few; but essentially the contributors were, in Watson's concluding phrase, "however indignantly," *The Dial*. Whatever the variety of relationships the Publisher's farewell announcement suggested, there remained one constant for the *Dial* staff: keeping contributors interested in remaining contributors. Obviously a dismissal such as Pound's by Scofield Thayer could not be a typical editorial activity if *The Dial* were to continue publication.

Relations with the two leading philosophers of the decade, Bertrand Russell and George Santayana, were still different from the intimidated formality shown to Yeats and the exacerbated intimacies of relations with Eliot and Pound. Both philosophers kept their equanimity as well as their distance, and both published a good deal in *The Dial* throughout the Twenties. As Santayana's disciple and quondam pupil, Thayer cherished the older man even while condescending to him. Thayer knew Russell personally, too, and visited the Russell household several times, but where with Santayana he could be easy and ironical, toward Russell, Thayer was relatively impersonal and polite. As Editor, he consistently played one man against the other and exploited the valuable fact that each was the leading representative, in the English-speaking world, of opposing views about that world.

The section headed "Book Reviews" in *The Dial* for November 1922 opens with Bertrand Russell's review, "Aroma of Evanescence," a discussion of George Santayana's collection of essays entitled *Soliloquies in England and Later Soliloquies;* it epitomizes Russell's dislike. He opposed Santayana's refutation of the "glib hopes" of liberals, and commenting on "The Irony of Liberalism" (originally published by *The Dial* in October 1921), remarked that one is compelled to conclude Santayana does not quite realize how profound is the effect of a really serious revolution. He condescended to Santayana's liking for the English character of "the 'gentlemen' who is mildly conservative and not too much in earnest. Intellectual England, Puritan England, the England of the various tribes of cranks and faddists, is recognized as existing, but regarded as a regrettable aberration." As the product of that latter England, Russell ended his review by asserting that most English-speaking readers "even when they admire most, will feel something which they cannot share" in the essayist's outlook, not so much Catholic as Catholic-and-Spanish. Perhaps the most interesting aspect of Russell's review is that it echoes the conscious liberalism of Thayer even while he was aesthetically closer to Santayana's attitude and decried the economic and social criticism of literature here indulged in by Russell. Readers of George Santayana's third volume of autobiography, *My Host the World*, may wonder whether in his character of Bertrand Russell as never being able to shake himself free from his environment and from the miscellaneous currents of opinion in his day,[1] Santayana was obliquely—and with a malice as urbane as his opponent's—taking long-range revenge. Certainly the attack on his former instructor at Harvard seems not to have greatly displeased Scofield Thayer. He considered Bertrand Russell to be England's greatest mind, and Russell continued to contribute to *The Dial*, indeed more often than did any other philosopher of the decade, and wrote well into its final six months of publication a total of thirteen essays and eleven reviews on an astonishing miscellany of books. This notice of Santayana's *Soliloquies* was the first work as a reviewer Russell contributed to *The Dial;* he returned in June 1923 in a lead review entitled "A Synthetic Mind" to express disapproval of Santayana's reissued five-volume *Life of Reason*, and in another lead review, "A New System of Philosophy," he castigated his opponent's *Scepticism and Animal Faith*, in the September 1923 issue.

Thayer's attitude, as Editor and contributor, evinced affinities with the thought of George Santayana, with whom he had studied at Harvard. The consideration not of men's handiwork alone but of the world itself as an aesthetic complex did not originate with Santayana, of course; the attitude is Kantian, Platonic too. Moreover, this point of view constituted but part of a total outlook with Santayana, complementing as it did his urbanity and emphasis on graceful style, his detached irony, his insistent cosmopolitanism. Thayer did not echo Santayana's reposeful equilibrium and disabused conservatism. Where the master was calm and immovable, the pupil was nervous and restless, where the older man was a conservative, the younger was a self-confessed socialist. This is far from saying that Scofield Thayer was a simulacrum of George Santayana; on at least two occasions Santayana referred to their differences. He concluded his remarkable autobiographical letter to Thayer of July 23, 1924: "*The Dial* is very amiable in printing my *Dialogues in Limbo*, which are probably caviare to the general; and I am glad to have them appear there, because although there is much in your contributors that I can't take very seriously, I like the spirit of freedom and of experiment to which you open the door." On August 8, he commented that it was pleasant to know that the Editor welcomed the *Dialogues*, "although I suspect you don't agree with the politics of my Socrates." On at least one other occasion, the pupil rebelled. He wrote to his mother from Paris at the end of July 1921, after an evening at Voisin's with Santayana and Raymond Mortimer, "Santayana is a most picturesque figure, but as I grow older and become more aware of myself and others, I find how really antipathetic he and I are. Indeed there was some friction between us before the evening was over." Yet this was the very evening on which Thayer induced Santayana to become a contributor to *The Dial* and received from the philosopher a promise of the well-known essay on Dickens, as well as other things to come. Besides confiding to Thayer the background of his novel, Santayana let it be know that he had an autobiography. Gilbert Seldes told the Editor (March 13, 1923) that Santayana had some manuscripts of "memoirs of Things and Places," which he would "publish posthumously" and Logan Pearsall Smith "will have much to do therewith."

It was partly through *The Dial* that Santayana exercised a direct influence upon the Twenties, deprecated by him in so many ways and in so much of his later writing. The trickle of influence flowed from Santayana, at Harvard and after, to Thayer; he contributed three of his *Dialogues in Limbo* to *The Dial* (March 1924; August 1924; March–April 1925) as well as various essays and reviews, notably for the June 1922 issue a set of "Marginal Notes" on Harold Stearns's compilation *Civilization in The United States* and for the October 1921 issue, the essay on "The Irony of Liberalism."

A third philosophical contributor, less eminent than Russell and Santayana, established a relationship with *The Dial*, through his correspondence with Thayer, that was fruitful in its consequences, despite an untoward inception. It was in Edgartown in the summer of 1924 that Scofield Thayer began an epistolary debate with Leo Stein, over Thayer's "Comment" for June 1924 concerning some remarks Stein had made about Picasso in *The New Republic* in its issue for April 23, 1924. Stein had written of Picasso, "As for his intellectuality, that is rubbish." Thayer quoted the passage disapprovingly, though not taking the space directly to refute Stein's argument, and then suggested that Stein come to America to discover the direction in which his talents lay and further suggested advertising, rather than art criticism, as a proper outlet for them. The swipe at Stein concluded the "Comment" satirically analyzing the policy of *The New Republic*, its avowal of "free and unfettered journalism," and the contrasting commercialism of its pages. Priding himself as he did on his expertise as an aesthetician, Leo Stein quickly wrote a letter to the Editor and took issue with him. The exchange, which was devoted to a disagreement over Picasso's place in the Movement, to the accuracy of an anecdote about Renoir that Stein had once related in Thayer's company, and to the accuracy of Thayer's recollection of the meeting, appeared as "Two Letters" in *The Dial* for July 1924. A second and final exchange with the same title was published in the October 1924 issue, and again it revolved about Picasso's comparative standing, with Stein opposing Thayer's belief that Picasso was the "chief ornament of our time"; again Thayer questioned Stein's notions as to just what constituted "intellectual interests." And again Thayer's emphasis was on an eclectic and cosmopolitan content, liberal in its bias. Perhaps this approach to the problem of content in art was, all things considered, the one by which Thayer would make fewest mistakes. (For he really was not knowledgeable in politics; in a letter of February 17, 1925, he wrote to Alyse Gregory about *The Commonweal* as "America's leading conservative weekly"! She replied that she thought it was an Irish journal.)

But what was at the core of the disagreement between Leo Stein and the Editor of *The Dial* was not liberalism as it affected politics so much as another, deeper opposition. "It does seem to me," wrote Scofield Thayer in an unpublished postscript (September 4, 1924) to the published correspondence between himself and Leo Stein, "that there lurks behind our more obvious disagreements a difference in our conceptions of the relationship between intellect and art, or, anyhow, between intellect and painting." And he requested Stein to "do us the honour of contributing to our pages an article upon this subject. I should of course hope the subject might be handled impersonally and not controversially. If I myself should disagree with your handling of the subject and should desire to publish my disagreement (or should indeed anyone else disagree with your article and wish to publish his disagreement) you may depend upon it any criticism in The Dial of such an article from your pen would be expressed in the same courteous and, I hope, impersonal and scientific manner in which you would yourself write."

After this handsome offer, Leo Stein wrote Thayer a detailed and explanatory and also a more friendly letter (October 17, 1924) outlining his "system of pragmatistic logic" and declining Thayer's offer; for the kind of article that Thayer suggested would not be worth while. Stein declared he had developed a mode of thinking on aesthetics that was too much apart from the conventional categories to be intelligible in a short exposition. For popular purposes one could only speak in popular terms, and there he would mean about the same thing that Tom, Dick, or Harry meant, nor did he think this particular issue of much importance. So far as Picasso was concerned, the question was whether he had improved his art by the inmixture of conceptual thought. That he did so is a matter of fact familiar to any one who saw him intimately in the years from 1907 to 1910. Whether one preferred to call mental energy intellectual energy was a barren terminological question that interested Leo Stein not at all, as in these matters description was merely psuedoscience and practically bunk. An imaginative expansion of personal experience was the only effective mode. But there were plenty of other and interesting things to write about, and Stein promised that on his return to Paris he would try to send *The Dial* something.

In June 1926, *The Dial* published the Editor's unsigned verses "Leo Arrogans" in conjunction with Adolf Dehn's two caricatures, *Leo Arrogans* and *Le Byron de nos jours*. The latter drawing portrays Scofield Thayer in dressing gown, quill in hand, presumably penning the satirical address taking his dilatory contributor to rather stern task:

> *My heart is angry at your small delays. . . .*
>
> *So you may play your tricks against the moon*
> *And be well gulled, and gull the gullible. . . .*

"Comment" for June 1928 was a kinder, and final, editorial reference. "It is his resolve, Leo Stein tells us, never to review a book unless essentially in sympathy with it and never to proffer his critical verdict without at the last again consulting the book to be sure that what he has written is apt and dependable. Though we are sufficiently like 'Prussolini' to feel we should, possibly, have the same impression of a book after writing about it that we had had of it before, we agree with Mr Stein in choosing, when we can, to analyse what we instinctively like."

Not until July and September 1927 did *The Dial* publish the "something" Leo Stein at last succeeded in sending. The first of these two essays was "Distortion," a discussion of the place and function of distortion in painting, with special reference to the distortion in the work of Cézanne. The second essay was "Reality," dealing with the necessity of the artist's knowing his identity in relation to the world about him. By 1927, however, Scofield Thayer was no longer active at *The Dial*, and there was no one to argue about Leo Stein's points with Thayer's zest and intense involvement. The time and thought spent on keeping up the correspondence and in eliciting, eventually, Stein's two essays go far toward refuting Pound's charge that *The Dial* was only interested in names.

Nor did the Editor's time and effort go, even primarily, into the kind of big-game hunting that bagged *The Waste Land*. He

Adolf Dehn *Leo Stein* JUNE 1926

stalked Eliot, with varying success, but he consistently published other poets. If a poet can be described as having been pushed to his first fame, then E. E. Cummings was thus pushed by *The Dial*, a progress that Charles Norman has detailed in *The Magic-Maker*.[2] Contemporaries as widely varying in their tastes as Ezra Pound and Alfred Kreymborg recognized Cummings as *The Dial*'s "arch-discovery," its "white-haired boy." *The Dial* materially helped Cummings and sealed its approval with the Dial Award for 1925, though for all the puffing his work did not reach a wider public for another two decades.

Perhaps more representative than Eliot and Cummings of the rank and file who contributed their work to *The Dial* is Mina Loy. Her experimental verse play *The Pamperers* was published in July 1920 in the first appearance of the section "Modern Forms." In August 1921 appeared her poem "Perlun," and in October, "Poe." Also she contributed three pictures to *The Dial*, two untitled water colors of women in April 1921 and a wash drawing, *Baby's Head*, in February 1922. "Notes on Contributors" for July 1920 identified her as Mme. Arthur Cravan, "a member of the Paris Salon," who "was born in England and has lived and travelled in both Europe and South America. She now resides in New York." In June 1926, *The Dial* printed Yvor Winters' appreciation, "Mina Loy," an attempt at literary classification. According to Winters, Mina Loy was one of the four outstanding poets of the group that published *Others*, along with Marianne Moore, William Carlos Williams, and Wallace Stevens: "She attacked the dirty commonplace with the doggedness of a weight-lifter. Nearly any one might have written her worst poems, and innumerable small fry have written poems as good. Her success, if the least dazzling of the four, is not the least impressive, and is by all odds the most astounding. Using an unexciting method, and writing of the drabbest of material, she has written seven or eight of the most brilliant and unshakably solid satirical poems of our time, and at least two non-satirical pieces that possess for me a beauty that is unspeakably moving and profound." Oddly, the clip-sheet for the issue omitted, probably by editorial intention, Miss Moore's name from the list of outstanding poets of the *Others* group.

In the period after 1912–13, Mina Loy was one of the more spirited and shocking poets of the New Movement. She participated in the early activities of the Provincetown Players, and Alfred Kreymborg published her verse in *Others* and thereby aroused the opposition of the opponents of the movement. Mina Loy is encountered in Kreymborg's autobiography *Troubadour* as "redoubtable" and "super-sophisticated." [3] Perhaps, as the writers of *The Little Magazine* suggest, Scofield Thayer met the poets of the *Others* group at a party one evening late in 1919 at Alfred Kreymborg's New York apartment—Kreymborg asserted that Thayer first met Marianne Moore there and procured her first contribution to *The Dial*: "England," published in April 1920—but to assert as they do that *The Dial* in its "poetic tone was really a continuation of the *Others* spirit" is so obvious an inaccuracy as not to need refutation. [4] Scofield Thayer had an entrée wherever he wanted to go, and he did not need Alfred Kreymborg to introduce him to Mina Loy, Marianne Moore, Lola Ridge, or any other ladies who contributed their verses to *Others* and later to *The Dial*.

Mina Loy was, in the early Twenties, an acquaintance whom Scofield Thayer saw occasionally in New York (where she and Thayer probably first met), Vienna (where he considered engaging her as his secretary), and Paris (where, so she wrote the Editor on September 19, 1921, she found lots of New Yorkers—Marsden, Djuna, Bobby, all reacting in their different ways—and managed to amuse James Joyce). Her sixth and final appearance in *The Dial* was in November 1922, with "Brancusi's Golden Bird":

> *The toy*
> *become the aesthetic archetype*
>
> *As if*
>
> *some patient peasant God*
> *had rubbed and rubbed*
> *the Alpha and Omega*
> *of Form into a lump of metal. . . .*
>
> *The immaculate*
> *conception*
> *of the inaudible bird*
> *occurs*
> *in gorgeous reticence . . .*

The publication of the poem illustrates another aspect of the relations of *The Dial* with its contributors. Often Thayer used photographs of objects and reproductions of pictures much as a lecturer

Adolf Dehn   *Le Byron de nos jours*   JUNE 1926

uses slides to illustrate points in his talk; the text, really, is ancillary to the art that it is concerned with. He had accepted Mina Loy's poem in April 1922 and had asked Gilbert Seldes to hold its publication until it could appear in the same issue with photographs of the work of Brancusi. Thus juxtaposed to "Brancusi's Golden Bird" in the magazine is a photograph of the gorgeous bird itself, gleamingly reflecting the photographer's magnesium flash, but erroneously credited to the collection of John Quinn. This elicited Thayer's complaint to the Managing Editor (November 28, 1922) that "The picture in question has *no aesthetic value whatever* and is *commercially suicidal.* As to the quality of "The Golden Bird," having seen only this picture I, of course, have no idea whatever." Seldes apologized for the error and admitted to the Editor (December 14, 1922) that "The Brancusi situation is sufficiently complicated here also. A Mrs Foster seems to have control of the photographs and as soon as she returns to town I shall try to make some arrangements with her for you to see what she has. It was she who was instrumental in getting us the Golden Bird, and I entirely mistook a kind remark of John Quinn's and superfluously gave him credit. Watson knows nothing better than Mrs Foster as a source."

In 1922 Brancusi had of course been known since the Armory Show to adventurous collectors such as John Quinn and the Arensbergs, but it was *The Dial* that put his work in wider repute. Besides Brancusi's golden bird praised by Mina Loy, *The Dial* published in February 1927 an essay, "Brancusi," by Dorothy Dudley, accompanied by a photograph of John Quinn's marble version of Mlle. Pogany, of the several Brancusi made, and a line drawing of a *Nude* lent by the Brummer Gallery. The essayist felt that a room with Brancusi's "geometry of forms in bronze, wood, and stone" was one without measurement, a room to feel happy in: "One had entered into something." Brancusi's art was the art of the future, inasmuch as once "rid of the religions and philosophies, art is the one thing that can save the world." In her views Dorothy Dudley was echoing the opinion of the artist himself, whom she quoted as saying that "In the art of other times there is joy, but with it the nightmare the religions drag with them. There is joy in Negro sculpture, among the nearly archaic Greeks, in some things of the Chinese and the Gothic. . . . Oh, we find it everywhere. . . . But even so, not so well as it might be with us in the future, if only we were to go out of all this." Such, his admirer insisted, was Brancusi's "lonely primitive faith" flashing in him.

Others felt less sanguine and less tolerant about Brancusi than did Mina Loy and Dorothy Dudley. Thayer had originally planned to include a photograph of one work by Brancusi in his folio *Living Art*, and he carried out his plan despite the sculptor's anxiety not to be reproduced any more, together with his insistence that only *his* selection of photographs be submitted through Dr. Watson to the compiler of *Living Art*. True, Watson believed this to be mostly a pose, he told Thayer (July 29, 1922), and was disgusted at Ezra Pound's chittering and kowtowing and apologizing when the two of them went up to Brancusi's studio to take a look at whatever might prove suitable. Thayer wanted only one photograph for reproduction, but for all his show of reluctance Brancusi ended by pushing two into the hands of Watson, who had pointed out several things he thought Thayer would like but must take what the master gave. "You win the victory," said Brancusi as though Watson had been beseeching him for a week. It was, according to Dr. Watson, a damned Pyrrhic victory. Thayer, apparently, agreed, for John Quinn's callipygian marble was the only example by Brancusi reproduced in *Living Art*, wherein the rear view appeared under the demure appellation of *Marble*.

The publication by *The Dial*, in November 1922, of the golden bird of Brancusi and its poem preceded by several years a *cause célèbre* in American art in the Twenties, the dispute in 1927–28 over whether the sculptor's *Bird in Flight* was to be allowed, as the purchase of Edward Steichen, to pass through the United States Customs without duty, as became a true work of art, or whether it must pay the ad valorem tax of forty per cent required of more utilitarian metalwork. Fortunately for the New Movement in art and for the peace of mind of its advocates, the three judges of the United States Customs Court ruled unanimously that the sculpture was "the original production of a professional sculptor and is in fact a piece of sculpture and a work of art," and as such entitled to free entry. Henry McBride testified on Brancusi's behalf at the trial and extensively wrote his view of the case in "Modern Art" for February 1927 and January 1928.

The Dial not only proved hospitable to the new writing but through regularly published letters from its foreign correspondents as well as the monthly chronicles of the arts, conscientiously attempted to keep its readers abreast of developments in the New Movement. Pound and Paul Morand wrote a "Paris Letter" for the purpose, just as Eliot and his successor Raymond Mortimer wrote a "London Letter." Rafaello Piccoli occasionally contributed an "Italian Letter," and at long intervals throughout the decade several correspondents wrote a "Russian Letter," the last of which was contributed by Maxim Gorki, from Moscow, and printed in March 1929, as the meager outcome of Thayer's effort in 1924–25 to secure him as correspondent. José Ortega y Gasset contributed the "Spanish Letter" for October 1924. Equally exotic were Stoyan Christowe's "Bulgarian Letter" printed in January 1929 and the "Prague Letter," two of these by P. Beaumont Wadsworth in December 1922 and July 1923 and one by Edwin Muir, as "Edward Moore," in April 1922. A final "Prague Letter" was by Otokar Fischer in December 1923; Fischer and Béla Balázs, who (from his exile in Vienna) wrote the "Hungarian Letter" in April 1923, were, according to Marianne Moore, "inactive" foreign correspondents. Translating the letters from abroad was, of course, an essential chore. Marianne Moore has noted that these "foreign letter translations–unsigned in accordance with *Dial* practice–should make the ghost of the magazine intensively apologetic to [Sibley Watson], to Scofield Thayer, to Kenneth Burke, Alexander Gunn, Eva Goldbeck, Hildegard Nagel, Ellen Thayer, and some two or three others." [5] Such a spate of newsletters did not pass unsatirized. In May and September 1921, as W. C. Blum, Sibley Watson burlesqued *The Dial*'s foreign correspondents in the "American Letter," the first of which was dated from "Traverse City, Mich., April 1921"; not to be outdone, Gilbert Seldes, as "Sebastien Cauliflower," contributed a third "American Letter" to *The Dial* for November 1922.

The *Dial*'s cosmopolitan spirit is also exemplified in the "Dublin Letter," as well as in the magazine's relations with Irish writers and artists. *The Dial* for many years preceding its transforming at the start of 1920 had followed the course of the Irish literary revival. Its greatest admiration was for Yeats; and despite the Editor's condescension to George Moore, he told his Managing Editor (September 24, 1921), "I want The Dial to be friends with Moore."

The first "Dublin Letter" appeared in May 1920; by Ernest Boyd, it dealt with the novels and plays produced by Irish writers in

Ireland and reflecting the national struggle then approaching its height. From March 1921 through May 1929 the literature and society of modern Ireland as it painfully took shape were the scene observed by "John Eglinton"—the pen name of William Kirkpatrick Magee—in his eight "Dublin Letters" and, from December 1926, six "Irish Letters." Appropriately the first of Eglinton's letters discussed the Irish Renascence and the post-1916 writers such as Daniel Corkery; and the final letter in May 1929 returned to this subject, giving consideration to the single personality who at the time best represented Ireland. Eglinton dismissed Burke, Goldsmith, and Carleton, because by 1929 the English ascendancy and the Protestant supremacy were vanishing; to the older generation of the late Twenties the only Anglo-Irish author held in esteem was Yeats, but Eglinton held that perhaps one day to the future generations Joyce would occupy this position—a sensible if not singularly percipient prophecy.

For a time during the mid-Twenties, Eglinton moved to London, and there was a hiatus in the "Dublin Letters." Scofield Thayer, in an attempt to fill the post of the Dublin correspondent, wrote to James Stephens on November 15, 1923. Recalling the "unique and superb short stories" Stephens had contributed to *The Dial* in 1920, the Editor asked for some shorter pieces—shorter, that is, than the *Deirdre* he had heard Stephens had just finished writing—and then proceeded to the real point of his letter, the request that Stephens consider the post of Dublin correspondent writing, as had Eglinton, "letters upon the artistic and literary life of Dublin and indeed of Ireland every few months—letters from one thousand to three thousand words."

Stephens contributed significantly to *The Dial:* in 1920, four stories, "The Boss," "Desire," "The Thieves," and "In the Beechwood," and a few poems, "The Last Word" in March 1923 and "Three Poems" ("Death," "The Rose in the Wind," and "The Main-Deep") in November 1924.

He also complied with Thayer's request and provided *The Dial* with four letters, the first two entitled "Irish Letter" in *The Dial* of April and June 1924, the latter two entitled "Dublin Letter" in August 1924 and April 1925. Perhaps Stephens' chief contribution to the "Dublin Letter"—and a very important one it was—was his announcement in *The Dial* for June 1924 (the letter dated as of

May, however) of an exciting new voice in Irish literature: "Our dramatist, Colum, from whom we expected great things, has become an American; our critic, Boyd, has become an American; and to be an American is at least as difficult an occupation as those they hurried from in Dublin. And now, for woe falls on woe, Yeats is a senator, Russell is an editor, Moore is a Londoner, Gogarty is a demi-absentee, and Magee"–i.e., John Eglinton–"a foreigner. Once more Ireland is exporting her saints and scholars, and is but ill-comforted in retaining her senators, her editors, her republicans and sinners–her kittle cattle. The arena is being left to the young folk, and some of them are writing verse that one must be even younger to read. Five years hence, or even next year under the stimulus of O'Casey, our new dramatist . . . they may be less tenuous." And Stephens' next letter, in August 1924, praised O'Casey's *Juno and the Paycock* as "in every way worthy of that delicate and delightful title" and as "Irish in every word of it, but it is magnificently more." But Stephens dropped his *Dial* correspondence, which after all was journalism rather than serious writing, and not until Magee returned from his sojourn across the Irish Sea did *The Dial* resume its "Irish Letter" in December 1926.

Padraic Colum, one of the expatriates from Ireland mentioned by Stephens, was for years the chief representative of the writers of the Irish literary revival directly connected with *The Dial*. Not only did he regularly review books such as Lady Gregory's *The Image and Other Plays*, as an Irish writer (in the November 1922 issue); also no contributor ever gave *The Dial* more faithful service. Colum had begun writing for *The Dial* when Martyn Johnson had taken over the magazine from the Browne interests of Chicago and, with Randolph Bourne and others, had become a contributing editor to Johnson's *Dial* in March 1917. Shortly before assuming Gilbert Seldes' duties as reviewer for "The Theatre" in February 1929, Colum had published in *The Dial* the Prologue to his comedy *Balloon* in December 1928; he, Cummings, and Edmund Wilson were the contributors to "The Theatre" who were playwrights as well as reviewers of plays. As one of the chief reviewers for *The Dial*, Colum turned his hand to writing about the classics of ancient literature as they were edited and translated in the Loeb Classical Library, and to the March 1929 issue he also contributed a sizeable review-essay, "Infinite Correspondences," dealing with the second volume of Spengler's *Decline of the West*, with citations from several other works on the philosophy of history such as Christopher Dawson's *Age of the Gods*. A dozen of his poems and a couple of his stories appeared in *The Dial* at intervals throughout the Twenties. Colum's intimacy with the staff of *The Dial* has been recalled by Marianne Moore, who mentions his casual visits to the offices of the review and the nickname given him by John Cowper Powys of the "fairy cardinal"—an allusion no doubt to his faith as well as his red hair.[6]

Colum as a friend of Joyce and of *The Dial* contributed to the April 1928 issue his preface, entitled "The River Episode from James Joyce's Uncompleted Work," to *Anna Livia Plurabelle*, the limited edition of an episode from the then unfinished and untitled *Finnegans Wake*, published by Crosby Gaige in 1928. Joyce himself—though he was the subject of reviews and critiques throughout the last ten years of *The Dial*—published only a single poem in it, "A Memory of the Players at Midnight," in July 1920. Despite Scofield Thayer's discriminating admiration of Joyce's work, most of it *The Dial* would not print out of fear of the censorship that confiscated *The Little Review;* but Thayer's financial help given to Joyce just after the Great War (through the intervention of Mary and Padraic Colum) and his continued interest in Joyce resulted in a meeting of the two men in Paris in 1921. Of their encounter Thayer wrote Alyse Gregory (July 30, 1921) that "James Joyce is much more Padraic Colum than reading Pound and Eliot one would have thought. The man is much more obviously ailing . . . . a Paris apothecary recently gave him inadvertently some acid for his eyes, the result being that he is mostly blind and strikes me as the most unhappy man I have ever seen. One is again aware how outrageously de trop refinement in this universe is." From the meeting nothing more tangible emerged than this informal editorial reminiscence.

In the middle Twenties, a younger generation of Irish writers made its appearance in *The Dial:* Liam O'Flaherty with a prose piece, "The Conger Eel," in January 1925; and Seán O'Faoláin with a story "Under the Roof," in September 1926. *The Dial* moreover was hospitable to at least one Irish artist as well as the three literary generations of Irish writers in their several ethnic varieties; Jack B. Yeats, the brother of the poet, appeared in four issues, with such drawings reproduced as his vignettes of Irish life, *New Arrivals at the Fair* and *The Old Harness Cart*, in March 1924, and such oils as *Fair Day, Dublin Newsboys*, and *The Funeral of a Republican*, in February 1927. Despite Padraic Colum's praise of the art of Lady Gregory as "the only playwright of today who writes comedies that have poetry in them," the only Irish playwrights to contribute to *The Dial* were George Moore, with his closet drama *The Apostle*, serialized in June and July 1923; William Butler Yeats, with *The Player Queen* and *The Cat and the Moon: A Play for Dancers;* and Padraic Colum with his Prologue to *Balloon: A Comedy.*

The German note—more specifically, the note of German culture as represented chiefly by writers and artists of the Viennese and Berlin circles—insistently rang through *The Dial* month after month, to the pleasure of its Editor and the improvement of its readers but also to the exasperation of the staff in New York, who kept pleading for more French and fewer German writers and artists to be represented in the review. There were objections, Sibley Watson wrote Thayer (March 10, 1923), to the "preponderance" of German and Austrian material in *The Dial;* two months later (May 12, 1923), Thayer completed the circle by telling Kenneth Burke—Watson's protegé on the staff and also the staff translator of contributions in German—that Watson "feels that we are running too much Teutonic stuff."

The staff had little cause for its alarm. Literarily, the weakest aspect of *The Dial*'s cosmopolitan attitude certainly was not its failure to publish French writing of the 1920's. From the first year, contemporary poetry from France was published: two poems ("Nocturne" and "Villonesque") by Guy-Charles Cros appeared in the original French, in September 1920; and in March 1921 were printed two poems by André Spire, "Dagmara" and "Midi," also in the French. And in July 1920, Sibley Watson's version of Rimbaud's *A Season in Hell* used both French and English, though his version of the *Illuminations*, in August 1920, was in English only. (One month, March 1921, even four of the "Briefer Mentions" were in French!—reviews of Paul Bourget's *Anomalies*, Valéry's *Album de Vers Anciens*, Duhamel's *La Confession de Minuit*, and the Comte de Gobineau's *Mademoiselle Irnois*.) In May 1921 Witter Bynner contributed a translation of Charles Vildrac's poems, "A Friendship" and "The One Song." But not until April 1929 did a poem by Paul Valéry appear, "Helen, the Sad Queen," in Janet Lewis's version.

There were, however, some essays by Valéry printed earlier in
their English versions: Natalie Clifford Barney's translation of "An
Evening with M. Teste," in February 1922; in June 1925, Lewis
Galantière's version of "A Letter from Madame Émilie Teste"; in
January 1926, a memorial piece, "Pierre Louÿs, 1870–1925"; "The
Method of Leonardo da Vinci: Note and Digression" in June (Part
I) and July (Part II) 1926; and in November 1927, in Lewis
Galantière's translation, the "Discourse in Praise of Anatole France
Pronounced by Paul Valéry on the Occasion of His Admission to
the French Academy." This issue of *The Dial* was something of an
hommage to the new Academician. The "Discourse" was accompanied by Galantière's essay "On the Poems of Paul Valéry"; J. H.
Lewis contributed "A Note on Paul Valéry"; and Alyse Gregory
reviewed Valéry's *Varieté*. It is worth noting that Valéry contributed to *The Dial* mostly after Scofield Thayer had, effectively at
least, relinquished its active direction to Marianne Moore; indeed the
first substantial notice of his work did not appear in the magazine
until June 1925, Edmund Wilson's review-essay, "Paul Valéry."

While Thayer was active as Editor, Anatole France, with much
publicity, contributed *La Vie en Fleur*. Thayer wrote Seldes
(July 30, 1921) that *La Vie en Fleur* was "the most important
acquisition, apart from Yeats' 'Four Years,' which I have yet made
for the Dial. . . . The translation of these memoirs is to be made by
the Dial, that is to say, by you or Watson or both." In the October
1921 issue, the first of the three monthly instalments was printed
with his portrait and, in "Notes on Contributors," the assertion that
the memoir "is, we believe, the first work of ANATOLE FRANCE to
appear in English simultaneously with its publication in French."
Edited by Michel Corday, "Last Fragments" by France posthumously appeared, in J. Lewis May's translation, in four instalments
(January–April 1926). Jules Romains' novel *Lucienne* was serialized
in five issues, July–November 1924, in Waldo Frank's translation;
the writer's portrait by Henri Le Fauconnier accompanied the first
instalment, as also did the translator's prefatory note. A much
slighter performance was Gilbert Seldes' translation of Louis Aragon's "Madame à sa Tour Monte . . ." printed in January 1922.

The only other French fiction of note published in *The Dial*
was by Marcel Proust, an anonymous English version of "Saint-
Loup: A Portrait" from *À la Recherche du Temps Perdu*, printed in

October 1920. Proust was pleased by this appearance of his work and also must have liked Ezra Pound's "The Island of Paris: Letter," which appeared in "Modern Forms" in October 1920. Describing the current literary scene in Paris, Pound mentioned André Gide, Alfred Vallette, Valéry (who "bears unquestioned the symbolic and ghostly plaid shawl of Mallarmé"), André Spire, Paul Morand (whose promise in *Lampes à Arc* is "simply fulfilled" in his *Feuilles de Température*, the title poem of which *The Dial* had published in the French in its preceding issue), the "young and very ferocious" (i.e., the Dadaists—Aragon, Philippe Soupault, André Breton, Drieu la Rochelle), Julien Benda, Remy de Gourmont—and Proust. In the same issue appeared Richard Aldington's appreciation, "The Approach to M. Marcel Proust." Almost two years later (May 15, 1922), Gilbert Seldes told Scofield Thayer that "Marcel Proust also speaks in extravagant terms of us in an inscription which I copy out for you: 'Au trés cher Dial qui m'a mieux compris et plus chaleureusement soutenu qu'aucune journal, aucune revue. Toute ma reconnaissance pour tout de lumière qu'illumine la pensée et réchauffe le coeur.' " On February 26, 1923, Seldes consulted Thayer about the advisability of printing a thirty-page portion of *La Prisonnière*, recently published in *La Nouvelle Revue Française*, but nothing happened. Proust's expression of gratitude was an extravagant tribute perhaps, but it earned two memorial essays: in March 1923, Malcolm Cowley's "A Monument to Proust" and in May 1923, Francis Birrell's more ambiguous "Marcel Proust: The Prophet of Despair."

Besides Ezra Pound's translation of Remy de Gourmont's *Dust for Sparrows*, a transcription from the critic's notebook that endured nine months of serialization (September 1920–May 1921) and that D. H. Lawrence called rubbish, there were many essays and appreciations on classic and contemporary French writers: to cite a few, Benedetto Croce's "Balzac" in September 1921; Gabrielle Buffet's "Guillaume Apollinaire" in March 1922; Jean Cocteau's "Cock and Harlequin: Notes Concerning Music," in January 1921; translated by Lillian Chamberlain, Paul Claudel's "A Glance at the Soul of Japan," in November 1928; and, more lengthily, Julien Benda's *Belphegor*, on "The Aesthetic of Contemporary Society," serialized in the last four months of 1920. The staff could not justly complain that the French were neglected in *The Dial;* under the circumstances, the Editor was adamant in his stand to keep on publishing translations from the German.

His bias was not narrowly Middle European, though most of his time abroad was spent in Vienna. He took part in the expatriate life on the Continent, went out a good deal socially, and did not wholly immerse himself in his editing and publishing affairs. He traveled to Paris and London and Berlin and spent a summer on the Baltic island of Sylt with his friends the von Erdbergs. Alfred Kreymborg saw Scofield Thayer in Munich, crowded as it was with Americans attending the theater and opera. The Editor lunched with Hugo von Hofmannsthal and gossiped with Franz Werfel, called on Schnitzler and attended a lecture given by Thomas Mann. Thayer thought Munich least changed of all European cities, since 1914; Vienna had become adulterated; the Prussian spirit of Berlin, Europe's chief source of raw energy, was biding its time.

Of the eminent Viennese writers, Hugo von Hofmannsthal was closest to *The Dial* through his personal acquaintance with its Editor. Thayer knew the von Hofmannsthals socially as well as through Hugo von Hofmannsthal's "Vienna Letter" written for *The Dial*. His first contribution, translated by Kenneth Burke from *The Book of Friends*, appeared in the July 1922 issue. The playwright published the first letter of his series in *The Dial* for August 1922; another followed in October; three more, in March and September 1923 and June 1924; then after Thayer's resignation as active Editor, only one "Vienna Letter" appeared, an account published in August 1928, detailing von Hofmannsthal's collaboration with Richard Strauss in *Die Ägyptische Helena* and containing a synopsis of the libretto, some comment on its meaning, and thoughts generally on dialogue, its function, and the lyric drama. One other contribution by von Hofmannsthal, in *The Dial* for August 1922, "Lucidor: Characters for an Unwritten Comedy," is of similar interest to his final "Vienna Letter," for "Lucidor" is the scenario of the opera *Arabella*, which a little later von Hofmannsthal and Strauss collaborated on. In May 1925 von Hofmannsthal's essay "Honoré de Balzac" was printed, accompanied by a photograph of Rodin's sculpture of Balzac.

Frau von Hofmannsthal, like all Vienna, was put out at Thayer's publication in *The Dial*, as the frontispiece for the March 1923 issue, of Kokoschka's portrait of Max Reinhardt. She did not hesitate—so

Thayer wrote Alyse Gregory (April 21, 1923) – to tell the Editor that it was a shame: "It is so dreadful that people in America should get such an impression of such a nice man just before he arrives. One should handle such people as Mr Reinhardt and Dean Briggs with gloves." (This was a glancing reference by Thayer to the resentment among certain quarters at Harvard at Ivan Opffer's cartoons of "Six Harvard Worthies," with a most unflattering head of *Le Baron Russell Briggs* among them, which had appeared in *The Dial* in June 1920 and which "Comment" had apologized for in November 1920.)

Perhaps in retaliation for Frau von Hofmannsthal's criticism, the Editor proceeded to give Alyse Gregory a verbal caricature of Hugo von Hofmannsthal, who "is now small and yellow like a Siamese. He says he is always so in the spring and that it is the natural course of nature. In the autumn he energizes and glitters and writes comedies for Pallenberg, comedies which make money and are awful. When I lunched with him the other day he stopped in the middle to take aspirin to quiet his nerves, but now in the usual March in April weather he is setting out on an automobile tour to quiet his nerves. I thought he was crazy when he told me and presumably showed it in my eyes, so he called my attention to the fact that he never drove more than five hours in the day. Baroque creature!" Of American critics of the drama, von Hofmannsthal remarked of Stark Young that no one could do that sort of thing so well in German; Thayer disagreed with this estimate (to Alyse Gregory: June 11, 1923) and much preferred Edmund Wilson's work for *The Dial*. Yet if von Hofmannsthal preferred another to the critic of "The Theatre," he thought highly of *The Dial* as a whole, feeling that it was "just the contrary of blasé and routinier." [7]

The other Viennese writer for whom Scofield Thayer had particular respect was Arthur Schnitzler. In its house advertisement for November 1923, *The Dial* announced as its two features for the next issue, Clive Bell's essay "Virginia Woolf" and Schnitzler's "The Baron von Leisenbohg," "Dr Schnitzler's acknowledged short-story masterpiece. Those who have read in THE DIAL previous stories by the great Viennese writer will appreciate the full importance of this announcement." "The Fate of the Baron von Leisenbohg" in Kenneth Burke's translation duly appeared, accompanied by Adolf Dehn's amusing and rowdy line drawings *Viennese Coffee House* and *Viennese Cabaret*.

Arthur Schnitzler's first story in *The Dial* was Pierre Loving's translation of "Crumbled Blossoms" in June 1920. Loving's translation of "The Greek Dancer" appeared in the September 1921 issue, and then came the serialization of *Doctor Graesler*. In July 1922 the first instalment appeared coincidentally with von Hofmannsthal's initial appearance as "the most distinguished living Austrian poet" (according to "Notes on Contributors") with a few extracts from *The Book of Friends*. But, although *Doctor Graesler* had been the featured contribution for that month, no note introducing it had appeared. This lack was remedied in September with Richard Specht's essay "Arthur Schnitzler" in Kenneth Burke's translation: "That Arthur Schnitzler is one of the few who know how to say this unsayable, or at least to make us feel its presence, that he is a giver of light and has told his contemporaries for the first time many conclusive facts about themselves . . . this is his significance in the literature of our days." The fifth and last instalment of *Doctor Graesler* (in Paul Bloomfield Zeisler's translation from *Doktor Gräsler, Badearzt*) immediately followed Mina Loy's paean to the scandalous Brancusi bird, in the November 1922 issue.

Luckily it *was* the last, for the Editor, then in Vienna and seeing Schnitzler a good deal, deplored what he viewed as extremely unfortunate handling of this novel by a man whom he ranked among the two or three greatest writers then living. As Thayer complained (November 17, 1922) to his Managing Editor regarding the possible publication in *The Dial* of another novel translated from the German—Hauptmann's *Der Ketzer von Soana*, translated by Bayard Quincy Morgan as *The Heretic of Soana* and serialized in April, May, and June 1923—"I must insist that the story be not published in the extremely unfortunate fashion in which 'Doktor Gräsler' was published. I remember that in regard to 'Gräsler' I insisted that it should appear in large pieces and the maximum number of parts that I gave was fewer than the number of parts in which it appeared. So in this case I take the opportunity since in another letter that I have just received from you you regret that I do not speak more decisively to state that I veto absolutely the publication of 'Der Ketzer von Soana' in more than three parts. My preference is that it be published in two parts." In his reply (December 21, 1922), Seldes thought he agreed with his Editor about serials not running more than three installments if possible: "As a matter of fact you arrive at it pragmatically, but I think that ideally we should accept nothing beyond three instalments, and few of these."

Another novel serialized at about the same time *Doctor Graesler* was running in *The Dial* was Sherwood Anderson's *Many Marriages*, which would run to six installments, concluding in March 1923. Thayer would be even more upset about it than he had been about the serialization of Schnitzler's novel. The Editor of *The Dial* at least admired Arthur Schnitzler as a novelist and only protested at what he considered the inept handling of the serialized *Doctor Graesler*. But, to Thayer, to run "any more serials from the pen of Sherwood Anderson, certainly in the course of the next few years," would be "catastrophical for The Dial." He continued to Gilbert Seldes (October 24, 1922): "He is a good short story writer and we must have his best short stories; otherwise we require nothing from his pen. We only want serials when they are by masters." No further longer fiction by either Schnitzler or Anderson appeared in *The Dial*, and only two more of Schnitzler's short stories after "The Fate of the Baron von Leisenbohg"–"Lieutenant Gustl" in August 1925 and "The New Song" in November 1925. Cuthbert Wright reviewed Schnitzler's *The Shepherd's Pipe* in December 1923 and *Doctor Graesler* in July 1925.

Besides Schnitzler, Hauptmann, and von Hofmannsthal, another distinguished writer to be translated from the German in *The Dial* was Thomas Mann. In March 1923, Mann was in Vienna, where he had just made a notable speech. "Thomas Mann took tea with me yesterday," wrote Scofield Thayer to Alyse Gregory (March 21, 1923), "and I have pursuantly to exhortation from New York obtained his permission to delay publication of *Der Tod in Venedig*"–which Kenneth Burke was translating for *The Dial*– "until next winter." *Death in Venice* was serialized in *The Dial* for March-April-May of 1924; its publication was one of the triumphs of Thayer's editorship. But to continue the Editor's letter: Mann "has agreed to write a new German Letter this month before his departure for a protracted trip in Spain. He got about $14 for his much advertised, much affected, and much quoted lecture here, said lecture being the German Letter I had turned away! I felt very sinister. Nevertheless he can afford a secretary, who always addresses him as 'Meister'!" As writer of the "German Letter," Mann contributed a total of eight letters, averaging a little oftener than one a year from December 1922 through July 1928.

In June 1927 appended to Paul Morand's "Paris Letter" was an extended footnote, Burke's translation of Mann's *Pariser Rechenschaft*, a speech given in Paris to inaugurate the postwar resumption of intellectual relations between France and Germany. Its being reprinted in *The Dial* is evidence of Mann's importance to the magazine; he was of course one of the major European writers *The Dial* published. Of his well-known works of the decade, besides *Death in Venice* appeared *Disorder and Early Sorrow*, serialized in October and November 1926; before meeting Thayer, Mann made his first appearance in *The Dial* with a story, "Loulou," in April 1921, and in December 1922 and January 1923 the translation by the Editor and Kenneth Burke of *Tristan* was serialized.

Just preceding "Loulou" in *The Dial* for April 1921 was Alec W. G. Randall's "Main Currents in Contemporary German Literature," and presumably Mann's story illustrated the tendency described by the literary historian. Randall's essay exemplified, again, the systematic interest in the German, or more broadly Central European, arts evinced by *The Dial* during Thayer's term as Editor. With Julius Meier-Graefe's essay on the fine arts in Germany after the Great War, with the dozens of pictures and photographs of sculpture, with the stories and correspondence and essays contributed by Central European writers and artists, *The Dial* more than any similar review in America or in England showed an intelligent and discriminating interest in the civilization that was then reorganizing itself on the ruins of the old Hohenzollern and Hapsburg empires.

According to Alec Randall, the most immediate effect of the revolution of November 1918 in Berlin was that it released certain rebellious poets and novelists from the restraint the War had laid upon them. But this was a mere mechanic effect; it indicated no permanent influence. And to the historian, the best proof of this fact was to be discovered by a consideration of certain contemporary novels and plays, such as Walter Hasenclever's *Antigone* and Heinrich Mann's *Der Untertan*. Randall went on to discuss many other figures—Ernst Toller, Max Barthel, Iwan Goll, Gustav Landauer, Fritz von Unruh, Arthur Schnitzler, Sudermann, Jakob Wassermann, Gerhart Hauptmann (whose *Der Ketzer von Soana* was "a little masterpiece"), Eduard Stucken, Wedekind, Stefan George (Reinhold Lepsius' woodcut *Stefan George* was reproduced facing a page of Randall's essay), Friedrich Gundolf's critical work on George, Hugo Salus, the "strange plays" of Oskar Kokoschka,

Franz Werfel ("in poetry we may select as typical the poems of Franz Werfel"), and Carl Sternheim, selected as the representative novelist of the postwar scene. It was from this movement—"before-the-war in its origins, let us be careful to point out in this case, too" —that the greatest changes might come, thought the essayist. For the young German writers were very active, and almost all were confessing the Expressionist creed, intelligently and for reasons that they were prepared to give: "If the main current of German literature to-day may be summed up negatively we could do it in a sentence: It is all that Naturalism is not."

Of these men only Schnitzler appeared importantly in *The Dial*. Heinrich Mann's story "Virgins" was published in the review in February 1924, in Kenneth Burke's translation, and Willi Geiger's portrait of the writer was reproduced in half tone in October 1925. Jakob Wassermann's story "Adam Urbas," in Marian Weigall's translation, appeared in December 1925. Otherwise the Expressionist writers of Central Europe, as named in Randall's essay, did not figure in *The Dial*, which published the Expressionist artists much more consistently.

Alec Randall also wrote another literary survey of the postwar German scene, this time of the drama, "Contemporary German Dramatists," published in *The Dial* for August 1921. He noted the position of supreme importance the stage occupied in the intellectual life of Germans before the Great War and still had in the early Twenties. The chief tendency since 1914 had been against Naturalism and the materialistic philosophy that inspired it. Even the older men such as Hauptmann, once the "high-priest" of Naturalism, had reacted; Randall also cited as anti-Naturalist the Symbolism of Hugo von Hofmannsthal, Sudermann's "romantic-realist" drama, the comedies of manners of Schnitzler, and the light comedies of Hermann Bahr. As for the younger men, the most hopeful writers came from that paradox of cities, Vienna: Anton Wildgans, George Kaiser, and Rolf Lauckner. Despite Randall's optimism about the state of the drama in Germany and Austria, *The Dial* printed no translations of postwar German plays among the few plays it published. Even those favorites of Thayer, Schnitzler and von Hofmannsthal, were published in *The Dial* as authors of stories and essays, poems and correspondence.

Writing from Berlin early in 1926, Scofield Thayer showed

his abiding preoccupation with the Germans and Germany, in a "Berlin Letter" published in *The Dial* for May 1926. Here he attempted to define the essence of Berlin after the Great War, changed as it was, like the other capital cities of Europe. "Berlin is a hole in the ice. Looking in you shall see how ice-cold water is, in this instance, black; and how profound, tortuous, and malefic ice-cold water without sufficient outlet can have become." Militarism had formerly been for Prussia the appointed if unworthy outlet: "There black water could flow. The natural, unregenerate man possesses natural, unregenerate activities: the natural, unregenerate Prussian possesses War. The virtues of war are the virtues of Prussia. The aims of war are the aims of men who know what they are after." Even though Prussian energy need not, considered in the abstract, attain fulfillment only in modern international warfare, such warfare was the thing next to hand. This militarism, then, was the fine elixir of Prussianism, the vital and essential fluid of "that most Prussian capital, Berlin." Its potent gland removed, Berlin was no longer Berlin, but about in line with other such less German cities as Milwaukee. Scofield Thayer foresaw that when "Prussia finds its feet, when Prussia again assumes Berlin, Prussian officials . . . will have bigger fights on than as to whether Herr Schillings shall or shall not continue *Intendant* of the Berlin Opera. I hope these fights will not be international. But they will be big. And there will be big Prussian talk, too." But, for the time being, Berlin was less gleaming: "a lost war is a lost war."

The staff of *The Dial* did not always respond affirmatively to the Editor's Middle European predilections. On February 20, 1923, Thayer wrote to Kenneth Burke announcing *The Dial*'s acquisition of a long thirty-page article by Sigmund Freud; however, in the ensuing correspondence (Thayer to Burke, April 14, 1923; Thayer to Burke, May 3, 1923), it turned out that Burke persuaded Thayer that the magazine could not print Freud's essay. The Editor was unhappy but accepted the verdict from the man who, after all, had the chore of translating from the German.

Nor did contributors always grasp eagerly the suggestion that *The Dial* would like to print their work. Wallace Stevens' group of poems entitled *Revue* had led the Editor to hope that further contributions would be forthcoming. Scofield Thayer wrote Wallace Stevens (November 7, 1923), asking for a group of poems to run with "a very fine review from Miss Moore of your poems, and also a very charming little essay by Llewelyn Powys, à propos of your poems." Stevens replied to Thayer (December 10, 1923), promising to submit something to *The Dial*, if everything went well. Thayer then sent to Stevens (December 14, 1923) a note requesting "the group of poems which you wrote me I may hope to receive from you later in the winter. . . . We are publishing Miss Moore's review of your book in the Dial for January. We are holding Mr. Powys' little essay upon you in order to publish it simultaneously with the group of poems which you write me I may hope to receive from you later in the winter." The "something" submitted—as in the case of Leo Stein, though with not such dilatoriness—was too long in arriving. In February 1924 *The Dial* printed Miss Moore's long and perceptive review, "Well Moused, Lion," of Stevens' *Harmonium*. And not until July 1924 did Stevens' "Sea Surface Full of Clouds" appear, preceded by Llewelyn Powys' appreciative essay "The Thirteenth Way" ("May we not be perhaps permitted to regard Mr. Stevens' own poetry as the thirteenth way of looking upon life—the thirteenth way of Mr Wallace Stevens, this 'tiptoe cozener' "?). But *The Dial* not often was thus rebuffed.

The Dial opened its pages to reviewers of varying ideologies but with the professional's attitude toward their task. Representative of the youngest reviewers was Malcolm Cowley; in November 1922, his review of "Two American Poets" discussed Conrad Aiken's *Priapus and the Pool* and Carl Sandburg's *Slabs of the Sunburnt West*. The work of both poets previously had appeared in *The Dial*; in fact, the poem that gave the title to Sandburg's volume had been published in *The Dial* for March 1922. Aiken had been associated with the magazine since 1916 as a contributor and, briefly, as a member of Martyn Johnson's advisory board of editors, and he had lingered at the new *Dial* for a few months in some capacity. Malcolm Cowley's thesis with regard to Sandburg's and Aiken's work under review was that the American renaissance in poetry was done, that "those old and grand days" of American poetry were over, or at least that their contagious excitement had subsided: "Masters dies slowly after the childbirth of Spoon River. Robinson embalms himself in a collected edition. No one appears to close the gaping ranks. There are no new American poets." To prove his point, after a thorough, and a witty, examination of Sandburg's new work,

Cowley contrasted him to Aiken. One poet was perceptibly of recent immigrant stock, despite his avowals of nationality; the other was of perceptibly established American stock despite his genteel and Anglophile background. It would be too simple to picture either poet as "American" at the other's expense. "Except as a party label there is no American poetry." There was no American poetry in the sense that there was French or Chinese poetry. America was not a point of view, Cowley asserted, but a subject merely. And calling as witnesses the examples of Sandburg and Aiken, he concluded that American poets did not exist but that there were capable poets in America.

Cowley was well aware of what he was about. The very day (August 3, 1922) he began work on "Two American Poets," he wrote Scofield Thayer that he intended to compose, of course, a review of Aiken's and Sandburg's latest, but chiefly an analysis of what the adjective "American" meant when applied to a poet: "It is a temporal rather than a spatial adjective; it belongs definitely to the generation of 1914; an earlier writer like Poe, or a later like Cummings is just a poet; Amy Sandburg Frost is an American Poet." *The Dial* consciously was publicizing the work of a newer literary generation than that of 1912–13–14, the groups of *Poetry: A Magazine of Verse*, the Armory Show, and *The New Republic;* the younger men such as Cowley and Kenneth Burke were consciously harking back to the tradition of Poe, the tradition occasionally appealed to by Gilbert Seldes, the tradition as well that T. S. Eliot was revivifying, among other contributors to *The Dial*, in his "London Letter" and his essays and reviews. Cowley's review thus exemplifies the way Randolph Bourne's transnationalism and Scofield Thayer's own cosmopolitan attitude toward the life of art were transmitted to the newest writers of the Twenties.

Generally speaking, the reviewers for *The Dial* also contributed to its front pages. Occasionally the Editor placed a review of major importance in the front; Santayana's "Marginal Notes" on Harold Stearns' *Civilization in the United States* led the June 1922 issue, for example. Such reviews, important in themselves or because of the work reviewed, were called "review-essays." Often the staff wrote reviews, and invariably the reviews in the "Book Reviews" were signed. Dr. Watson used "Sganarelle" and "W. C. Blum" as his pseudonyms, but the rest of the staff signed their own names.

The department of "Briefer Mention," however, was—as the editorial "Comment" usually was—anonymous.

Just which contributor wrote which review paragraph in "Briefer Mention" the unpublished editorial papers in the Dial collection do not specify, but the manuscript list of contributors to the November 1922 issue does give their names and the number of paragraphs written by them: Gilbert Seldes, 1; Lisle Bell, 5; Ben Ray Redman, 2; Helen Ives Gilchrist, 1; Robert J. Roe, 1; Gerald H. Carson, 1; and Stanton A. Coblentz, 1.

The twelve paragraphs reporting on twelve books in the "Briefer Mention" for November 1922 begin with Joseph Hergesheimer's *The Bright Shawl* ("Joseph Hergesheimer has written, and written remarkably well, a straightforward, unpretentious and beautiful romance"); include work as disparate as Kathleen Norris's *Certain People of Importance* (which had—"despite the defects of its ambitions—an incontestable solidity and worth") and A. M. W. Stirling's *William De Morgan and His Wife* (Mrs. Stirling "displays an admirable talent for research, together with an almost unbelievable ineptitude as a biographer"); and conclude with Robert Nichol's *Guilty Souls* ("The author of this play gives the effect of attempting to carry a greater weight than his shoulders will support").

This list for the November 1922 issue itself is a distinguished one, and the contributors to "Briefer Mention" also included Padraic Colum, Gorham Munson, Edmund Seaver, Nathan Asch, Winthrop Parkhurst, Edward Sapir, Kay Boyle, Babette Deutsch, Pierre Loving, Alice B. Parsons, Kenneth Burke, and Malcolm Cowley in 1922 and 1923. In a letter dated June 2, 1928, Marianne Moore replied to Henry Goddard Leach's compliments on the quality of "Briefer Mention," saying that recently *The Dial* had liked best the briefer mentions contributed by Padraic Colum, Henry McBride, John Cowper Powys, Alyse Gregory, Charles Trueblood, Lisle Bell, and Gilbert Seldes.

The principle of selection for "Briefer Mention" is obvious: it included everything worthy of being noticed by *The Dial* but not extensively reviewed—the remnant of the old Chicago *Dial*'s compendious effort. Actually the principle of selection was capricious; *This Side of Paradise* was not reviewed at all; *Certain People of Importance* was approved of, with qualification, in "Briefer Mention";

while the translations of the Loeb Classical Library were customarily reviewed at length in the main section of book reviews. What is certain is that the paragraph-reviews in "Briefer Mention" were executed and received with labor as diligent and editorial taste as discriminating as were reserved for any other section of *The Dial*. "Briefer Mention" was a grab-bag, to be sure, by its nature, but it was a grab-bag of craftsmanly miniatures.

The Dial obviously was interested in its contributors, but it was equally as fascinated by the intellectual and aesthetic fashions that they espoused and that inspired their contributions. It was triumphantly the synthetic ability of Thayer and his staff to bring together and to relate significantly the artistic effort of their contemporaries. More often than not, the artists and writers ignored all the lines of demarcation created and used by scholars to distinguish one art form from another. Such was the case with one of the important preoccupations of the Twenties: the primitive. For *The Dial* the primitive meant primitive art, principally that of the Americas, but also to some extent the primitive art of Africa, and the naïf art of modern Western culture. This combination of the anthropological with the aesthetic is one of the consistently maintained interests of *The Dial*, and one meets it in the book reviews, as for example, Edward Sapir's "A Symposium of the Exotic," in the November 1922 issue. Sapir here considered the collection by various hands, *American Indian Life*, edited by Elsie Clews Parsons. Sumptuous though the volume was, its pictures Sapir found disappointing; yet despite its disarming modesty it gave "more than a hint of how compelling an imaginative treatment of primitive life might be." Sapir was interested in the question, to what extent can we penetrate into the vitals of primitive life and fashion for ourselves satisfying pictures on its own level of reality? And, to a limited extent, so was *The Dial*. The limitation, of course, was the self-imposed limitation of the aesthetic, for *The Dial* treated the primitive artifact primarily from the standpoint of its interest as an art object.

For example, as early as the first issue of the monthly *Dial* edited by Scofield Thayer, in January 1920, there occurs Walter Pach's essay on "The Art of the American Indian," with its proclamation that there was "more than one voice crying out in the world to-day that in the earlier forms of society values were attained that our present proud condition has lost." So well received was Pach's

essay that the issue of March 1920 reproduced three Indian water-
colors—Fred Kobotie's *"Na-Ka-Vo-Ma": Hopi Snake Dance*, from
the Sia Pueblo *The Legend of the Deer*, and, also from the Pueblo
Indians of New Mexico, a depiction of the Corn Dance. "Notes on
Contributors" stated that the three pictures were all from the collection of Mabel Dodge Sterne, later Mabel Dodge Luhan.

Undoubtedly the major as well as the most historically significant example of Indian art *The Dial* reproduced in 1920 was the
American Museum of Natural History's great Mayan Chac-Mool,
the frontispiece of the October 1920 issue. "Notes on Contributors"
for the issue stated: "Chac-Mool is said to be the Drunken God or
Dionysus of the Mayas, who flourished in Yucatan about 500 A.D."
When Gilbert Seldes drew up an important publicity brochure to
attract readers and subscribers to *The Dial*, the Chac-Mool was one
of a dozen or so objects and pictures that had been reproduced in
the pages of *The Dial* and that were chosen to represent the best
art that appeared in the magazine. In October 1921 the frontispiece was a photograph of a *Head in Diorite*, also labeled as from the
American Museum of Natural History; "Notes on Contributors"
stated: "The Head in Diorite was found in the Valley of Mexico.
Its precise significance and origin are matters of conjecture. The
original of the Head is in Mexico City." Although scholarly opinion
of the 1960's holds such art as the Chac-Mool and the Mexican (perhaps Toltec?) *Head* reproduced in *The Dial* to be the sophisticated productions of civilized peoples, the staff of *The Dial* in the
early Twenties apparently classed them as "primitive" along with
the three Indian water colors reproduced in the March 1920 issue.
These pictures done by "untaught young Indians," Walter Pach
announced, were "Primitives in the true sense of the word, their
form and content deriving from an immediate response to the scenes
they depict, the simple means of execution being suddenly raised to
their intensity of effect by the intensity of conviction and enthusiasm
of the artists." A similar picture—similar in the presentation, that is
—was the line drawing of Chief Rain-in-the-Face reproduced in
November 1921 and made, according to "Notes on Contributors,"
by an Indian chief who was visiting the Carlisle Indian School in
1882 and who had tried, without the aid of an interpreter, to de-
scribe to authorities the home life of his tribe. As late as August 1928
The Dial reproduced a companion drawing to that of Rain-in-the-

Face: Marianne Moore's tracing, made when she was at Carlisle, of four Indian horsemen entitled *Sioux Drawing—1882*. She told Sibley Watson (June 20, 1928), when submitting the drawing to him, that making a line a little heavier would improve the primitiveness; the original had been in pencil or crayon. The editorial "Comment" for the same issue alluded to the profound respect of the plains Indians for "primitive resourcefulness, loyalty, and domestic aestheticism." These virtues and the domestic aestheticism of the American Indian, then, were worthy of notice to *The Dial*. They are qualities totally different from those inherent in the Mayan Chac-Mool and the Mexican sculptured head; indeed, these Indian drawings from the plains have little in common with either the water colors done by the untutored young Indian painters in New Mexico or the complex and civilized votive art of pre-Hispanic Central America. Rather, the reproduction of all of these Indian artifacts, simple and sophisticated alike, expresses a fashion of the Twenties, the dawning recognition of the artistic worth of the artifacts of all cultures in all ages and places, and concomitantly the tendency to substitute one set of values for another, to pass off aesthetic values as religious values.

One discerns this growing realization and its accompanying tendency also in the fact that *The Dial* reproduced Negro sculptures from Africa—ritual heads and figures—as well as the primitive art of America of pre-Columbian and modern times. Scofield Thayer had dealings with the famous Parisian art dealer Paul Guillaume, as is shown by their unpublished correspondence of 1923–24 in the Dial Papers. From Guillaume's collection, in the September 1923 issue, two of these Negro sculptures—a wooden figure and head jointly titled *Negro Sculpture (Pahouin)*—were photographed, before the collector's voyage to America in 1925: striking evidence of the influence he would exert on *The Dial* and through *The Dial* on American taste. The June 1928 issue reproduced a wood *Pahouin Ritualistic Head (Gabon)* from the "Collection Rutherston." A third of a century later such sculpture would find a considerable place in many homes and most museums.

Edward Sapir and Walter Pach gave voice to the attempt by the Twenties to search for and to capture the spirit of the primitive—to recover the elemental freshness that they saw in the exotic American Southwest. The interest shown by *The Dial* in the "primitive" painting of New England relates to this same attempt. The reproduction of the seventeenth-century "Early American" portrait of *Madame Freake with Baby Mary*, in *The Dial* for March 1925, may express interest in the infantine or simple antiquarianism, but the reproduction, in *The Dial* for November 1925, of three "Early American" pictures—*Beneath a Willow Tree*, *Whittier's Home*, and *Portsmouth Harbor*, undated but obviously of the earlier nineteenth century—this interest in art so naïf and fresh, is it not another aspect of the search for the primitive or at any rate for what it saw as primitive by a decade that already felt jaded?

A further extension of this fascination with the naïf is the reproduction in *The Dial* of pictures by the French "primitive" painter, Henri Rousseau—*La Carriole de M. Juniet* in the issue for May 1922; in that for January 1923 an untitled painting elsewhere called *Le Repas du Lion;* and the famous *La Bohémienne Endormie* in the issue for March 1926. The magazine also published Albert Dreyfuss's essay on Rousseau, "A Modern Primitive," in July 1926. *The Dial* thus consistently showed its liking for Rousseau, whom in May 1922 "Notes on Contributors" described: "HENRI ROUS-SEAU, called Le Douanier, was born in 1844 and died in 1910. He was a government official living in the outskirts of Paris, and it was only near the end of his life that his work as a painter became known, partly through the enthusiasm of Guillaume Apollinaire." As in other ways, *The Dial* was, with its interest in the primitivism of the naïf, following the lead of the most advanced artists and aesthetes rather than actually initiating a new taste.

In its quest for the primitive, *The Dial* followed the fashion for the Hispanized Indians of the Southwest, both in choice of subject and choice of style. The subject appears in the May 1926 issue in Elizabeth Shepley Sergeant's "The Wood-Carver," two scenes from a play in nine scenes entitled *Sangre de Cristo*. The significance of the play lies in its attempt to portray the psychological process by which a native wood-carver who lives at the head of a remote canyon in Mexico carves his images; thus the aesthetic fashion for the primitive *santos* is revealed along with the more scientific curiosity about primitive peoples—their crafts, customs, beliefs, and attitudes. Dealing with similar subject matter, the magazine published in June 1928 and April 1929 Lowell Houser's linoleum cuts done in the manner of the then new Mexican School of Rivera and his fellow artists; Houser's *Cristo, The Fisherman,* and *Guadalupe Dancers,* with their recollections of Mayan and Aztec techniques, must have seemed as novel as Cubist or primitive works. *The Dial* printed D. H. Lawrence's essays "Indians and an Englishman" and "Taos" respectively in February and March 1923. Here one of the great paleface aesthetes tells of his response to redskin artists, but while he admits that "these old men telling the tribal tale were my fathers," Lawrence concludes that "My way is my own, old red father; I can't cluster at the drum any more." A more flippant version of the same attitude occurs in the casual aside of the American artist Marsden Hartley in his essay "Vaudeville," in March 1920: "I have but recently returned from the vaudeville of the centuries. Watching the kick and the glide of very ancient performers. I have spent a year and a half down in the wonderful desert country of the Southwest. I have wearied, however, of the ancient caprice, and turn with great delight to my old passion, vaudeville." And Hartley's appreciation is appropriately followed by the three Indian water colors from Mabel Dodge Sterne's collection.

Just how serious or sincere *The Dial*'s involvement with primitive American art may have been, is a problem. The interest of *The Dial* in the primitive art of the American Indian furnishes a warning for the wary. Among the purported translations of Indian poetry that appeared in *The Dial* was a group by Amy Lowell, "Songs of the Pueblo Indians," published in September 1920: "Women's Harvest Song," "Basket Dance," "Women's Song of the Corn," "Prayer for a Profusion of Sunflowers," "Prayer for Lightning," "Flute-Priest Song for Rain." Such an elaborate presentation of a poet whom *The Dial* published but did not affect—Amy Lowell, after all, belonged to the earlier literary generation of poets—might seem to strengthen the case for *The Dial* as a champion of the new interest in primitive art. But this is not true. Just after the publication of "Songs of the Pueblo Indians," Scofield Thayer wrote Ezra Pound (September 26, 1920): "The Amy Lowell I disliked as much as you. The stuff was accepted because we are considered un-American and Indian songs are American, so is Amy. The public who love to be humbugged fell for said songs flat." In the light of that remark, it is clear that *The Dial* exploited the new fashion for the primitive and for collecting and admiring the primitive, at any rate where the arts of the American Indian were concerned. Nevertheless by exploiting a fashion, *The Dial* did influence American taste in the arts. Perhaps not in poetry or in fiction and memoirs: the artists, the poets, the novelists would have written from and about Taos and Taxco regardless of what *The Dial* advocated. But in the fields of the fine arts—painting and sculpture mostly—*The Dial* accomplished more than the mere exploitation of fashion. It made primitive art, in a very real sense, "respectable," by taking it out of the American Museum of Natural History and endowing it with the same status that a painting by Picasso or a poem by T. S. Eliot possessed.

EIGHT

Art and Artists
and Entrepreneurs

Facing the first lines of *The Waste Land*, the frontispiece of the November 1922 issue was Robert Delaunay's water color, *St Séverin*. Of Delaunay and his work, "Notes on Contributors" said: "Influenced by the works of Henri Rousseau he turned to the new painting. He is the creator of the absolutely pure abstract painting. His influence on the present generation of French painters is everywhere obvious." One in a series of studies of the Parisian church of St. Séverin, Delaunay's picture in dark blues was a clear analogue to the poem, and it remains paired with *The Waste Land* to memorialize the editorial taste and insight of the Dial staff, in thus publishing together the harmonizing works of two such pioneering artists. An answering harmony of text and picture, through which the individual relevance of each, the individual qualities of each, are better seen, was a basic intention in the editorial use of art in *The Dial*. Achieving the result was no easy task.

St Séverin was the third color reproduction published in *The Dial* and was one of a large group of pictures that Scofield Thayer had secured in Berlin, through Herwarth Walden, publisher of the Expressionist review *Der Sturm* (1910–32). Writing from the Adlon late on September 24, 1921, Thayer told Gilbert Seldes that he had just met the master mind of the Sturm Group and in Walden's private collection had discovered far more interesting objects than there had been in the Sturm public exhibition he had previously visited. Djuna Barnes, the Editor of *The Dial* learned, had been there the day before and was deciding which pictures to reproduce in *The Little Review;* Thayer therefore took the greatest pleasure in picking up all those pictures that were first-rate for reproducing. The lady in question had neglected to ask for reservation rights, so Walden agreed definitely to give no other journal in America but *The Dial* the right to reproduce the pictures the Editor chose. He spent the whole afternoon with Walden and took in the neighborhood of two dozen pictures, a group he specified as representing all the best work being done by the more conservative contemporary artists east of the Rhine including Russia.

The pictures Thayer secured from the Sturm headquarters were notable for two additional reasons. First, a good half of them were of a nature that would permit their reproduction on the regular paper of *The Dial*, that is to say, they were either woodcuts or drawings of a quality easy to reproduce on the mat paper of the text of the magazine. Second, others were chosen to be used in *The Dial* as examples of a new method Walden and his partner had recently evolved for cheaply reproducing paintings in color. Thayer contracted on the spot for four of Walden's paintings to be reproduced by this process and to be run in *The Dial*. Each picture would be printed in 10,000 copies on paper of the right size for tipping into *The Dial*. Thayer anticipated getting the whole lot of four for very little, but anyhow, *coûte que coûte*, these pictures must be reproduced in color and sent. It rested, concluded the Editor, with Seldes, Walden, and Samuel Craig to put the matter through with the least expense.

Thereupon ensued a tortuous, bewilderingly involved, and seemingly endless correspondence between *The Dial* in New York, Walden in Berlin, and Thayer in Vienna. As Seldes truthfully put the matter to the Editor, "The Sturm is not commercially intelligent." Walden mailed a printing of 30,000 reproductions of pictures and objects to *The Dial* in December 1921, which did not arrive in America for three months. But the bill Walden sent amounted only to about forty-six dollars, because of the wild fluctuations of the German mark in those years of inflation. The first of his work to be used by *The Dial* was a photograph of Oswald Herzog's *Geniessen*, as the frontispiece for the issue of January 1922. *The Dial* did not, however, give *Der Sturm* proper credit for the work being used in America until at last in the "Notes on Contributors" for the May *Dial* the four drawings for woodcuts by Jacoba van Heemskerck that had been reproduced in *The Dial* for March were credited to *Der Sturm* of Berlin.

With the issue of September 1922, the first color reproduction by Walden was published as a *Dial* frontispiece, Franz Marc's *Horses*. In October a rather off-color reproduction of Chagall's water color *On Dit* was the frontispiece; and Delaunay's *St Séverin* was the last that Walden executed for *The Dial*. Inasmuch as his prices hiked steeply upward when Adolf Dehn, Thayer's emissary to *Der Sturm*, started negotiations for a second batch of Walden's pictures for *The Dial*, and as Thayer was disappointed with the color reproduction of *On Dit*, the decision arrived at through correspondence (Seldes to Thayer: April 17, 1922. Thayer to Seldes: April 30 and May 14, 1922) was against using any more colored reproductions from *Der Sturm*, so that *The Dial* finally published only three of the four Thayer had first ordered. The practice of using inserted colored pictures as *Dial* frontispieces was not resumed until the issue of February 1924, when Julius Meier-Graefe's print of Chagall's *The Market Place* was published.

In 1922, however, Thayer was not satisfied to publish miniatures, in color, of pictures. His Managing Editor would soon learn what the Editor's latest preoccupation was when they encountered one another in Europe. Once debarked from New York and aboard ship, Seldes unsuspectingly informed the Editor (in a letter postmarked aboard ship as January 13 and from London as January 15, 1923) that he was sailing for Europe to get some "REST, and in order to rest and particularly to rest the Bean which in association with the Nerves is very wobbly, I am trying to settle my mind," and he proceeded to try to settle, while on board the *Manchuria*, some unfinished business. Should *The Dial* accept Joseph Conrad's new novel for serialization—probably it was his "famous Napoleonic romance"? (Seldes, on later inquiry, told Thayer on March 19, 1923, that it was sold to *The Pictorial Review!*) Seldes declared against the Conrad, not that he was not "good enough, because I rather fall for his later stuff; I mean that I don't consider TD as so deeply a fiction magazine."

The rest of the letter was concerned with the itinerary of the

Managing Editor on the Continent and with problems relating to his journeys. The Theater Guild was paying for a trip from Berlin to Prague, while *The Dial* was paying Seldes a regular stipend. Actually, Seldes hoped to cut the expenses of his European stay by running errands for the Guild and for *The Dial*, while he wrote a book with a title that has become a cliché—*The Seven Lively Arts*. He did indeed write his book, even while he busied himself with the affairs of *The Dial*. By the fourth week in May 1923 the manuscript was completed, and Clive Bell, with perhaps exaggerated foresight and amiability, said the work might be the book of the epoch.

Bell, incidentally, had just taken Gilbert Seldes calling on Picasso for the purpose of ascertaining whether, as *The Dial* had alleged in its "Notes on Contributors," for July 1921, the painter's *période bleu* had preceded his *période rose* and, actually, whether such periods had ever existed. "Pablo HISSELF," wrote Seldes in a Poundian moment (May 24, 1923)—though Ezra, at outs with *The Dial* for sacking him from his job as Parisian correspondent, cut the Managing Editor dead—had verified the assertion that the rose period had followed the blue period in the Picassoan *oeuvre*.

Elated by this verification and by Bell's praise, Gilbert Seldes told his Editor that he would shortly be submitting "a copy of the longest and best essay in the book: Toujours Jazz which I would like you to publish in your interesting magazine The Dial. Seriously it would please me if you liked it well enough. And thought it appropriate. The section devoted to an analysis of the jazz bands of New York ought to be condensed for Dial publication to about a paragraph. And it could be shortened a little elsewhere. Since I so infrequently submit to you, will you honour me with a ready response. I may be able to place it elsewhere. Vanity Fair has about 2 pieces a month for the next six months, and it wasn't written for them any how." *The Dial* duly accepted "Toujours Jazz" and published it in August 1923, intact save for a few words about Mr. Ted Lewis; and two other chapters of *The Seven Lively Arts*, "The Demoniac in the American Theatre" and "Before a Picture by Picasso," which is the conclusion, also appeared in *The Dial*, in, respectively, September and October 1923 (but the magazine's "Demoniac" became the book's "Daemonic").

Thirty-five years after writing "Before a Picture by Picasso," Gilbert Seldes described the circumstances of his visit to the painter's studio in May 1923, with Clive Bell. In his comments added to the second edition of his famous book, Seldes identified the picture as that one of Picasso's generally called *The Lovers* and deprecated his own youthful taste.[1] In that spring of 1923, however, the young Managing Editor told his Editor (May 24, 1923) that he had just seen Picasso's "chef d'oeuvre. Really, a great work, just done. Superb. Simply. 'On dirait en Amérique que vous avez retrouvé le véritable chemin,' said I to him when he asked me what they would think. 'C'est ce que je pense, moi,' said Bell. Noble moment. We embraced. But really, au fond, the picture is Picasso's best thing, and greater than anything I've seen of contemporary painting anywhere." Perhaps in his enthusiasm about Picasso's return to the true way of sentimental representation, Seldes was invoking the memory of the Editor's recent ferocity about the commercially suicidal photograph of Brancusi's *Golden Bird*.

Apparently, in a letter now lost, Scofield Thayer suggested that this new masterwork by Picasso be reproduced in *The Dial;* there exists Seldes' undated reply that Picasso's permission to use "his lovely picture in my book" had only that day been given— "since the chapter explaining the relation of the major to the minor arts is called 'Before a Picture by Picasso.'" The author was happy to yield his precedence to *The Dial*, however, and it would publish the picture as a frontispiece before October. Seldes promised to send on the manuscript of the pertinent chapter, which he did, together with a photograph of the Picasso painting; but *The Dial* never published *The Lovers*. As for Picasso, the Editor, when he came to Paris, was invited to call on the painter at 23 rue de la Boëtie, two doors above Paul Rosenberg's gallery where inquiries about purchasing any work by Picasso must be addressed. Picasso himself was *on ne peut plus aimable!*

Thus Gilbert Seldes wrote his book in Paris in the spring, in 1923, supporting himself largely with his stipend from *The Dial*. His fifty dollars a week from *The Dial* as Managing Editor was for another reason, however, than for making useful contacts to secure material the magazine would publish. He was acting for *The Dial* in a more diplomatic capacity.

As early as the first week in March 1922, Scofield Thayer was obviously exercised about the allegedly "degenerate" pictures *The Dial* was given to reproducing. The Business Manager, Samuel

Craig, had written Thayer that sundry bookmongers continued to refuse to advertise in *The Dial* because of its pictures and had suggested the omission of all inserts from the regular numbers and, instead, the quarterly or annual publication of an "artistic" supplement to contain reproductions of works of art. Otherwise, *The Dial* could not, within the next year at any rate, become self-supporting. The dilemma has been dramatized by Sibley Watson in an anecdote. The photograph of Gleb Derujinsky's sculpture of Leda and the Swan appeared as frontispiece in the December 1921 issue. Henry Holt the publisher was aghast when he saw it; Dr. Watson recalled that Holt exclaimed, "Why, it's coitus!" and promptly withdrew his firm's advertising.[2] Adding a third horn, Thayer contended he could not continue his support of *The Dial* if its current deficit were not soon curtailed, especially as he was not in complete sympathy with so much of the work that, he alleged, Watson desired to publish in it.

Sophia Wittenberg–Lewis Mumford's wife and a member of the staff of *The Dial*–would be coming to Europe for the summer. The experiment with Herwarth Walden's Der Sturm press had not succeeded, and further colored frontispieces for *The Dial* must be printed in Vienna rather than in Berlin. From these three diverse bits–Thayer's dissatisfaction with *Dial* policy, Mrs. Mumford's proposed trip to Europe, and Walden's failure to satisfy *The Dial*–a coherent picture formed, and the Editor began to see, he told Sibley Watson, how it might be worth their while to take advantage of events that might be made to work together for *The Dial*. (Of the thirteen pages dictated, typed, and dated March 5, 1922, Thayer regretted to Watson "that this letter should seem rather scrappy and that things which go together are not always in the same paragraph.")

First, being in Vienna, where colored reproduction could anyhow be done better than anywhere else in the world, the Editor would be able to direct the inception of a *Dial* folio of contemporary art. Second, Sophia Wittenberg could bring abroad with her three or four pictures and as many negatives of sculptures. Thayer therefore had already got in touch with the best people in Vienna, and had obtained innumerable figures, and had had innumerable conversations with printers, with a view to expediting his new project. It appeared that a folio to contain ten colored reproductions of modern painting, ten reproductions of drawings, and ten photographs of sculptures by the best people and in every way got up in the very best manner would cost in Vienna from five to ten dollars per copy for an order of a thousand copies. An order for five hundred copies would probably cost between eight to twelve dollars per copy.

The Editor admitted his realization that those who had understanding for modern art were not numerous nor particularly monied; nevertheless he thought *The Dial* might ask fifteen or twenty dollars for such a folio and get that price from a few hundred people. Moreover, such a folio would have permanent value and might sell as well two years after publication as when it was issued. Should it sell satisfactorily, *The Dial* might issue successive similar folios annually about Christmas time, and even as early as Christmas time of 1922 the first of this projected series might be ready, provided before the end of March Watson gave the Editor a free hand immediately to order it and to make the first payment on it. Also, if the folio were wholly successful and if *The Dial* in the winter of 1922–23 had as much trouble with advertising as it still seemed to have in early 1922, the publication of the folio would provide the opportunity for the review gracefully to withdraw pictures from its pages and to confine itself to the publishing each month, as frontispiece, the photograph of some contributor.

Well then, suppose the folio when issued did not succeed? *The Dial* need not publish a second one, and Scofield Thayer felt confident to be able eventually in years if not in months to sell enough copies so that anyhow the review should not lose money, though of course those concerned would lose time and thought over the matter. (By a slip, Thayer wrote that "we should anyhow lose money"!) Aside from its intrinsic value, the importance of the proposed folio was that it would be very helpful to *The Dial*, especially as its pictures had been so much criticized not only by Mr. Craig's friends but also by the friends of Mr. Pound. In such a folio Thayer proposed to include only pictures of first-rate aesthetic importance and should therefore by publishing it establish the fact that *The Dial* knew what a first-rate picture was.

The projected folio would resemble several German and Austrian folios of modern if not contemporary art such as that issued annually by the Marées Gesellschaft in Berlin and sold in New York by Brentano's or the *Französische Meister des XVI–XVIII Jahrhunderts*, published by the same Staatsdruckerei in Vienna from which Scofield Thayer had obtained his figures and sold at Brentano's for thirty or forty dollars. The drawings of the *Dial* folio would be reproduced exactly as the drawings in the Viennese *Mappe*, but the paintings would of course be even more elaborately reproduced.

The Editor desired to include therein the following works of art: two or three paintings by Matisse, one or two paintings by Picasso, one painting by Demuth, one painting by Marin, one painting by Chagall, and one painting by Derain; one or two drawings by Matisse, one or two drawings by Picasso, one or two etchings by Picasso, one drawing by Forain, one caricature of Moses by Boardman Robinson ("what he is up to, I forget"; in fact this was *The Hands of Moses*), one or two drawings by Lachaise, Wyndham Lewis's *Starry Heavens* (published as *The Starry Sky* in *The Dial* for August 1921), and one drawing by Kokoschka. Of sculptured objects, there would be, necessarily, photographs: Lachaise's *La Montagne* and his "small figure of a woman in black stone which Lachaise has I hope by now finished and which you and your friend Lady Rothermere found not without reason to be rather Beardsley" (Thayer apparently called a similar bronze figure *The Mountain* and did not give this black sandstone sculpture a title; both were published in the folio as *The Mountain*, the bronze as No. 9 and the black stone as No. 10, respectively front and rear views being printed); one of the Archipenkos Watson had received from Der Sturm group in Berlin; a work by Maillol; some work by Epstein ("two photographs of work" by him); Alfeo Faggi's *St. Francis* ("everybody agreed the St. Francis was the best thing that Faggi exhibited"); and Wilhelm Wauer's *Skater*. The list, as Thayer gave it now, was necessarily indefinite. What was definite was the number of examples of contemporary art to be included—ten paintings, ten drawings and etchings, and ten photographs of sculptures.

Throughout his long letter outlining the subject and format of the projected folio to Watson, Thayer stressed its international quality at the same time that he stressed the coming of age of American art by the early Twenties. All the artists, whatever their national origins, would be represented on the basis of the excellence of their work reproduced or photographed. True, the Derain favored for the folio had already been reproduced in a German folio, but this publication would scarcely be seen in New York, and besides, any reproductions of this reproduction would imply that this was the best work

Derain had done. The Germans might not buy the folio because only Kokoschka and Wauer would be represented in it. And the Editor realized he should be favoring the Americans in including five American artists and only two German, but he felt that this would be legitimate and indeed appropriate for *The Dial* to do.

To be as international as possible, it might be worth while to include one of those woodcuts by that Dutch woman of whose work Thayer had had Der Sturm group send four examples to his review; she was, in fact, Jacoba van Heemskerck. It might be nice to include something by the artist of *La Matinée angoissante* –Giorgio de Chirico's picture, reproduced in the December 1921 issue–also for the sake of internationalism, as well as something by Vlaminck "for the sake of Belgium." The *Dial* folio should then have represented France, England, America, Holland, Belgium, Germany, Austria, Italy, and Spain.

Thayer expressed his awareness that among this company Alfeo Faggi and Boardman Robinson were not as great artists as Derain, Marin, and Lachaise and indeed any other artists represented in the folio, but he had to have a second American sculptor, and after Lachaise, Faggi, especially in his *St. Francis*, was second choice; and, using the word *caricature* in its most expansive sense, Thayer wanted one American caricaturist and knew no better American caricature than the one with Moses in it. By fitting his final choices among these tentative selections into his scheme of ten paintings and ten drawings or etchings to be reproduced and ten sculptures to be photographed, Scofield Thayer said he thus should consider that he himself had represented in his folio the very best of the very best living artists of all nationalities.

The bases on which the intrinsic value of the folio would rest were two. First, Thayer was confident of his taste and of his ability to produce a distinguished publication. He was on the spot in Vienna to take advantage of Central European expertness in printing luxurious *Mappen* and to take advantage, also, of the favorable rate of exchange between the inflated Krone and the relatively stable dollar; moreover, he looked upon himself as the connoisseur best fitted to handle the proposed task. There were very few, Thayer told Watson, who were as conversant with American art who had since the late war seen as much European art as had the Editor of *The Dial* during his stay in Paris, his stay in Berlin, and now in Vienna. (There were almost as many first-rate things in Berlin as in Paris.) Thayer himself would be the one to undertake all the infinite bother the folio would cause, and as he would also be the one held generally responsible for its contents, he should not be willing to compromise with his own aesthetic judgment as to what should go into it. He hoped, however, that his taste and Watson's were still sufficiently related so that there would be no serious cause for difference here.

The second basis for the worth of the *Dial* folio was its special value as being the first definite recognition of the fact that contemporary art in America was at last on a footing of equality with the best in Europe. For that reason if for no other, Thayer said he would be unwilling to represent any American artists except the five he had previously mentioned to Watson. If, however, he were forgetting any artist whom Watson felt it imperative to include, of course he wanted to know the name of the artist and the work, which if unfamiliar he could judge from a photograph.

Acting as couriers for *The Dial*, Sophia Mumford and "her energetic spouse" would, then, have to bring to Europe, for reproduction in Vienna, some negatives of sculptures; one painting by Marin —not his most characteristic work but his best—to be chosen by a committee composed of Watson, Rosenfeld, and McBride; one painting by Demuth (in order of preference, the painting of a mill by a mill-pond that had been reproduced in *The Little Review* about a year and a half earlier, the painting reproduced in *The New York Times Book Review* a year and a half previously, or the painting of black velvety chimneys owned by William Carlos Williams and especially liked by Watson); Boardman Robinson's caricature of Moses; if Watson could get around John Quinn's various complications, the painting by Picasso of a woman sitting at a table, which the *Dial* had reproduced as its frontispiece in July 1921 (printed as "Property of John Quinn" and "From the Loan Exhibition of French Painting at the Metropolitan Museum of Art"); and Wyndham Lewis's *Starry Heavens*.

The Mumfords would bring these things to Paris to Thayer's aide in the project; he named Alfred Kreymborg or Mina Loy as possible candidates for this job. There the aide would confer with Pound and Gertrude Stein (who had "one or two Picassos which I should want to include provided she could be prevailed upon to let them out of her apartment") and with their help would collect such other paintings as would come from Paris. In Berlin, the aide would confer with Dr. Robert von Erdberg, Thayer's intimate friend and an Undersecretary in the Ministry for Cultural Affairs of the German Republic, as well as with the men at the Walden and Flechtheim galleries. The two best Matisses were in Berlin, and Thayer should try to get them to Vienna. He himself owned "the best drawings of Picasso and the best etchings of his which I know." But the aide would probably have to visit other cities to collect particular things, though of course one would try to avoid unnecessary traveling. Another difficulty was that en route—and especially en so many routes—some pictures and negatives might be lost. *The Dial* therefore must stand the risk of such loss and of making it good to the owners; but if the owner of a picture agreed with *The Dial* in writing as to its value, in case of a loss the review would not be out for more than a certain sum.

Such were the dangers as well as the virtues of this plan the Editor of *The Dial* so suddenly announced to his partner in New York. Watson acquiesced; and when he took his family to Europe in the summer of 1922, he brought over several things for the burgeoning folio, including a drawing by Lachaise and one of Marin's water colors. As might be expected from the tentative scheme Thayer outlined to Watson, the selections changed, most through the choice of the compiler, but some through force of circumstances.

By April 23, 1922, Thayer was breaking the news of the folio to his friend Raymond Mortimer and was proposing not only something by Wyndham Lewis but something by Duncan Grant as well. Other possibilities were Sickert or any other "of the less known young men" for the folio, "which begins more or less with Matisse and omits Zuloaga and Sargent," and which was to be quite international. The only possible English sculptor seemed to be Epstein, an American by birth. But perhaps Mortimer might help Thayer at least select a Grant, when he came to England in the autumn. To Mortimer on June 5, 1922, Thayer again wrote that he wanted "for me and The Dial three or four photographs of the best things of Grant and of such ones as allow themselves to be photographed without too much loss. . . . some works of Grant not fresh from his brush, but that have already been exhibited somewhere in London, either yesterday or five years ago."

In *The Dial* for November 1922 were reproduced three pictures by Duncan Grant—*The Acrobats*, here listed as owned by Lytton Strachey, a female *Nude*, the property of Bernard Adeney, and a *Landscape: South of France*, loaned by the artist. These pleasant but, for *The Dial*, unexciting pictures were the work of an artist who, though born in the Scottish Highlands, according to "Notes on Contributors," studied in London and Paris, was first influenced by Simon Bussy, exhibited in London as a leading member of the London Group, and also exhibited in Paris at the Galéries Vildrac. The intimation in the Notes is that Duncan Grant was something of a protegé of Clive Bell: "In Since Cézanne, Mr Clive Bell has written much of Mr Grant." It was Raymond Mortimer, however, who first mentioned Grant in *The Dial* in his "London Letter" in March 1922, as well as in his essay entitled "The Movement," a review of Clive Bell's *Since Cézanne* published in the August 1922 *Dial*. It was Mortimer also who was instrumental in acquiring Grant's water color *Woman with Ewer* for the Dial Collection from the artist. Raymond Mortimer selected the picture in Grant's studio, keeping in mind the possibility of its being reproduced in the folio; he wrote Thayer (November 12, 1922) that the picture chosen had been painted during the war and was very characteristic and, in his own opinion, truly beautiful. It had no name, but he suggested *Woman with Ewer*. Grant's prices then were rising, Mortimer added, as everything he showed was bought at once, and he was not a large producer. It was reproduced in color as the frontispiece for the September 1924 issue, as well as in the folio.

The letter of April 23 to Raymond Mortimer shows two further changes. Thayer dropped his plan to print the folio in Vienna; for he told Mortimer that during July he hoped to arrange the practical details in Berlin, where the folio probably would be printed. He also dropped the notion of employing as his aides in the project Alfred Kreymborg and Mina Loy. Nor did he make use of the services of the Mumfords; instead, in the summer of 1922 Sibley Watson brought to Berlin some of the required works, and Gilbert Seldes not only acted as an aide but also brought over a second lot in January 1923.

As for other aides, perhaps the most important in the actual selection of pictures and sculptures was Raymond Mortimer, whose taste Thayer held in unique respect. In the case of Marin's water color, *Lower Manhattan*, the selecting committee consisted of James

Sibley Watson, Paul Rosenfeld, and Henry McBride; however, the picture by Marin that they selected, a *Seascape*, now in the Dial Collection, was, or so said Henry McBride, switched by Alfred Stieglitz with the result that, as Thayer discovered to his dismay, the wrong picture got into the *Dial* folio. Attempting to smooth the matter over, Dr. Watson wrote Thayer on April 23, 1923, that Stieglitz had had no official part in the selection of the Marin, though he may well have hypnotized Paul Rosenfeld and certainly Watson himself. This hypnotic influence still continued, but why mention it in the portfolio? Thayer apparently agreed, as in the Preface to the published folio, when he gave credit to various owners, he merely thanked Stieglitz as the owner of *Lower Manhattan*. Otherwise, he himself seems to have assumed the task of selecting the works for his project.

For the immense amount of research that went into the notes for the folio Thayer employed Gilbert Seldes, Raymond Mortimer, and Robert von Erdberg. The compiler and his assistants succeeded signally in accumulating much original material relating to the artists whose work appeared in the folio. They gained this material at first hand, for Thayer insisted on obtaining relevant information regardless of effort or expense. In its day it was a remarkable collection of facts pertinent to what Mortimer, in the jargon of those years, called "the movement."

Raymond Mortimer was at this time beginning his association with *The Dial*, an association that would continue until the final months of the review. Most of his writing for *The Dial* was literary journalism. In eight "London Letters" at intervals between March 1922 and February 1929 he discussed aspects of English literary and artistic life. The letter discussing the Bloomsbury group, published in the March 1928 *Dial*, is one of the earliest descriptive analyses of that "dangerous company." Fittingly it was accompanied by a half tone of Duncan Grant's portrait of Lytton Strachey noted marginally as the property of Clive Bell. As an essayist, Mortimer appeared little in *The Dial;* he wrote an essay on the Baroque, published in the December 1920 issue, and a study of Thomas Moore as the most successful expounder of the literary fashions of the Romantic Age, published in the October 1921 issue. Most of his energies, when they were devoted to *The Dial*, were expended on book reviews and on helping Scofield Thayer compile his folio and the Dial Collection of pictures and objects. Raymond Mortimer amiably helped *The Dial* along in London by spreading good will for it, but when Scofield Thayer pressed him to come to America as Managing Editor, he pleasantly and firmly refused. Under the circumstances of this mutual affection and respect, Mortimer and Thayer worked together during the preparation of the folio.

Early in their association, on May 9, 1922, Raymond Mortimer described his taste for contemporary art to Scofield Thayer as informally as Thayer had described the project of a *Dial* folio. Mortimer thought Grant the only painter to be put in—presumably the only *English* painter. He did not know how many Russians and Americans were to be represented, but the French seemed to him so much the most important and to deserve proportional representation. Mortimer confessed his ignorance of Central European work, but such as he had seen had not inspired him with enthusiasm. Sickert was out of the question; he was a good artist, but spiritually a contemporary of Degas. The only other conceivable painter was Gertler; but Mortimer admired more than loved his work. He should not put in a Lewis painting, but a drawing, and he was not sure that Roberts did not do *that* better. The only conceivable sculptor was Frank Dobson. As for his notions in general about the folio, Raymond Mortimer admitted his increasing distrust of any art that approached the stunt. It was so easy to surprise the attention and so difficult to retain it, and, he fancied, the greater the initial shock the less long the impression was likely to last. He wanted painting to be subtle, to permeate, not to bludgeon. Mortimer held that such an album as Thayer projected must gain much of its value from the fact that it expressed an individual taste, and he should be sorry to do more than indicate which way the search for appropriate works might least wastefully be made. For instance, he did not know which of the modern French Scofield Thayer cared for. As for himself, abstract painting very rarely appealed to him, and such painters as Gris and Léger left him cold. Metzinger he wanted a chance to see more of. Derain he admired inordinately. Friesz he had worshipped for a while, but his ardors were now beginning to cool. A Segonzac nude exhibited in London recently had raised his opinion of that painter enormously. As for the English, Mortimer could get no reproductions of English painters. Anyway, Grant was libeled by anything that was not colored.

Thayer's answering agreement with his friend's observations

(May 14, 1922) was wellnigh complete. The fact that Duncan Grant was libeled by anything that was not colored relieved him of the need to take seriously the photograph of Grant's untitled landscape reproduced in Clive Bell's *Since Cézanne*. Thayer agreed as to the unfitness of including a painting by Wyndham Lewis and pointed out that he had intended only a drawing. "Abstract painting does not appeal to me either," he admitted. "I do not propose to include Gris or Léger or Metzinger or Braque. I want the folio to be as international as possible. But I quite agree with you that there are more good painters in Paris than in the rest of the world today."

Beyond its intrinsic interest, the exchange is important, because it shows in succinct embodiment the rationalizations and prejudices of the editorial policy of *The Dial* on art and the criticism of art. Where Scofield Thayer and Raymond Mortimer agreed was in their admiration of work done by the artists since Cézanne, up to a point. This point was not a point of time simply, although it was chronological to the extent that "the absolutely pure abstract painting," to use the phrasing of "Notes on Contributors," came into being about 1910–12 with the experiments of Dove, Kandinsky, Mondrian, and Delaunay; but this point also had to do with the painter's technique, and Thayer and Mortimer disliked abstract art as a technique. Thayer liked much of the work of Picasso and Brancusi, but he reserved his enthusiasm for the more obviously representational work of these men. He agreed that Paris had "more good painters than in the rest of the world today." In consonance with his pronounced general opinions, Thayer disliked what was happening to art in postwar Germany and said the best modern German art had been created prior to the Great War. The chief differences between the taste of Mortimer and that of Thayer lay first in Thayer's appreciation of much of Expressionism and, inconsistent with his declared attitude, his procuring, for publication in *The Dial*, work that had been done after 1914 in Central Europe. Second, Thayer appreciated that side of modern art that approached the stunt when such art was also decorative. *The Dial* was about thirty years ahead of popular opinion in its continued and consistent publication of the German Expressionists and in its daring to shock readers and advertisers with some of their flashier work. In at least these two respects, Scofield Thayer displayed independence of taste, in formulating, with Sibley Watson, the aesthetic policy of *The Dial*.

The trouble was that *The Dial* neither led nor followed ad-

vanced opinion in another direction. Because of Scofield Thayer's
dislike of abstract painting, almost no examples of this increasingly
important and popular tendency appeared in *The Dial;* in fact, the
only abstract painting that comes to mind as having been reproduced in *The Dial* is E. E. Cummings's *Noise Number 13*, reproduced to accompany the selections from *Him.* It may well be
that such a picture appeared because of the unusual editorial leniency
toward Cummings, who was, wrote Alfred Kreymborg, *The Dial's*
arch-discovery.[3] In sum, the limitations on reproductions of pictures
and on photographs of sculpture in both *The Dial* and *Living Art*
were fairly conservative. There are the expressive distortion and
fantasy of Marc Chagall in his *It Is Written.* Thayer told Gilbert
Seldes (October 13, 1921) that the artist was "today looked upon
amongst the more modern painters of Central Europe as the greatest
of living artists." There are intimations of Cubist experimentation
with volume and light in Demuth's *After Sir Christopher Wren*, a
favorite painting by one of Thayer's two favored American painters,
the other being John Marin; "our two best painters," remarked the
Editor. Purchased from the artist himself in 1921, *After Sir Christopher Wren* hung over the fireplace in the editorial office; the frontispiece for the February 1921 issue was not Thayer's picture but one
with the same title that later belonged to Ferdinand Howald, and, to
add to the confusion, Thayer's picture occasionally is entitled *New
England.*[4] When approached to give biographical data for the folio
in which his tempera was to be reproduced, Demuth replied en-
dearingly (to Gilbert Seldes: November 13, 1922), "Please pardon
me—I just forgot it, really, I did, I dont understand it,—as I'm as
anxious as the best of 'them,'—towards fame (so called) or publicity."
Understandably, six weeks later Thayer wrote to Alyse Gregory, on
getting a false report that Demuth was dying (December 29, 1922),
that he was "the only painter in America about whose work I much
care." That pictures by Chagall, Demuth, and Marin were reproduced
not only in *The Dial* but also Thayer's folio, sealed the Editor's
approval.

Perhaps the extreme verge to which Thayer ventured was the
work of some of the group shown at 291. To illustrate his lengthy
essay on "American Painting," for the December 1921 issue, Paul
Rosenfeld chose a conservative portrait of Albert Pinkham Ryder
by Kenneth Hayes Miller, because in Ryder's work "for the first

time, paintings speak to the American of what lies between him and his native soil," and, in Miller's portrait, "One sees the presence of a man born to gigantic power which he could direct." The three later painters chosen by Rosenfeld as bringing the "entire man . . . to the composition of their works" were John Marin, Arthur Dove, and Georgia O'Keeffe. Dove's *The Cow* was chosen by Rosenfeld as the second picture to illustrate the essay. Rosenfeld chose, as the third illustration to accompany "American Painting," Georgia O'Keeffe's *Black Spot*. Of O'Keeffe, "Notes on Contributors" said that her "work has never before been reproduced. She was born in Wisconsin and before coming to New York she taught art four summers in the University of Virginia and for two years at the West Texas State Normal School. In 1916 and 1917 she had exhibitions of her work at 291." Along with Dove's *Storm-Clouds in Silver*, O'Keeffe's *Alligator Pear* appeared in the August 1925 issue; and Demuth's *Poster Portrait of Georgia O'Keeffe* and his *Poster Portrait of Arthur G. Dove* also appeared. The Editors in their "Comment" for the month were "consciously indulgent, perhaps, towards certain of Arthur Dove's idiosyncrasies—towards 10-Cent Store Still-Life and Mary Goes to Italy; examining his Storm-Clouds in Silver, and his Garden, Rose, Gold, Green, however, we agree that we'd 'rather have the impossible than the possible,' that we'd 'rather have truth than beauty,' that we'd 'rather have a soul than a shape'; the soul and truth sometimes conveniently as in this case, having 'beauty' and a 'shape.' Wary, yet eager snappers-up of the uninsistent master-piece, like certain fish, we sometimes pre-empt something that we may afterward reject; and nearly always prefer precisely those works for which the author himself, cares least." The Editors less am-biguously praised O'Keeffe: certain of her "petunias and Portraits of a Day check the impact of precursory consent. The unvariegated burning brass of her autumn leaves, however, assures us as an interpreter of her work has said, that she 'wears no poisoned emeralds.' Her calla lilies, gladiolas, and alligator pears, have upon them, the lustre of mosques, of lotus flowers, of cypress-bordered pools. They have the involute security of Central African, of Singha-lese and Javanese experienced adornment." The pastel *Alligator Pear* had previously attracted Thayer, who wrote to Charles Demuth on March 14, 1924: "Obediently I pilgrimaged uptown to the Stieglitz-O'Keeffe double ring show. I did like some of the

O'Keeffe's better than any I had seen before I went abroad. And I liked best the one Miss O'Keeffe told me you liked best, in the corner farthest away from the corner in which your pictures were hung, and representing a pear lying on its side and with the stem pulled out, leaving a particularly precise hole. This is in pastel, and mostly black and grey and white, but with a slight bluish shadow behind the pear. Perhaps you remember it. We have taken a photograph of this for reproduction in the DIAL." Neither Dove's nor O'Keeffe's pictures in *The Dial* are more abstract, in their ways, than Brancusi's *Golden Bird*, but unlike Brancusi neither artist was represented in *Living Art*.

Reproduced neither in *The Dial* nor in Thayer's folio were the abstractions of Delaunay (except for the representational *St Séverin*, he did not appear in *The Dial*), Kandinsky, and Mondrian; nor did the intentionally pathological fantasies of Paul Klee appear in the folio and its parent review. When Glenway Wescott sent in a manuscript and photographs of Klee, Thayer wrote back (November 12, 1923) that he differed "absolutely in re: Paul Klee. I saw, of course, much of his work in Central Europe, and never saw anything about which I cared much." The relative conservatism of Thayer's taste meant that even by the middle 1920's the magazine and the forthcoming folio would not publish the artists in the vanguard.

The great folio, which would be called *Living Art*, took form slowly. Thayer's optimism about producing his publication in time for the Christmas book-buying trade of 1922 was not justified. Not until the middle of July 1922 had he secured the services of a suitable printing firm, and when he did, it was located not in Vienna but in Berlin. "I should particularly like to have you with me in Berlin— apart from the pleasure of being with you—because I have just ordered at the Marées Gesellschaft a folio of contemporary art to be made up for the Dial," Scofield Thayer wrote Raymond Mortimer. "Some of the pictures are not yet selected, and my reason for being in Berlin in the autumn will be to collaborate with Meier-Graefe in determining several important points in regard to the folio. Your help would be of infinite value to me." This was on July 20; plans had again changed, and Thayer would not, apparently, travel to England for the autumn of 1922.

Mortimer did come over to Berlin, in September, and there the two friends made their selections for the folio with the publisher,

Julius Meier-Graefe, head of the Marées Gesellschaft and of the printing firm, Ganymed Anstalt. The remainder of 1922 and nearly the whole of 1923 for Thayer were occupied—when he was not editing *The Dial*—with the preparation of *Living Art*.

Before an American connoisseur with money, all Middle Europe, especially Germany and Austria, lay recumbent from the economic blows of the inflation as well as from the knowledge of defeat. Both *The Dial* and *Living Art* essentially, even rather brutally, profited from these conditions. There perhaps would have been a *Dial*, if not at all the same *Dial*, had its Editor not lived in Vienna and traveled through Europe, for two years in the early 1920's, but there probably would not have been a *Living Art* of any sort, not only because of costs but also because Thayer formulated *Living Art* on the model of the contemporary German and Austrian art *Mappen*.

Despite the advantage of Thayer's command of relatively stable dollars, the publication of *Living Art* was held up by the difficulties of the inflation-raddled exchange, and by problems other than those caused by rocketing marks and Kronen. The process of compilation moved haltingly from obstacle to obstacle. Of the artists whose work was to be represented, some such as Alfeo Faggi and Charles Demuth actively co-operated by sending their own biographical data; interviewed by Raymond Mortimer, Wyndham Lewis and Frank Dobson obligingly gave him the needed information, as also did Lachaise when queried by Gilbert Seldes. But some of the artists were maddeningly vague about their work, and reliable information was difficult to obtain. Picasso would not give his pictures titles, so no "official" titles existed. Picasso told Raymond Mortimer to get all the facts about himself from the study by Maurice Raynal; however, on looking over the book, Thayer complained to Gilbert Seldes (March 17, 1923) that he had found it contained "very few facts and not sufficient for a Contributor's Note." Forain could *not* be persuaded that Scofield Thayer was not a *boche* and therefore was never induced, even after months of effort by Thayer and his aides, to agree to have one of his pictures reproduced in *Living Art*. There was, too, the human fallibility of those engaged in producing the folio; the staff of *The Dial* were dilatory in sending on to Thayer the accurate and necessary information about laws dealing with international copyright and regulating the importation to America of books produced in Europe.

Julius Meier-Graefe, at that time a leading interpreter and entrepreneur of the New Movement in Germany, had aesthetic scruples about the folio, at least in the form in which its compiler insisted it be printed. While associated with Thayer, Meier-Graefe wrote for the July 1923 *Dial* a prophetic and unheeded essay, "German Art after the War," in which names later fashionable, together with some not well known, are discussed: Hans von Marées, Max Liebermann, Lovis Corinth, Max Slevogt, Karl Hofer, Franz Marc, Max Beckmann, and Wilhelm Lehmbruck among them. The accompanying illustrations were examples of work by Hans von Marées, Lovis Corinth, William Sommer, and Karl Hofer.

Meier-Graefe was as strong-minded as was Scofield Thayer and had as high an opinion of his own aesthetic judgment; inevitably his employment by Thayer had its times of stress. The person who smoothed matters over whenever the going became rough was Dr. Robert von Erdberg, Thayer's friend in the Ministry for Cultural Affairs in Berlin. Von Erdberg welcomed Thayer's decision to write him about every business matter the compiler of *Living Art* discussed with Meier-Graefe. "Meier-Graefe is too much of an artist to be reliable," wrote von Erdberg (February 21, 1923), when Thayer complained (February 16 and 17, 1923) of Meier-Graefe's *Schlamperei* and said he had lost all confidence in Meier-Graefe's executive ability. Von Erdberg continued, soothingly: "If he were reliable, he wouldn't be Meier-Graefe. But let us take him as he is and be pleased with the pleasant characteristics, which he after all possesses in such rich measure. I do not know about his command of the English language, but I suppose if he is tardy, the only reasons are the ones indicated above."

To von Erdberg fell the tasks not only of acting as Thayer's representative in Berlin but also of obtaining permissions from the artists represented in the folio who were not American, English, or French; and von Erdberg also obtained legal opinion as to who had the right of reproduction in the case of pictures and objects, the owner of the work or the artist.

By April 27, 1923, Scofield Thayer was at last in a position to mail Robert von Erdberg a definitive list of pictures in the order in which he wished them to appear in *Living Art*. There were three divisions. The first consisted of "Oil paintings, tempera, watercolours, etc.," and they were to appear in the order listed: Paul

Signac, *La Rochelle;* Pierre Bonnard, an untitled painting regarding
which Thayer noted, "Please obtain correct title from Meier-Graefe
and inform me" (this finally appeared as *Village*); Henri Matisse,
Nasturtiums and the "Dance" II; Maurice de Vlaminck, an untitled
water color regarding which Thayer noted, "Please obtain title from
Flechtheim and inform me" (as printed in the folio, the title was
Rue à Nesles); André Derain, *Les Collines;* Pablo Picasso, *Le Bain
des Chevaux;* John Marin, *Lower Manhattan;* Charles Demuth,
After Sir Christopher Wren; Duncan Grant, *Woman with Ewer;* and
Marc Chagall, *On Dit* (given the title in print of *It Is Written*). The
second division was a list of *Graphiken*, or as the title in the folio
went, "Drawings and Engravings": Jean-Louis Forain, *Enfin ç'a
y est*, for which was substituted in the folio as published André
Dunoyer de Segonzac's *The Morin in Spring;* Edvard Munch,
The Last Hour; Boardman Robinson, *The Hands of Moses;* Gaston
Lachaise, *Woman's Head;* Jules Pascin, "A Pen and Ink Drawing,"
which was published with the title of *Maltese Family*, and at last
selected after Raymond Mortimer's dismaying initial peek at his
pictures and a subsequent declaration to Thayer (February 11,
1922) that most of them were in colors, or obscene, or in some way
unsuitable for reproduction in *The Dial;* Wyndham Lewis, *Head
of a Girl;* Marie Laurencin, "Portrait," which was published as
A Girl; Pablo Picasso, *Le Ménage des Pauvres;* a second Picasso,
a drawing bought from Flechtheim, published as *Pen and Brush
Drawing;* and a third Picasso, *Pencil Drawing.* Of the *Plastiken*,
published in the folio as "Sculpture," Thayer listed Aristide Maillol,
Coureur Cycliste; the same artist, *Femme Accroupie;* Wilhelm Lehmbruck, "Kneeling Figure," titled in *Living Art* as *Kneeling Girl;*
Ernesto de Fiori, *Male Figure;* Constantin Brancusi, *Marble;* Alexander Archipenko, *Female Figure;* Frank Dobson, *Female Torso;*
Alfeo Faggi, *Saint Francis;* and front and back views, respectively,
of the two sculptures here commonly entitled *La Montagne*, by
Gaston Lachaise. Thus before May 1923 the contents of *Living Art*,
save for the substitution of Segonzac's picture for the Forain, had
been selected and placed in order.

The rest of the preparation was concerned with the writing by
Thayer of the Preface, preparation of the notes on the artists repre-
sented, and selection of type and design of format. Finally, Adolf
Dehn, the artist whose works after Picasso's were most often re-

produced in *The Dial*, helped as courier between Vienna and Berlin; with his aid as well as with von Erdberg's continued supervision, the Ganymed Press completed its job. But so time-consuming were these measures that *Living Art* did not appear in America until the middle of December 1923.

Through the summer of 1923, Thayer planned the final steps of *Living Art* with Meier-Graefe, von Erdberg, and Gilbert Seldes, even to the publicity and the handling of foreign sales of the folio. Early in June, Seldes and Thayer were congratulating themselves on having secured the services of Clive Bell to write up the folio, for *The New Republic* as well as for whatever English journal the reviewer preferred.

Thayer did not consider Maurice Raynal the best man to puff the publication in France but was very glad (June 8, 1923) Seldes had secured Raynal, "because the more the better and he has anyhow some standing. But you should try to get someone else less of a cubist and more of a humanist than Raynal. I have included in the folio no piece of cubist art not caring for that type of art myself and not indeed valuing it highly, as I presume you know. I fear that for this reason Raynal may find the folio disappointing, reactionary, genteel, or what he will. Particularly in the case of his protegé Picasso I have included only representative painting and draftsmanship. Cannot you then nose out someone more appropriate also to write up the folio in Paris?" Thayer said that he himself would write about the folio and doubted whether it would be appropriate for *The Dial* to publish any other criticism of *Living Art* than this of his, especially as the critique might run to two numbers, "presumably the December and January numbers." The Editor also inquired whether McBride or Thomas Craven might be invited to do a regular review of the folio in *The Dial*, which would appear early, "that is, in the September, or at latest in the October number." Finally, Thayer asked, "Cannot you get Rosenfeld to write the thing up for Vanity Fair which is our most important selling possibility? I believe Vanity Fair likes his work and I feel his type of writing more adapted to this folio than to some of the things he insists upon writing about as for example, the unhappy Randolph Bourne who is now in process of ambergrication. I shall write Mortimer to try to get Fry, and also to write the thing up himself." (The reference to Randolph Bourne's "ambergrication" was a slap at the acceptance, by the staff in New

Boardman Robinson *Roger Fry* MAY 1923

York, of Rosenfeld's memorial essay "Randolph Bourne," which did not appear in *The Dial*, however, until December 1923.)

By July 19, Thayer told Gilbert Seldes that he had met Fry in London, and Fry had agreed to review *Living Art* for *The Burlington Magazine*. Berlin was not a suitable market for such a costly and lavish item as the Dial folio, but Thayer had made arrangements for it to sell in London "at about £ 8 or about $40 and about 25% of this is to go to the dealer," and he suggested that Seldes make similar arrangements in Paris. The Segonzac was being substituted for the Forain, and the last of the pictures taken to Berlin for reproduction in *Living Art* were being readied for their return to America or to individual owners. But the American copies of *Living Art* did not get through customs until early December 1923.

Thayer set sail for New York before the end of July 1923, but Seldes had to remain behind, though unwillingly, to act as courier between Berlin and Paris, and to settle matters. Gilbert Seldes now felt that he must make economies of his strength and mind, just as the backers of *The Dial* felt, in turn, that they must make financial economies in operating their review. With his final weeks of service to Thayer and *The Dial*, in correcting proofs of *Living Art* and generally tying loose ends of the project together, Seldes completed his period of intimate, and official, association with *The Dial* as a member of its staff.

Beginning with the preparation for the November 1923 issue, Scofield Thayer again assumed personal direction of *The Dial*. While Thayer was still in Europe, Sibley Watson had written (March 15, 1923) a general letter dealing with the managerial need of a Strong Man at *The Dial*—not Gilbert Seldes, not Raymond Mortimer, not Alyse Gregory—but maybe Kenneth Burke or Van Wyck Brooks? (Thus it was that in 1925, recalling Watson's suggestion, Thayer sounded out Brooks about becoming Editor of *The Dial*.) Thayer returned as the strong man, no doubt, and Alyse Gregory it was who came to work as Managing Editor, on December 18, 1923. By that date, *Living Art* had been sent to a number of people, although its publication had come too late for the Christmas trade. To publicize the new folio, Thayer planned an exhibition of the cream of the Dial Collection of pictures and objects, at the Montross Gallery in New York, January 26 through February 14, 1924.

As the experiment with Herwarth Walden, to print frontispieces in color for the review, had failed, *The Dial* returned to frontispieces in half tone in December 1922 and did not again publish any in color until February 1924. As early as May 5, 1923, Thayer wrote Kenneth Burke that "Meier-Graefe telegraphed me . . . that it would be impracticable without a great increase in the cost of reproduction to have pictures reproduced on whole Dial pages. I have therefore authorized him to make the reproductions as was previously done by Sturm. They must be pasted on our regular paper as was done in that case." Further instructions to Burke followed (June 27, 1923) that the colored frontispieces were to be run "regularly every month beginning with their receipt in America." Chagall's *The Market Place* resumed the policy of publishing, most months, a frontispiece in color, some of which were reproductions of pictures in *Living Art*. Julius Meier-Graefe's Ganymed Press printed these miniature color reproductions, among *The Dial's* best known and most attractive features; tipped in as frontispieces, they appeared until November 1927, when the last small picture, a Cézanne *Still Life* from the National Gallery in Berlin, was published. Along with the new, or resumed, policy of frontispieces in color, *The Dial* announced officially the publication of *Living Art* and the exhibition of the Dial Collection of pictures and sculptures.

1923, which culminated in the publication of *Living Art* and the exhibition of the Dial Collection, was also the year in which Scofield Thayer sponsored a new series of essays on contemporary art. The first was Thomas Craven's long historical analysis, "The Progress of Painting," published in two parts, in the issues for April and June 1923, and contending that "The history of painting from the death of Rembrandt to the advent of Impressionism is a curious void." It would give trouble later. In July 1923 appeared Julius Meier-Graefe's "German Art after the War," and in October 1923 *The Dial* published Walter Agard's "Aristide Maillol," accompanied by photographs of Maillol's three sculptures here entitled *Adolescence*, *Flora*, and *Girl*.

The Editor was disappointed not to have secured Roger Fry's attack on John Singer Sargent, but in November 1923, Fry contributed as a substitute an essay on Sargent, "The Wertheimer Portraits," illustrated by half tones of the works discussed: *Asher Wertheimer*, *Hylda Wertheimer*, and a group portrait of *Essie*,

Ruby, and Ferdinand, Children of Asher Wertheimer. (The critic remarked acidulously that "this marvellous series of portraits represents a social transaction quite analogous to the transactions between a man and his lawyer.") In December, Fry contributed an essay "Salamanca," illustrated by one of his own pencil drawings, *Spanish Scene*.

As the leading essay for the February 1924 *Dial*, the issue specifically intended to publicize *Living Art*, Lawrence Buermeyer contributed "Some Popular Fallacies in Aesthetics," which opposed the aesthetic theories of Roger Fry and Thomas Craven, theories that *The Dial* openly sympathized with. Buermeyer objected to their theories at three points. Fry and Craven were alike in making "form" the touchstone of the value of a painting and in repudiating the importance of a picture's subject-matter. Both Fry and Craven shared a tendency, "unavowed but clearly apparent, to judge all art since the Renaissance by the standards of that time," and therefore, according to Buermeyer, they denigrated art that did not take into account the laws of perspective, such as the work of Henri Rousseau and that of the Cubists. Craven, especially, was blind "to the aesthetic quality of painters whose work is not primarily or at least obviously concerned with depth and mass," and he failed "to grasp the true merits even of the modern painter whom he most highly recommends – Cézanne."

Thomas Craven contributed, in his turn, a riposte to Buermeyer, which appeared in *The Dial* for March 1924 as "Psychology and Common Sense." Craven here restated his devotion to a "tri-dimensional conception" of space: "In plain language it opens the flat doors of decoration and plunges us into the profound and moving realism of immense depths." Buermeyer's was the "conventional attitude of the dealer and the curator." Again he avowed his contempt for Impressionism, a school that "brought forth inimitable daintiness of surface" but contributed negligibly to design; and again he emphasized the art of the Italian Renaissance as affording the widest suggestive field for study.

A final communication from Buermeyer in the April 1924 *Dial*, entitled "Mr Craven's Reply," professed all his previous dubiety and called Craven's reply an "offense against the canons of good manners and good taste in the public print." Privately Thayer and Craven agreed not to reply. The argument thus concluded without settling any problems and indeed only raising some further ones. Having left Princeton, Lawrence Buermeyer during this period was connected with the Barnes Foundation at Merion, Pa., and his article had originally been submitted to *The Dial* by his employer, Dr. Albert C. Barnes, in the latter part of October 1923, though Buermeyer stated: "I first read his articles before I had any connection with the Barnes Foundation, and formed my general judgement of them then." As both the Editor and Craven knew, Buermeyer's attack in his original article was leveled not so much at Roger Fry as at Thomas Craven, who pointed out to Thayer that the very strictures Buermeyer laid upon Fry were ones that Craven had pointed out in "Mr Roger Fry and the Artistic Vision," his review of Fry's *Vision and Design*, published in the July 1921 *Dial*. It was the review and its backers that Barnes was attacking; the controversy between the critics was part of his grand strategy. Perhaps, as Daniel Catton Rich has said, Dr. Barnes was obtaining his revenge on *The Dial* because Watson and Thayer had not reacted positively to Barnes' proposal—made through Watson to Thayer (April 13, 1923)—that he would pay $2,000 to the magazine for an award in art criticism with the stipulation that it be conferred upon Craven "through The Dial." [5]

The controversy has relevance in the succinct summing up of his attitude toward the New Movement by the critic and theorist whom Scofield Thayer admired more than he did any other American then writing in the field. Craven's defense of volume and depth with his emphasis on line and form and total design, and along with his devotion to the traditional values of the Renaissance, was very much an echo of Thayer's praise of Munch, Matisse, and Picasso and Thayer's decrying art that he termed Cubism and abstractionism.

While *The Dial* for February 1924 was intended to publicize *Living Art* and the Dial exhibition at the Montross Gallery, there was a further purpose too. The publicity attendant on the exhibition at the Montross Gallery would precede the Dial Collection to Worcester, Thayer's home town, and thence to Smith College. Fear that "a conservative public might be prejudiced" (as Thayer put it to Hermann Riccius: March 4, 1924) caused the Worcester Art Museum to withdraw a large Braque oil of a nude woman, entitled *Standing Figure*, and a Picasso drawing when the collection was shown in Worcester from March 5–30, 1924, as the "Exhibition of the Dial Collection of Paintings, Engravings, and Drawings by Contemporary Artists." Thayer's indignation was aroused when John C. Johansen, then in Worcester to paint a "life-sized" portrait of President Wallace Atwood of Clark University, called *The Dial*, in an interview printed in *The Worcester Telegram*, "an intellectual sewer." Thayer retorted to the insult in one of his most combative "Comments," in May 1925, taking to task not only the artist for his opinion but Clark University for its President. From Worcester, most of the works went on to Smith College. There a Chagall, unspecified, was withdrawn, and to Thayer's regret the Smith College Museum did not exhibit the collection as a whole; but he rejoiced to Hermann Riccius (April 18, 1924) that "they seem appreciative of it. You do not mention whether the folio was on sale and whether the card which the DIAL should have sent them was conspicuous upon or above the folio." Although Thayer offered his collection for exhibition elsewhere, the museum and gallery directors variously declined.

Securing a favorable reception for *Living Art* was equally difficult a task. In an "Announcement" for February 1924 replacing his usual "Comment," the Editor related the Dial Collection to *Living Art*, wrote about the show of the Dial Collection, and urged his readers to go to the Montross Gallery. Several pictures in the issue were reproduced from *Living Art* besides the color frontispiece of Chagall's *The Market Place:* Boardman Robinson's *The Hands of Moses*, Segonzac's *The Morin in Spring*, Marie Laurencin's *A Girl*, Edvard Munch's woodcut *The Last Hour*, Pablo Picasso's *Le Ménage des Pauvres* and his untitled pencil drawing of two female nudes, and a photograph of Maillol's plaster *Femme Accroupie*. In fact, every illustration in the February 1924 *Dial* was a smaller counterpart of a reproduction or photograph in *Living Art*.

Besides writing his "Announcement," Thayer saw to it that both the house art critics concerned themselves with the folio. Thomas Craven emphasized, in his book review of *Living Art*, the personal taste that formed the selection comprising the folio. Admitting this factor, Craven said, no one with the remotest familiarity with the fundamental issues at stake would question the character of the undertaking or deny the validity of the achievement, a collection offered solely for its aesthetic value, without bombast or special pleading, with no purpose to antagonize the preferences of others. *Living Art* defined the contemporary status of plastic expression; its pictures must be considered as a definitive repudiation of the cursed fetish of naturalism. Craven selected for especial praise Matisse's *La Danse aux Capucines*, as he called it, which he liked better than Matisse's later work, as "more objective, closer to the light and air of actual vision." True, the eclectic nature of Picasso was not adequately shown by the four examples of his work presented by *Living Art*, and the absence of the mechanistic classicism of the Cubists was objectionable; although the "classicists" such as Maillol and de Fiori were successfully represented, Wyndham Lewis and Derain, "names militantly associated with the modernist idiom," as represented here were the least important artists of the collection. Yet Craven realized such personal reservations testified to the immense fertility of the field, and he advocated more such declarations as *Living Art* "in order to encourage the public, the artist, and the buyer, and to emphasize the importance of the period."

In "Modern Art," Henry McBride emphasized the technical excellence of the reproductions rather than the personal taste behind the selections; yet he too stood in wonder before several of the pictures, as much for their re-created beauty as for their original excellence. In particular, McBride praised the reproductions of Picasso's *Le Bain des Chevaux*, Marin's water color *Lower Manhattan*, and Chagall's *It Is Written*. Like Craven, McBride devoted the greatest amount of space to Matisse's *Nasturtiums and the "Dance" II:* "Matisse is undoubtedly one of the great painters of modern times and there are scores of his canvases that must seduce all those who succumb to virtuosity in painting, but in the Danse he throws all enticements to the winds and simplifies to an extent that would put even Giotto to shame." When McBride had first seen the mural in Matisse's studio—i.e., *La Danse*, of which a portion forms the background of *Nasturtiums and the "Dance" II*—"I was not precisely bowled over by it, preferring many other things in the studio to it, but now, of all the collection by which this folio has suddenly enriched me, it is this Danse aux Capucines I have chosen for my wall; and it glows there in a vital, relentlessly arresting way through all the day and through all changes of light." The attention paid to Matisse's picture could not but have pleased the Editor, who had once told Gilbert Seldes (March 6, 1922) that it was "the best painting Matisse has painted."

Having failed to secure Maurice Raynal as the French critic

to review *Living Art*, Thayer printed Élie Faure's review in October
1924. Like Craven, and indeed like every reviewer in or out of
The Dial save McBride, Faure differed from the compiler in his list
of selections. He cited five omissions, "the French painters Marquet
and Braque and the sculptor Despiau, the German painter Kokoschka, and the Polish sculptor Lipschitz"; but he also held that in
Living Art the publishers presented "almost all of the participants
in that spiritual surge, filled with the deep poetry of mysticisms and
myths in gestation, which is turning upside-down both the Old World
and the New." To people not familiar with "these singularly un-
academic forms," study of the folio might cause astonishment or even
indignant stupefaction. *Living Art* was just this tangled rout of
shapes and colors, and to unaccustomed eyes it looked like anarchy.
"Yet within it a new order is confusedly evolving."

Outside *The Dial* praise of *Living Art* was considerably more
measured than it was in the reviews Thayer commissioned. John
Quinn wrote about his reaction. Like the critics, but at least privately,
he told Thayer (December 18, 1923) he disagreed about the artists
represented and, twisting the knife in the wound, added that he
owned better works by some of the artists, which he would have
been glad to lend. Elizabeth Luther Cary reviewed the folio at
length in *The New York Times Magazine* (January 27, 1924) and
thought no better means than *Living Art* had been devised to the end
of making the public, which "delights in hating modern art," look
at this art. Miss Cary praised Signac's *La Rochelle* and the four
Picassos, but little else. To her the most "valuable plate in the collection" was Picasso's untitled drawing of two female nudes, because
it was "the kind of thing for a student to memorize in order to free
himself from the bondage of 'good drawing.'" But she thought a
"much better Matisse than the well-known 'La Danse aux Capucines'
could have been found for the purpose, one with his arabesques in
black to keep the color more within the frame," and Derain's *Les
Collines* was "very synthetic, but without much fullness of expression,
a good thing to choose, since it would be difficult to go wrong with
it." She spelled Thayer's first name as "Schofield," yet in discussing
Segonzac's *The Morin in Spring*, she said the title itself was curi-
ously wrong: "A pen-and-ink drawing of a Spring morning (why,
with such efforts and such successes, should a proofreader have
balked at the spelling of so simple a word as 'morn')." [6]

The Editor of *The Dial* almost immediately wrote to the reviewer (January 29, 1924) to complain about her alleged correction of the presumed balky proofreader, for the word in question, *Morin*, was correctly spelt. It "is a river in France." And he added: "Would you further be so very good as to correct the error in the spelling of my name? No doubt this is merely the oversight of a proofreader." The chiding of Miss Cary was to be public as well as private and epistolary. "Comment" for March 1924 devoted its two pages to her "gentle and balanced paragraphs," with particular attention being paid to Miss Cary's gaffe in confusing *Morin* with *Morn*. Thayer concluded: "THE DIAL is taking up a modest collection for the benefit of the New York Times. It is our desire to enable this ambitious contemporary to purchase an atlas of France."

Also, Clive Bell's review "Modern Art and How to Look at It," in *Vanity Fair* for April 1924, displeased Thayer by complaining, like Craven's and Faure's, that certain indispensable artists had not been represented in the folio. The tone of the Editor's consequent riposte may have been dictated further by his disappointment that Bell was *Vanity Fair*'s reviewer, rather than Paul Rosenfeld, who had been Thayer's nomination to Gilbert Seldes—though Thayer, after all, had considered Bell adequate for *The New Republic*. "Comment" for May 1924 began by describing *Vanity Fair* as one of the five readable magazines in the United States—*The Dial*, *The Nation*, *The New Republic*, *The Yale Review* being the others, with *The Atlantic Monthly* and *The Saturday Review* being held up as examples of "non-alcohol, non-caffeine, non-bones, non-everything personally pre-sterilized and pre-peptonized nutriment." It was nonetheless in such a magazine that Bell, with Gilbert Seldes one of the "twin gilded bantams" ruling Frank Crowninshield's roost, had obtusely regretted Thayer's failure to include "nine more Parisian artists—all of whom, as well as the more important Georges Braque (whom, I take it, Mr Bell forgot) making an even ten, I could easily have included by merely raising the price to one hundred dollars and selling dog-carts to go with the folio. Mr Bell would have slightly facilitated these generous and sweeping inclusions by the expulsion of one German-Italian, one Scandinavian, one Englishman, and two Americans. This *international* folio of contemporary art would then have been, aristocratically, 72% Paris Pure: in fact it registers, apologetically, only 46% Parisian." Besides his offense at

Bell's partiality for the School of Paris (" 'a babbles of Bonnard")
and certain British cliques ("Contemporary London rejoices in this
pester"), Scofield Thayer was especially put out at the slurs,
open or implied, against Wyndham Lewis, Alfeo Faggi, Boardman
Robinson, Ernesto de Fiori, and Edvard Munch, and recommended
a Cook's Tour to Scandinavia to Clive Bell, where he might discover the mastery of Munch.

Scofield Thayer had wanted Roger Fry, who was the most
important person directing policy in *The Burlington Magazine*,
to review *Living Art* in that periodical. R. R. Tatlock, however,
wrote the review; his reservations echoed those of Craven and Faure.
It was impossible to perform acceptably the task, as Thayer had
said in his Preface, of representing "the leading artists of our time."
The compiler had "in fact frankly represented his own taste rather
than attempted to express that of art critics in general."

There was an important and consolatory review by Forbes
Watson in *The Arts* for January 1924–a journal Thayer praised
in his "Comment" damning Clive Bell at such length. Forbes Watson
lauded the enterprise of the Dial Publishing Company in bringing
out "the handsomest portfolio of contemporary art that has been
produced in this country," a fine if inaccurate tribute. He admitted
that it was a little difficult to see why certain painters had been included in a list that was not "comprehensive" and objected to the
pictures by Duncan Grant, Chagall, and Wyndham Lewis. But the
main purposes of the folio had been achieved: "One of these purposes
undoubtedly was to present reproductions after contemporary artists
of such exceptional quality that they would give as complete a statement as possible; another purpose was to select a sufficient number
of the works of contemporary European and American painters to
indicate the scope of the vital art of today." The reviewer thought
it would require a good many portfolios to complete the work *The
Dial* had started, and he congratulated the review on the solid
encouragement it had given to living art. He also noted that unfortunately the expense of *Living Art* would make it impossible to
attain "wide circulation" (how could this have been attained anyway,
with a possible sale of 400 copies?), but "libraries and art schools
and a certain number of individuals will undoubtedly take the
opportunity which the portfolio offers to survey the field of contemporary art."

A house advertisement in *The Dial* for February 1924 quoted

Henry McBride's observations and also those of "Mr Alfred Stieg-litz, the connoisseur and photographer," who wrote: "Living Art is an achievement, a triumph in reproduction. I do hope that the Art Museums and the larger libraries of the country will avail themselves of the opportunity to procure copies of this genuine achievement. The price is certainly most reasonable." Thayer had estimated to Hermann Riccius (December 17, 1923) that the profits of "the folio" (as he usually termed it) would be "several thousand dollars" if 400 of the total printed of 500 were sold ("about 100 copies have to be given away"). Albert Boni was distributing copies for a net of 15% and persuaded Thayer to raise the price per copy from forty to sixty dollars. In a letter dated July 29, 1924, Thayer told Henry Gerstley: "Incidentally, your 'guess that the portfolio is not selling very well' is wrong. Our business manager reports to me that we have sold over a thousand dollars' worth a month for the last few months." Month after month *The Dial* advertised its great folio, and by the spring of 1925 *Living Art* had been reduced to forty dollars. "In order to dispose immediately of the few remaining copies which The Dial possesses, the price of this folio has now been reduced from sixty dollars to forty dollars," announced a house advertisement in the back of *The Dial* in May 1925, and in subsequent issues.

The artists included in the folio were less analytical than the critics and simply expressed their gratitude and enthusiasm for Thayer's service to contemporary art. On December 20, 1923, Boardman Robinson thought the quality of the "great portfolio" admirable in the extreme and its dimensions appalling. It would force him to move into a larger place. "Is it possible that people capable of buying such a work exist?" he asked the Editor. In her undated, brief bread-and-butter note answering Thayer's gift of the folio, Marie Laurencin called it magnificent and averred that it gave her great pleasure. Charles Demuth wrote to Thayer (December 26, 1923): "It is beautifully done. . . . In my own case, it is like getting my 'tempera' back!—really. It hardly seems honest." And Demuth did hope *Living Art* would meet the appreciation it deserved. Alfeo Faggi, too, thanked Scofield Thayer (December 28, 1923) not only for the *magnifico folio* but also for the vitally and well-reproduced works of art in it, among them his *San Francesco*. These thanks must have contrasted refreshingly to the weightier qualifications voiced by the critics.

For all the attention *Living Art* received, and for all Scofield

Thayer's protestations that the folio was selling satisfactorily, the fact remains that it did not. *Living Art* as a unit did not possess sufficient attraction for even 400 persons in America and Western Europe. Its taste, was, as R. R. Tatlock alleged, a frankly personal taste. Now one can make no objections to the folio on this score, but a personal taste is not usually a representative taste, and Scofield Thayer consistently held that his taste in compiling *Living Art* was representative. Yet on at least one occasion he confessed the opposite: he would include no Cubist work in his folio, and for that reason such a critic as Maurice Raynal might find *Living Art* "disappointing, reactionary, genteel, or what he will." That *Living Art* was the product of a highly personal taste—a sophisticated and exclusive taste—rather than of a taste more representative if perhaps less discriminating probably influenced some connoisseurs against purchasing the folio. Thus both the material and the aesthetic limitations of *Living Art* precluded its having an immediate sale of even 400 copies.

What must also have hurt was the opposition from within the New Movement itself, not just from Albert Barnes and Lawrence Buermeyer, who might be dismissed for various personal reasons from serious esteem, but from such allies as Clive Bell and Roger Fry. Even the reservations of Thomas Craven must have been difficult to take with equanimity. Especially apposite here were the words of A. A. Orage, written before the conclusion of the second year of the monthly *Dial*, and quoted at length in a house advertisement in the June 1922 issue. Orage had remarked the American *Dial* as "perhaps the most fully realized of all the promising literary magazines now current in the world. It is in all probability considerably in advance of the American reading public for whom it is intended, but it is all the better on that account. Culture is always called upon to sacrifice popularity, and, usually, even its existence, in the interests of civilization." [7] (Significantly the final sentence was omitted in the advertisement's quotation.) But *The Dial* had sought popularity, had attempted to pay its own way through advertising and increased circulation. Unsystematically and sporadically, it had even temporized with advertisers. The fact that *Living Art* did not succeed as its compiler had hoped it might, was ominous for *The Dial*. No second annual of the folio was apparently considered, and pictures in *The Dial* thus continued to be a necessity. Indeed nobody ever seems to have suggested that they be dropped, once the folio had been published.

Dr. Watson told Charles Norman that "The more copies of the magazine we published, the more we lost. When the circulation went up to 22,000—the high watermark [*sic*]—we lost too much and let it sink back to 4,000, a normal run. Towards the end of the Twenties this seemed a natural number." [8] Their first flush of enthusiasm had died, and now the backers of *The Dial* must proceed to pay the deficit of their review without any illusion that somehow it might become other than it plainly was—in Elizabeth Peabody's epithet applied to the first *Dial*, the "Organ of the Free," but also of the Few.

NINE

To the End of the Twenties

WITH THE PUBLICATION of its issue of February 1924, *The Dial* reached fruition. From that number to the final issue of July 1929, there would be but one major change, the resignation of Scofield Thayer as Editor in June 1926. Marianne Moore, who had come to work at *The Dial* in April 1925 and had become Acting Editor in July 1925, thereupon assumed the title of Editor.

Some months later, *The Dial* had spent its force. At least, so *The New Republic* asserted, on the occasion of the announcement of the Dial Award for 1926 to William Carlos Williams. He, on the contrary, felt ebullient gratitude and wrote a poem in consequence, "Lines on Receiving The Dial's Award," which was published in the March 1927 *Dial* and reprinted with slight textual changes. "He was, of course, pleased?" asked Edith Heal in 1958. "So pleased," replied the poet, "I wrote a poem about it. There was a patient who knew that I liked to collect old bottles—but read about it in the poem," with its concluding lines:

> An old empty bottle in my hand
> I go through the motions of drinking,
> drinking to THE DIAL and its courtesy [1]

The gratitude expressed in these "Lines" was merited. Williams had made his first appearance in *The Dial* in August 1920 with a group of "Six Poems": "Portrait of a Lady," "To Waken an Old Lady," "The Desolate Field," "Willow Poem," "Blizzard," and "Spring Storm." His interviewer, Edith Heal, asked Dr. Williams whether "Portrait of a Lady" had been suggested by either Henry

James or T. S. Eliot; but after reading it, she laughed with the poet and agreed that it could not possibly have been suggested by the work of either gentleman.[2] Williams was as consistently published by *The Dial* as any poet in the Movement, nineteen poems of his having appeared in its pages by the time he received the Dial Award.

On being offered the Dial Award, on November 29, 1926, Williams wrote the Editor that "Surprise and delight have so upset me after the unexpected announcement in your letter just received that I really do not know how to frame a letter that would properly convey to you my feelings and thoughts at this time and it would be too childish even for your friendly eyes, and there would be too much to say and no satisfaction, were it not all said, so please accept this note of thanks as an Esquimo might perhaps out of gratitude present his friend with a bone fishhook or the like." He noted Miss Moore's intimation of the need for a little haste and said that in another twenty-four hours he would write again and more fully. Gallantly Dr. Williams concluded that "Had such news come from anyone else than you the pleasure of it could not have been so complete." [3]

Apparently Williams gave *The Dial*, at about the time he was told of his nomination for its award, the poem entitled "Paterson," published in the February 1927 issue. He told Edith Heal that he had written a poem called "Paterson" as far back as 1926, which had been singled out for mention by *The Dial* when he received the Dial Award. Like so many memories of that bygone period, the Twenties, this one too is inaccurate. As the eulogist for the occasion, Marianne Moore had constructed an essay largely woven of quotations and allusions drawn from Williams' poems, but she did not mention "Paterson," though undoubtedly it had been received at *The Dial* for some time. Nor did Kenneth Burke mention "Paterson" in his appreciative essay, "William Carlos Williams, the Methods of," immediately following the poem in the February 1927 *Dial*. (Incidentally, Williams emphasized to Edith Heal that the early poem in *The Dial* did not touch on his later theme for his long masterwork.[4])

In March 1927 Williams contributed a group of "Three Poems," one of which was his "Lines on Receiving The Dial's Award"; and, following the verses, the Editor published her own essay, "A Poet of the Quattrocento" (not collected in her *Predilections*). She insisted that "One sees nothing terrifying in what Doctor Williams

calls a 'modern traditionalism,' but to say so is to quibble. Incurious-
ness, emptiness, a sleep of the faculties, are an end of beauty; and
Doctor Williams is vivid. Perhaps he is modern. He addresses himself to the imagination." Encouraged by his Dial Award, and the
eulogy in the Award issue and Burke's and Miss Moore's laudatory
critiques, Williams contributed, besides "Paterson," ten more poems
published in the review in 1927–28, and a portion of his novel *A
Voyage to Pagany*, as selected by Marianne Moore, appeared in the
June 1928 *Dial* as "Five Prose Sketches," with the author's permission even though he told Miss Moore that the effect produced
did not give an impression of the book, "tho' it does give a taste of
the writing." [5]

Williams, it is clear, was one of the chief contributors to *The
Dial* throughout the Twenties; toward the end of the decade, he
figured more prominently than ever in the review, receiving the
accolade of a critique by Ezra Pound illustrated by Eva Herrmann's
drawing, in the November 1928 issue.

It was the Dial Award to Williams, made with all the fanfare
of three consecutive monthly eulogies, that brought on the attack in
The New Republic. This editorial presented an arraignment of *The
Dial* that has endured, and for that reason worth examining in
some detail. Under the heading, "A Number of Things," *The New
Republic* for January 5, 1927, published a paragraph entitled "The
Dial Award." After naming the previous recipients of the Award, including Dr. Williams, the anonymous editorialist admitted that it
would be difficult to find another literary prize of which the record
seemed so consistently satisfactory: "in every case the award has been
made to a writer of unmistakable originality and importance who was,
at the same time, not in a position to profit by the rewards of popularity. To have brought such a group of writers to notice and to have
made it possible for them to do independent work is a valuable contribution to our letters: perhaps no other magazine has matched it."

But then came the indictment, which voided all the preceding
praise. All of these writers, said *The New Republic*, "were represented in the pages of the Dial during the first year of its present
phase, 1920—as were also most of its other important contributors.
And it is almost impossible to think of any interesting new American
writer who has appeared since that time whom the Dial has encouraged. Yet, the supply of these charter contributors will presently
become exhausted: with all respect to Doctor Williams, one is not

sure that the prize-winning material of the Dial is not already beginning to run thin. What will the Dial do for deserving writers after another two or three years, if it continues as implacably as in the past to decline to interest itself in the original work of new artists?"

Reaction to that paragraph was not immediate on the part of the Dial group. Gilbert Seldes was the first to reply to the allegation, with a letter printed by *The New Republic* for February 9, 1927, in its "Correspondence" under the heading "The Dial and the New Writers." Seldes protested, both as a former managing editor of *The Dial* and a current associate of *The New Republic*, the "semi-editorial reference." The accusation of implacable hostility to new writers did not exactly follow, and it was not in accordance with the facts. Seldes specified that he was writing as a comparative outsider— one may guess that he wanted to exonerate himself with the staff of *The Dial* more than with readers of *The New Republic*—but, as an outsider, he found three to seven names on each month's contents page, not only new to *The Dial* but unknown to him. It did not follow that these new writers were great artists; if one happened not to like their work, he might accuse *The Dial* of bad judgment but not of not admitting the work of new writers. The editors answered that *The New Republic* did not say *The Dial* never printed the work of new writers, but that it did not "interest itself in the original work" of new writers and that it had scarcely, since 1920, encouraged a single *interesting* American writer who had come upon the scene since that time. And there the matter rested for awhile.

Then, in its September 1927 issue, *The Dial* replied officially, through "Comment." The anonymous writer—one suggests Sibley Watson rather than Miss Moore—summarized the observation of *The New Republic* of the previous January and drew the conclusion from it that new writers whom *The Dial* had published were not interesting, together with the hint that interesting new writers had been encouraged by other people and that *The Dial* had missed them. What, "Comment" asked rhetorically, was an interesting new writer? He might fall into one of three categories:

1] A writer who is interesting for some reason other than his writing. Thus the most interesting writer is often oneself and after that one's friend. But we shall not undertake to argue the matter on this plane.

2] A writer who has lately written something interesting. We naturally feel that our contributors are interesting in that way.

3] A writer who will later make a considerable name for himself in an appropriate quarter. In practice an argument between stubborn people about a new writer can be settled only, if at all, at a time when the writer is anything but new.

"Comment" then got down to the business of selecting and categorizing the writers who had been new during the preceding seven years and were, by late 1927, of such reputation that both *The Dial* and *The New Republic* must agree that they were also interesting. First in importance came the writers one had never heard of and should not hear of until *The American Caravan* turned them up, annually, in October. Then came the writers who made one jealous. But the directors of *The Dial* did not need precisely to knock their heads together for not having encouraged Miss Loos or Mr. Erskine, authors respectively of *Gentlemen Prefer Blondes* and *The Private Life of Helen of Troy* and similar historical novels. Did anyone recall to the advantage of *The Dial* or to his that it had published, when he was a new writer, stories by Michael Arlen? Here, however, "Comment" was being less then candid, for *The Dial* had published, in its August 1920 issue, Arlen's brief comedy "The Ci-Devant." (Incidentally, Arlen's playlet, which consists of Lady Beryl Trafalgar's telephone conversation with an unseen and unheard former lover, anticipates in its dramatic situation Jean Cocteau's similar brief play of 1930, *La Voix Humaine*.) Proceeding in its vein of irony, "Comment" went on to mention a second writer, Gordon Young, whose melodramas for *Adventure* magazine had been improving steadily for some years. And what could *The Dial* have done for him?

Ernest Hemingway, admitted "Comment," was another matter. His book, *The Sun Also Rises*, had more warmth in it than one was accustomed to find in a dozen American successes together. Fortunately he reached a level from which he could kick encouragement downstairs. What "Comment" did not tell its readers, however, was that on at least three occasions Ernest Hemingway, encouraged at first by Ezra Pound, had submitted poems and stories to *The Dial* in the early and the mid-Twenties and that once the Editor and twice Alyse Gregory had rejected Hemingway's work, with politeness but with, nonetheless, definiteness, and without an invitation to submit future work.

Alexei von Jawlensky   *Head of a Woman*   FEBRUARY 1926

The final editorial paragraphs once again explained the attitude of *The Dial* toward its contents, its contributors, and its public. To "Comment" it remained inconceivable that *The New Republic* should not have thought a single new contributor to *The Dial* interesting. Perhaps it was with the "encouragement" of *The Dial* that fault was found and not with its contributors at all. For whatever character *The Dial* might have was the result of a selection not so much of writers as of writing. This more usual way of running a magazine that pretended to general interest was apt to prove more encouraging to the reader than to the writer, since it aimed at ensuring that the magazine contained things that would be interesting to read. Admittedly, things that were interesting to write some times came to be rejected. On the other hand, magazines that were edited by their contributors—this was a palpable hit at the coteries of the little magazines—could and must give their contributors the run of the place, and to be given the run of any place could be, for a time, a great encouragement to a writer. Such magazines were often more immediately encouraging to interesting new writers, not to mention movements, than were magazines like *The Dial*. But in the long run the reader too was important. Many writers would continue to appear first in small "group magazines." In contrast, the business of *The Dial* was to furnish a not too scattered public for what writers wrote well, as others would see that they had a larger public whenever they chose to be tiresome. "Comment" reminded its readers that it was impossible in the world of letters to act or to refuse to act without stirring up a hurricane of catcalls, of which *The New Republic*'s were not always the merriest. Lists of interesting new American writers of the preceding seven years would be gratefully received, "Comment" concluded.

In its "New York Diary," under the heading "The Decline of the Dial," *The New Republic* for October 12, 1927, replied to "Comment" at some length. First of all, the diarist admitted one exception to the allegation that it was difficult to think of a single interesting new writer whom *The Dial* had encouraged and who was not among the original group of writers published in 1920. This exception was Hart Crane; he had been well represented in *The Dial* and was not among its original contributors, supposedly; but here *The New Republic* was wrong. As early as April 1920, *The Dial* had published Crane's "My Grandmother's Love Letters," and "Notes on Contributors" for the issue had selected Hart Crane for mention as "a young man of twenty, engaged in business in Cleveland, Ohio. Poems of his have appeared in The Little Review and various magazines of verse."

Then *The New Republic* proceeded to name distinguished American writers who had emerged since 1920; John Dos Passos, Ernest Hemingway, and Lewis Mumford, in prose; and in poetry, Louise Bogan, Elinor Wylie, Léonie Adams, Allen Tate, Phelps Putnam, and John Crowe Ransom. These men and women had written books that had been reviewed favorably in *The Dial*. All had submitted manuscripts to *The Dial*, but only Mumford and Dos Passos had received acceptance, and that of the scantiest. As for Hemingway, *The Sun Also Rises* was not the beginning of his literary career, and at the time when he was still unknown and writing the vignettes and short stories that afterwards appeared in *In Our Time*, *The Dial* did nothing to bring him before the public. As for the writers appearing in each year's *American Caravan*, here *The New Republic* thought *The Dial* very much in error to suppose it had never heard of them; *The Dial* could recognize amongst the members of *The American Caravan* not a few names whom it certainly would not be seeing there for the first time and to whom it might have been expected in the past to show itself a little more hospitable. Nor had *The Dial*, said the New York diarist of *The New Republic*, lately been doing well by some of its original writers—William Butler Yeats, for example, who had been formerly one of the review's most important contributors and was probably the greatest living English poet, but whose recent poetry, though published in London periodicals, had been going begging in America as far as *The Dial* was concerned.

In conclusion, *The New Republic* said that its objections were not to the editorial policy of Marianne Moore, a very distinguished person and herself one of those original and important American writers whom *The Dial* discovered in its first year and to whom it had since appropriately awarded prizes. Miss Moore was not responsible for the recent policy of *The Dial;* from all that could be seen by a tolerably assiduous reader of *The Dial*, the magazine was not a whit different under Miss Moore's editorship from what it was under Mr. Thayer's. The only difference appeared to be what was a genuine misfortune for its readers—that, now that Miss Moore had become editor of *The Dial*, she no longer published any poetry in it. In any case *The Dial* needed somebody's attention: it was no longer serious. It should play an important role in American journalism—a role that no other magazine could play—and it had begun by performing this role splendidly. But it had been a long time since *The Dial* had seemed "anything more than a random throwing together of literary scraps—some of them queer, some of them insipid and now and then one—but increasingly less often—of exceptional interest."

The Dial never replied to this wholesale condemnation. Perhaps it should have done so, citing chapter and verse in its rebuttal of *The New Republic*. It could have done so. What seems incredible, more than three decades later, is the list of names *The New Republic* gave as proof of the fact that *The Dial* had not encouraged interesting new writers since 1920, when the original Dial group appeared. Lewis Mumford had been associated with the old fortnightly *Dial!* Dos Passos had been represented in *The Dial* by an essay on Antonio Machado in June 1920, accompanied by his translation from the Spanish of ten of Machado's poems; by two poems ("Jardin des Tuileries" and "On Poetic Composition") in June 1921; and by reviews of *The Enormous Room* (in July 1922) and Pio Baroja's *The Quest* (in February 1923). As regards Hemingway and the six poets *The New Republic* cited, *The Dial* might well have a bad conscience about having refused their work, but the truth was that the editors did not like the work these writers presumably submitted. The papers in the Dial Collection contain correspondence with Dos Passos, Hemingway, and Elinor Wylie but with none of the other writers *The New Republic* mentioned.

As for new writers, Scofield Thayer had encouraged George Dillon in 1925. And after 1925, *The Dial* continued to print, by way of encouraging, the work of many new writers and foreign writers new to American readers. Among the writers of prose fiction new to *The Dial* in the years 1926–29, appears the work of Azorín, translated from the Spanish by Katie Lush; Roark Bradford; Claude Cockburn; John Collier; Daniel Corkery; Walter D. Edmonds; Albert Halper; Oliver La Farge; and Meridel Le Sueur. Among the poets new to *The Dial* in these years are works by John Collier again; Mark Van Doren; Bravig Imbs; Orrick Johns; Leo Kennedy; Stanley Kunitz; Archibald MacLeish; Theodore May-

nard; Charles Norman; Sterling North; Frank O'Connor, as translator of "The Song of Liadain" from the Middle Irish; Ruth Pitter;
Rainer Maria Rilke, in translation by Freddie Döhle Lee; A. J. M.
Smith; L. A. G. Strong; Jean Toomer; and Louis Zukofsky. Here
is writing by a group of names as distinguished and as interesting
as the list submitted by *The New Republic*, with the important
exception of Hemingway, and newer by the better part of a decade.
The authors of *The Little Magazine* have said that *The Dial*
discovered only Louis Zukofsky and Albert Halper; however, this
statement is probably not ascertainable and is not substantially true.[6]
What is significant is the fact that *The Dial* always encouraged interesting writing and in doing so, encouraged new writers.

But, said *The New Republic* in its indictment, *The Dial* was
not "serious." Its contents were mostly a random throwing together
of literary scraps, some of them queer, some of them insipid, and now
and then one—but increasingly less often—of exceptional interest.
This canard echoed Gorham Munson's accusation in the first number of *Secession* back in the spring of 1922. *The Dial* had attempted
many times to answer the charge and had explained repeatedly that
it was interested in formal excellence in the arts, not in experiment,
not in ideology. If it gave its Awards to living writers, and if those
living writers were what some academicians called "Experimentalists," the coincidence was perhaps inescapable. The directors of
The Dial were, however, encouraging excellence rather than experimentalism or any ism whatever. They were not interested in any
fancied ideological consistency. To be sure, they may have made
mistakes, and some of the pictures and poems and stories in *The
Dial* do indeed seem queer. The point is that *The Dial* did strive. It
did try to abide by the high aesthetic standards it professed, and it
published the best, according to its lights, available to it.

The arguments about the failure of *The Dial* resolve into three
assertions: it was a hodgepodge of conflicting ideologies; it did not
encourage new, which is to say, experimental, writers; and it refused
to publish Ernest Hemingway. (The other names on the list *The
New Republic* drew up do not significantly matter.) Let it be
admitted, first off, that *The Dial* erred regarding Hemingway. At
least it erred with its eyes open. On the other two counts, *The Dial*
and *Secession* and *The New Republic* simply did not see eye to eye.
The Dial, as Scofield Thayer pointed out at the time of his resigna-

tion, owned to no aesthetic dogma. *Secession* and *The New Republic* did—or, rather, *Secession* had its special aesthetic dogma concerning the encouragement of experimentalism, and *The New Republic* had its special political dogma. Theirs was a short cut to culture; no wonder *The Dial* was suspect.

Matters worsened, too. The new age dawning would be vociferously political, and vociferously ideological in its politics. But *The Dial* was nothing if not aesthetic. From a monthly printing of about 18,500 copies at the end of 1922, the monthly printings plummeted to 10,000 by the end of 1925. The Audit Bureau of Circulation stated in 1925 that the new paid circulation in *The Dial* was 10,844—about 844 copies more than *The Dial* was printing in November 1925. For the last four years of the Twenties, *The Dial* gave out no official circulation figures, but Dr. Watson's estimate of 4,000 seems near enough the mark. Undoubtedly a confusion exists here between the aims of *The Dial* when Scofield Thayer was actively its Editor and the aims of the review after his departure— between the attitude of the proprietors in the earlier years of the Twenties and their attitude toward the end of the decade. This contention is borne out by Watson's further statement to Charles Norman that "Our annual deficit was usually around $30,000; but some years it was $50,000." The larger deficits surely occurred during the first period of publication, when both Thayer and Watson seemed to believe that in order for *The Dial* to show a profit or at least to break even, they must be willing to lose some money in the process of publicizing the magazine and lifting its circulation to the desired level. Essentially, the failure of their scheme meant the failure of their review to achieve its main purpose of attracting a sizable number of cultivated readers. In the last three years of publication, circulation wavered dismally between 2,000 and 4,000 copies a month. Only bravado or a transcendence of fact lay behind the assertion in the September 1927 "Comment" that *The Dial* was a magazine pretending to general interest.

Its very integrity, its insistence on printing things that would be interesting to read, was of course its undoing. Toward the close of the Twenties nobody, it seemed, very much liked *The Dial*. Among the "Periodical Reviews" in its second issue (December 1927), the young *Hound and Horn*, edited from Harvard, declared with undergraduate vigor and assurance:

Magazines grow old early; so after nearly eight years a lovely soft shawl of calm settles over the shoulders of the *Dial;* she meditates variously but mainly in a staid fashion—on Chinese Poetry, William James, Walter Pater, Anatole France, and Tolstoi—so far so good. With years her taste in poetry grows editorial and sentimental.

The Dial used to be exciting; it is now—not exactly dull or dreary—but quiet, careful; its ardor is very thin. It has its own variety of 100% reputation to maintain.

Yet there are enough fragments left to reward the purchaser. *Leander* by Malcolm Cowley, *Powhatan's Daughter* by Hart Crane, *In Love?* by D. H. Lawrence do considerably more than keep the pages turning. *The Briefer Mentions* continue useful and the longer reviews able. But, in a way, we think of that *faux bon* the *Dial* speaks so contemptuously of in its advertisements; with honourable exceptions.

Indeed, by 1928 the day was ebbing for *The Dial.* Paul Rosenfeld told Marianne Moore (March 9, 1928) that his year of sabbath, away from the chores of the "Musical Chronicle," had seemed so close to the peace of heaven that it was impossible for him to break it. He must leave *The Dial* once for all, and his withdrawal was anything but an unconsidered step. In her acceptance (March 13, 1928) of Paul Rosenfeld's resignation as the contributing editor-critic of the "Musical Chronicle," the Editor was graceful, but perhaps inadvertently she cast a darker tone in her note when she said that "we can hardly realize that you are abandoning the staff of The Dial." Less than a year later Gilbert Seldes left. Of the three original contributing editor-critics, only Henry McBride stayed at his post until the end, flanked by Padraic Colum as Seldes' successor and Kenneth Burke as Rosenfeld's.

Even writers who had most greatly benefited by the generosity of Thayer and Watson now turned against the review that had helped them to attain renown. William Carlos Williams wrote Ezra Pound on August 11, 1928, that Scofield Thayer seemed to have all but nothing to do with the management of *The Dial* then, from what he could infer from a talk he had had with "Mary Ann" (Marianne Moore). The rumor that Williams had heard, that *The Dial* was up for sale and might be bought by "G.," was perhaps no more than a rumor. He had not heard the rumor again. If *The Dial* were sold and bought, the change would surely mean the retirement of its Editor, who would not sell out but would probably go back to the library—on starvation wages. Williams admired Marianne Moore: she received little credit for her fight in New York but stood aces high with him for what she was doing, not, though, for what she was able to accomplish, unfortunately. Among the publishers, Williams wrote Pound, *The Dial* was a dead letter: "It almost means that if you are 'one of *The Dial* crowd' you are automatically excluded from perlite society as far as influence in N. Y. goes." Yet, admitted Williams, he felt so disgusted with *The Dial* for its half-hearted ways that he was almost ready to agree with anyone concerning its worthlessness. Though Marianne Moore—whom he again excluded from his condemnation—was quietly doing all she could to warp things toward a better policy, she would not succeed. If Watson sold *The Dial*, Williams vowed he would positively, for once in his life, stir everything about himself in an effort to have the former Publisher of *The Dial* back Ezra Pound's little magazine *Exile*, which was meagerly supported.[7] These confidences suggest that rumors about the imminent retirement of Thayer and Watson from *The Dial* were noised abroad, that Pound asked Williams to verify them, and that Williams talked with Marianne Moore in an effort to ascertain just what would happen to *The Dial* now that both its directors were no longer closely in touch with their review.

Dr. Williams' disgust with *The Dial* for its half-hearted ways did not, however, prevent him from continuing to contribute to it, nor did Pound's apparent agreement with Williams prevent him from praising Williams publicly in *The Dial*. Pound and Williams shared this attitude with others less indebted to *The Dial*.

There was, too, an attitude similar to that expressed by the young Harvard men who started *Hound and Horn* in 1927. *Hound and Horn* saw a betraying of the cause by *The Dial;* but the "cause" was no longer the "Movement." *Hound and Horn* by its existence attested the success of the movement *The Dial* had stood for, however, and it patently imitated *The Dial* in format and in critical policy. That is to say, *Hound and Horn* included pictures as well as stories and verse and critical pieces in its pages; its editorial "Comment" and its chronicles of the arts (in art, music, and theater) obviously imitated those of the older magazine; and it carried into the 1930's the attitude established first in America by *The Dial*, the critical habit of looking at the work of art rather than at the artist and his milieu, the desire to publish original writing that would be interesting to read for its own excellence rather than for considerations extraneous to art. The editors of *Hound and Horn* nevertheless did not pay tribute to the directors of *The Dial*, who had really blazed the way that future periodicals of art and letters would follow—the way in fact such reviews and magazines still travel, but with comparative ineptitude and uniform dulness. Some of the people who contributed to *Hound and Horn* had contributed to *The Dial:* Marianne Moore, Kenneth Burke, Constantin Brancusi (with *The Golden Bird* again!), S. Foster Damon, Louis Zukofsky, Paul Valéry, Yvor Winters, T. S. Eliot, Charles Burchfield, Malcolm Cowley, and E. E. Cummings. As the authors of *The Little Magazine* have well said, these contributors made *Hound and Horn* a worthy competitor and successor of *The Dial.*[8]

That *The Dial* was imitated by its rivals and that these would carry on and exploit the tradition established by *The Dial* was a fine irony: the parent review died, its lesser imitators were legion. Its devices and techniques were used and used again as commonplaces of the journalism of the small reviews and quarterlies. Some of the things *The Dial* had disseminated seemed, moreover, to be reaching the general public. In May 1929, "Comment" noted that Ezra Pound had been writing in *The New York Herald-Tribune:* "Ezra Pound may proffer too readily Stendhal's remark that it takes years for anything to reach the general public, and he is not afraid of repeating what he has said before; but a discussion by him in The Herald-Tribune—How to Read, or Why—is a lively, or better say a living, thing, and not undistinctive rhetorically in its dual method of emphasis by over- and by under-statement." On the other hand, much of the distinguished writing that *The Dial* had published was already forgotten and unread by the end of the Twenties. Ten years after Sibley Watson had published in *The Dial*, in June, July, and August 1920, his brilliant, and pioneering, translations of Arthur Rimbaud's *A Season in Hell* and *Illuminations* and had discussed the poet, in "Some Remarks on Rimbaud as Magician," with "quietness amounting to scandal," Caresse Crosby could find a dozen versions in English of Rimbaud's *Le Bateau Ivre* and dozens of the "Voyelles," but only a small number of English versions of the early poems, and no rendering at all of *Une Saison en Enfer* or of the more esoteric work.[9] Even to the 1960's, the dozens of examples of German Expressionist work *The Dial* reproduced—such as Franz Marc's *Horses* and Oskar Kokoschka's *Max Reinhardt*—seem novel, so soon forgotten were the pictures in *The Dial* and so far in advance of their contemporaries were Thayer and Watson and their staff.

Nearly ten years of striving, of success and failure, of partial, hesitant acceptance by the American public and quick indifference came to an end in July 1929. Scofield Thayer had become ill about 1927, and, in the long run, his illness was an important factor in the decision to discontinue *The Dial*. It is remarkable that, comparatively inexperienced though she was at the outset of her editorship of *The Dial*, Marianne Moore worked with such efficiency for the four years she sustained the review.[10] Certainly Miss Moore and Dr. Watson kept *The Dial* going through the latter Twenties.

Miss Moore has explained the end of *The Dial* as the result of a combination of factors: by 1929 Dr. Watson was absent from New York for months at a time; editorial consultations were difficult; and "what had begun as a spontaneously delightful plotting in the interest of art and artists, was becoming mere faithfulness to responsibility."[11] Also, Scofield Thayer was not happy about the editorial policy of *The Dial*. He had submitted to its Editor a poem to be published in his review, and she had returned the verses, explaining she believed them not to be of publishable quality. This perhaps was the final small factor in deciding Thayer to pull his interest out of *The Dial*. William Carlos Williams to the contrary, Thayer and Watson apparently never seriously considered selling their Dial stock to someone else. They had never been concerned to profit from their venture.

The news of the closing of *The Dial* was painfully given out and as painfully received. On May 16, 1929, Marianne Moore had to inform Henry McBride suddenly that she had had to permit the Corn Exchange Bank to acknowledge his galaxy of briefer mentions submitted, for responsibilities had not come singly or lightly to those at *The Dial*. "After the July issue, *The Dial* is to be discontinued; so with the exception of a briefer mention of the book of woodcuts"—McBride's review of Roger Avermaete's *La Gravure sur Bois Moderne de l'Occident* was printed in the final issue; at last a paragraph in "Briefer Mention" can be identified by its author!— "we must plan for nothing further. We are hoping that our decision to close will not be known in general until the formal announcement in the June issue. . . . I cannot say how much I wish that instead of sending you these doleful items I could be enquiring of you respecting a free afternoon when you could have tea with us."

The doleful news was disheartening to other members of the Dial group. On May 29, Padraic Colum, writing from Westport, told Marianne Moore he felt so mournful about the discontinuation of *The Dial* that he did not know how to write her: "I can honestly say that I feel as if a bit was gone out of my own life. Writing for The Dial was not like writing for any other periodical. I know I shall never have again such sympathetic editors. My own loss is a great one, but even if I had not been attached to The Dial through writing for it I should feel at a loss because of the defeat of so gallant an intellectual adventure. . . . I shall always look back on the time I wrote for The Dial as to my good days." The loss must indeed have been a deep one for Colum, as he had been an important contributor not only to *The Dial* of Thayer and Watson but also to the fortnightly *Dial* of Martyn Johnson. Padraic Colum had been one of the contributing editors to Johnson's *Dial* and twelve years later was still on the staff in much the same capacity, as the contributing editor-critic writing "The Theatre."

Alyse Gregory may not have learned the news about the closing of *The Dial* until she read it in the June 1929 issue; or, again, it may be that mail to England written in the latter part of May did not reach her until the middle of June. On June 13, 1929, she wrote Marianne Moore upon learning the sad and final news, in which she discerned but two consoling factors, one that Miss Moore would now surely turn her creative energies to writing, and the other that *The Dial* had not been sold to someone who would change its whole tone and lower its literary standard. But it was a great loss, and one that people were sure not to realize.

When the news was made public, reaction in the New York press was more casual. On May 31, 1929, *The New York Times* announced: "The Dial to Suspend / Publication to Halt with July Issue / No Reason Given for Move." The news release was brief:

> The Dial, a magazine of arts and letters, will suspend publication with the July issue, Dr. James S. Watson Jr., president of the publication, announced last night. No reason for the publisher's

decision was announced. Dr. Watson was not certain whether offers of purchase would be accepted.

The magazine has devoted itself to finding and publishing promising and meritorious work and has not sought success as a best seller. It has been generally reported that the publication did not make a profit.

Although started in Chicago in 1880 as a conservative review, it assumed a liberal point of view on moving to New York in July, 1918. In January, 1920, it was taken over by Scofield Thayer, who retained the editorship until July, 1926. Since then he has been adviser, turning over the editorship to Marianne Moore. Throughout this time Dr. Watson was associated with him.

During the last eight years The Dial has made an annual award of $2000 to the writers who the editors considered had made the outstanding contribution to American letters during the preceding year. The magazine published early writings of John Dos Passos, Edmund Wilson Jr., Lewis Mumford, Hendrik Van Loon and Evelyn Scott.

The reporter who wrote this piece had made a conscientious attempt to get his facts straight, and he succeeded except for his closing paragraph. One may well wonder, too, about the accuracy of the labels "conservative" and "liberal" as applied to *The Dial* to distinguish its various periods. It was always liberal, but not always political; but, then, perhaps from one point of view, not to be primarily concerned with politics is to be conservative. There were more substantial inaccuracies in the *Times* item. The Dial Award was never given to the writers who the editors of *The Dial* considered had made the outstanding contribution to American letters during the preceding year. Rather, Thayer and Watson gave the Award each year on the basis of the recipient's total production and in order to enable him to pay a few bills; the Dial Award was in no sense a prize and involved no obligation on the part of the recipient. As for the list of writers whose early work *The Dial* published, Edmund Wilson and Evelyn Scott received the welcome encouragement the review offered, of regular publication; but despite the incontrovertible fact that Lewis Mumford, John Dos Passos, and Hendrik Van Loon did publish a few things in the monthly *Dial*, they were certainly not representative contributors.

That same day the *Times* printed an editorial on the passing of *The Dial*, poetically entitled "If O'er The Dial Glides a Shade." For nearly eight years and a half, so the piece inaccurately began, Mr. Scofield Thayer had had the pleasure—if costly, far outweighing the cost—of publishing and much of the time editing a magazine molded to his heart's desire. Its originality, eccentricity, brilliancy, its competence and its willfulness in arts and letters, its delight to spoof and *épater*, had endeared it to faithful readers, too many of whom, perhaps, had sought it in the reading room and had abstained from the subscription desk. *The Dial*, as the *Times* viewed it in retrospect, had been hospitable to much native and to more foreign talent. Its foreign correspondents and contributors had been interesting or distinguished. If it had had a fault, it was that its imports were too much the work of old clever hands. Its great merit was that it had taken what it wanted and wasn't made to sell. *The Dial* was not made to please anybody but its owner. It was highly intelligent, even in its obscurities or peculiarities of choice. The *Times* was sorry to learn *The Dial* would be discontinued after the July issue, and it concluded with the hope that "sometime Mr. Thayer will renew his experiment to enlarge the field of the arts and rasp the nerves of the stolid. He cannot be surprised that, as Mr. D. H. Lawrence writes in 'When I Went to the Circus,' in the May Dial:

THERE WAS NO GUSHING RESPONSE,
AS THERE IS AT THE FILM."

The generosity of the *Times* contrasted to the tone of *The Herald-Tribune* in its editorial the next day, entitled "Another 'Dial' Dies." *The Herald-Tribune* first observed that another of the great names in the history of American magazines disappeared with the passing of *The Dial*. It enumerated the various *Dials* of Margaret Fuller, of Francis Browne ("The Chicago 'Dial'"), of Martyn Johnson ("the paper which Robert Morss Lovett, Thorstein Veblen, Clarence Britten and others edited here in New York in armistice days"), and of Scofield Thayer ("the strange 'Dial'"). Of this last *Dial*, *The Herald-Tribune* remarked that its illustration went to the extremes of eccentricity and its prose ran the gamut, and it combined worship of the new with adoration of the old. The editorial gave an "impressive" list of contributors—Spengler, Thomas Mann, Benedetto Croce, Maxim Gorki, Paul Valéry, Anatole France, Remy de Gourmont, William B. Yeats, George Moore, Arthur Symons,

George Santayana, George Saintsbury, and Ford Madox Ford. But these were not young men, and *The Dial* had let it be understood —possibly through the esoteric mysteries of its "art," possibly through the odd awards of its annual prizes—that it was the apostle of the young. And of these newer and more native talents, *The Herald-Tribune* cited Sherwood Anderson, E. E. Cummings, and (why? except possibly the editorialist had read the news item in the *Times* of the day before) John Dos Passos and Evelyn Scott. *The Dial* had also printed pages and pages of unintelligible prose and poetry by scores of bright young men and women whose names already had been forgotten; and the reader had had a profound suspicion that a great deal of their newness was merely self-conscious posing. The editorial comment and the criticism of *The Dial* had seldom helped to understand or to appreciate these contributors. Possibly, concluded the editorial, this very catholicity of taste kept *The Dial* from being an exciting magazine. It had no tang of its own. It never condescended to journalism, and, after all, the not altogether despicable art of journalism consisted in discovering a public that wanted what the editor liked to feed it. As a last bit of second-guessing helpfulness, *The Herald-Tribune* pointed out that a little less receptivity to all the forms of newness, however empty, might have left more evident the indubitable skill of the editors of *The Dial* in importing the work of the ripe talents of Europe.

However regrettable the hostility of *The Herald-Tribune*, its attitude was undoubtedly as widespread as the well-bred nostalgia of the *Times*. The gratuitous sitting in judgment over a dying contemporary, the deliberate twisting of the contents of *The Dial* into "pages and pages of unintelligible prose and poetry by scores of bright young men and women," the unjustifiable allegations that *The Dial* had no tang of its own and was too receptive to all the forms of newness however empty—these constitute the reactionary complement to the more private complaints of William Carlos Williams and Ezra Pound. Yet *The Herald-Tribune* did see the nominal link between the various *Dials* even if it did not observe the invisible link between them: the continued growth of an American aesthetic tradition, culminating in the movement of the Twenties.

The end of the line was the "Announcement," signed with Sibley Watson's initials, "S. W." on the last page of *The Dial* for July 1929:

THE
DIAL

JULY 1929

VOLUME LXXXVI   NUMBER 7

50 cents a copy

Nine and a half years is a rather long time for one management in the present journalistic mêlée. On the edge of quitting we want to express our immense gratitude to the distinguished men and women who, with us, have edited and helped edit THE DIAL since 1920. These are: Stewart Mitchell, Gilbert Seldes, Alyse Gregory, Kenneth Burke, Marianne Moore. We are also grateful to our readers, always bearing in mind that although a magazine can get along somehow without readers it cannot exist without contributors —who were, however indignantly, THE DIAL.

Surely such a statement goes far to discount Dr. Watson's suggestion that *The Dial* lacked contributors and therefore must cease publication. But whatever he meant—and it is another reason to add to the several that account for the end of the review—*The Dial* was now finished. It existed only as an historical fact for future exegesis.

There had been the Transcendentalist quarterly of Margaret Fuller and Ralph Waldo Emerson, one bloom of the garden that was the flowering of New England. Its four years had been lonely and unremunerative, but it had encouraged the growth of native poetry and criticism and appreciation of letters and the arts. It had criticized what was most dignified in Puritan modes of thought as not favorable to beauty and bravely had condemned the habits of an industrial community as not propitious to delicacy of sentiment. The succeeding *Dials* of Cincinnati and Chicago, under Moncure Conway and Francis Browne, had carried on the intellectual traditions of the mid-nineteenth century, and under Browne the Chicago *Dial* had succeeded in becoming, as its Editor wrote, an intelligent guide and agreeable companion to the book-lover and book-buyer who wanted but was unable to keep informed of the character of the vast literary current constantly flowing around him. Its standard was the known capability and fairness of its reviewers, whose judgments carried with them the weight of the best available authority for the particular work treated. Its editorial comments were made with conscientious freedom of expression.

But times change, and manners. What had once been revolt had become tradition; what once inspired a generation before the Civil War softened into Alexandrianism. And this phase passed. In a decade of turmoil and revolution *The Dial* once more was transformed into the Organ of the Free, in the hands of the Humanity and Reform Men. From Chicago *The Dial* was moved to New York, in all the feverish upset of the end of the First World War, to cry the political and sociological and economic beliefs and slogans of Randolph Bourne and John Dewey and Thorstein Veblen. But this phase passed too.

The beginning of the Twenties was also the beginning of a new *Dial*. The old fortnightly of Browne and of Johnson was now a monthly review of literature and the arts, directed by Scofield Thayer and James Sibley Watson. Louise Bogan has described the beginning publication of this *Dial* as a key event.[12] It was indeed. *The Dial* of the Twenties broke away from the preoccupations of its recent past and lived instead by the rule of the arts. In its pages, both European and American, and even Asian, writers, the novelists and poets and artists, the critics and scholars and historians, discussed and debated every aesthetic trend and many of the philosophical and sociological trends of the decade. *The Dial* was uniquely authoritative because it was uniquely urbane and tolerant of differences. It was not slipshod in its editorial thinking, it was not indifferent; it had convictions, and these were the convictions of the editors of the original *Dial:* belief in freedom of expression, in the supreme importance of the arts, in the viability of excellence from whatever period and whatever direction and whatever source. But excellence for Thayer and Watson and their staff was excellence of form, not an imposed conformity of ideas.

Because of that belief, *The Dial* of the Twenties rejected the narrow concept of Americanism that Emerson and Margaret Fuller and Francis Browne, too, had had to combat in their times. Both the New England *Dial* of the 1840's and the Chicago *Dial* of the turn of the century had attempted to incorporate something of the spaciousness, the full play of mind, the easy and confident dignity their editors saw in the great European reviews of the nineteenth century. Their achievement in this respect was imperfect because, through no fault of intention, the tone of the American *Dials* was provincial. Thayer and Watson first gave America a review of the kind that their predecessors had envisioned, a periodical as beautiful as it was intelligent, urbane and cosmopolitan only because it incorporated in its conception the best, according to its directors' lights, that was possible in America.

Money, a great amount of money freely and steadily given, made this *Dial* possible, but money without vision and intelligence and taste and incredibly selfless devotion to an ideal of culture would not have produced *The Dial* of the Twenties. As the Editor himself said, when he resigned, no aesthetic dogma dominated *The Dial*, but on the other hand, as one anonymous "Comment" asserted, the writing in the review must be interesting to read. Beauty and ease of format were also essential, whatever the cost. Contributors were respected, their wishes heeded, sometimes at considerable expense. The older writer might appear side by side with the younger, more experimental writer, but they could not be said to jostle one another. Rather, their juxtaposition revealed new aspects of the commonwealth of art. Similarly, the appearance of European writers alongside American writers revealed the cosmopolitan excellence and regional virtues of both groups.

The aesthetic revolution of the New Movement, with its consequences incalculable even decades later, was received hospitably into *The Dial*. Here the later reader may discern the existence of a *Dial* coterie; but many times the spirit of *The Dial* was the rapport of men who knew one another only through the admiration the critic entertained for the poet's verses. This was at the root of the new criticism of *The Dial*, this emphasis on the poem rather than on the man who composed it or on the influences of the school or group upon him. Most notably exemplified in the early years of *The Dial* by Eliot's early essays, the new approach was also to be seen in Gilbert Seldes' reviews in "The Theatre," in Scofield Thayer's "Comment," in Sibley Watson's pseudonymous essays, and in the correspondence, essays, and reviews of Kenneth Burke, Padraic Colum, Marianne Moore, and Ezra Pound. The pictures in *The Dial* received a similar consideration; the work of art was the focus of the critic's observation, not the life of the artist or sculptor or the school to which he belonged. Through the Twenties, the new aesthetic evolved.

The Dial by the very fact of its continued existence created a public, small perhaps, but informed and intelligent, alive to the implications of the movement *The Dial* publicized. It was an influential public, too, and a discerning one at least as regards the new directions in the fine arts of pictures and sculpture and music and in poetry and criticism, and the drama. This was the public that perpetuated and elaborated the discoveries and revolutionary changes of the movement of the early Twenties, so that the ensuing decades have only seen an exploitation of the taste disseminated by *The Dial* and shared by a few thousand people. During the 1930's and '40's the aesthetic impulse of this group was not dominant. The aesthetic movement of one decade gave way before the political struggle of the next. A national and social bias dominated the arts. But the influence of *The Dial* has been long-lived, and despite the vicissitudes of its approach to arts and letters, it made, through the readers it attracted and affected, a substantial and lasting contribution to the growth of the arts in America.

But what of *The Dial* itself? Is its importance more than historical? Has it any essential value in and for itself? How few periodicals of the past are now interesting to read! Whatever in them has retained its interest has been collected, anthologized, embalmed in textbooks. The case of *The Dial* is different. Some things in *The Dial* were topical, some were of indifferent worth; yet almost every issue is still fascinating to dip into, not only to read but also to look at. And that interest does not depend on one's sudden recognition of greatness, as with a Yeats or Eliot poem, which he may come upon. Rather, such an interest grows as the reader becomes aware of the interplay of illustration and text, the rapport between the work of art, be it picture or poem or story or play, and the review or critique of it. *The Dial* is still interesting just as any excellent work of art transcends the mannerisms of its immediate milieu; and *The Dial* possesses a distinctive unity that arises from a correspondence and harmony of its parts, from care and craftsmanship in execution, from attention to the most niggling detail as well as to the grand architectonics of structure, and from the intention of Scofield Thayer and Sibley Watson and their staff to create a journal of surpassing artistic worth. *The Dial*, too, has wit and sparkle; it refused to try for the bad metaphysics, the solemnity, and the false decorum that so blightingly mark current reviews and quarterlies and that have taken, in them, the place of courage, good humor, and sure taste.

If it owned relatively few of the supernatural virtues, *The Dial* surely possessed the virtues of this world in abundance—*ordre et beauté, luxe, calme, et volupté*, as Baudelaire wrote in another context. *The Dial* still remains the greatest American magazine of arts and letters of our century.

LIVING ART

Charles Demuth   *After Sir Christopher Wren*   FEBRUARY 1921

Marc Chagall *It Is Written* OCTOBER 1922

Henri Matisse *Nasturtiums and the "Dance" II* JULY 1922

(*Top*) Paul Signac *La Rochelle* AUGUST 1924

(*Bottom*) André Dunoyer de Segonzac *The Morin in Spring* FEBRUARY 1924

Alfeo Faggi *St. Francis* NOVEMBER 1926

Maurice de Vlaminck *Street in Nesles* MARCH 1924

THE DIAL

Charles Burchfield *Spring Thaw* APRIL 1920

Gaston Lachaise *The Peacock* APRIL 1921

Jacques Lipchitz   *Harlequin with Clarinet*   NOVEMBER 1920

Robert Delaunay   *St Séverin*   NOVEMBER 1922

Franz Marc *Two Horses* SEPTEMBER 1922

Henry Le Fauconnier *Stefan Zweig* JANUARY 1923

Max Liebermann   *Richard Strauss*   AUGUST 1922

Jan C. Juta   *D. H. Lawrence*   FEBRUARY 1923

Boardman Robinson *H. G. Wells* SEPTEMBER 1923

Oskar Kokoschka *Portrait of Max Reinhardt* MARCH 1923

Rockwell Kent *Voyagers* MAY 1924

Reinhold Lepsius *Stefan George*

Pablo Picasso *Mother and Child* MARCH 1923

Pablo Picasso *Pierrot* AUGUST 1924

(*Top*) Pablo Picasso
Heroic Head of a Woman
MARCH 1929

(*Right*) Pablo Picasso
Classic Head
SEPTEMBER 1926

(*Left*) Adolf Dehn
In the Park
JANUARY 1926

Max Weber *Gesture* APRIL 1925

Marie Laurencin   *The Party*   AUGUST 1925

Edouard Vuillard *At Table* SEPTEMBER 1925

Elie Nadelman *Horse* OCTOBER 1928

THE DIAL COLLECTION

Ivan Mestrovic
Madonna and Child   JANUARY 1925

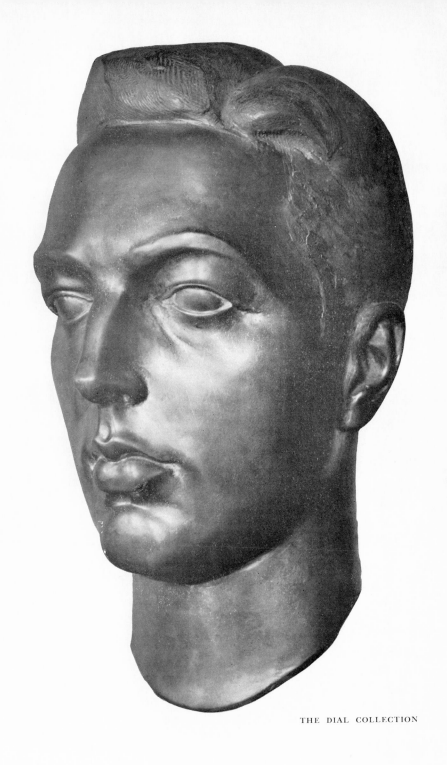

Gaston Lachaise *Scofield Thayer* JANUARY 1926

Gaston Lachaise *E. E. Cummings* JANUARY 1926

Gaston Lachaise *James Sibley Watson* JANUARY 1926

Pierre Bonnard *Dressing Room* MARCH 1926

Gustav Klimt   *Two Reclining Nudes*   1959

Egon Schiele   *Seated Nude Girl Clasping Her Knee*   1959

Oskar Kokoschka   *Portrait of a Viennese Art Dealer*   1959

Oskar Kokoschka *Bust of Woman with Hands Clasped over Her Head*

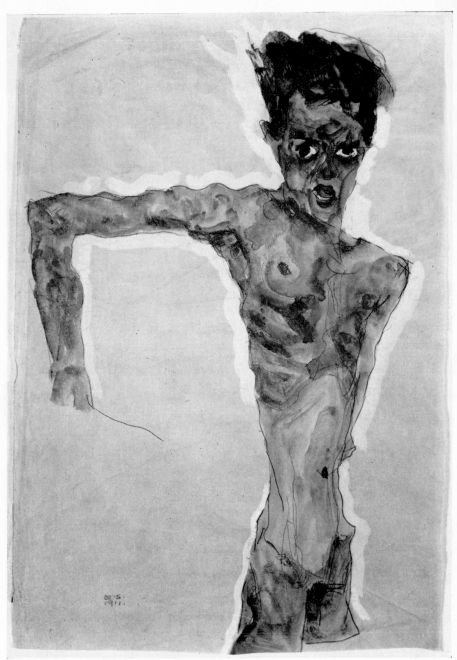

Egon Schiele   *Self-Portrait*   1959

Ernst Barlach   *The Listeners*   1959

(*Right*) Marc Chagall *Susanna* 1959

Marc Chagall *Water under the Moon* 1959

Jean Marchand   *Reclining Figure*   1959

Georges Braque   *Standing Figure*   1959

Aristide Maillol   *Woman with Crab*

Pablo Picasso *Woman Bathing*

Edvard Munch *The Day After*

Edvard Munch *Night Café*

Auguste Renoir *Two Bathers*

Aristide Maillol   *Seated Nude Leaning on Her Left Hand*

Boardman Robinson *One-Step*

Emma Löwenstamm   *Arthur Schnitzler*

Gaston Lachaise   *Seated Woman, Arms Upraised*   1959

NOTES / INDEX

1. LX (August 15, 1916), 113. I have not been able to discover Martyn Johnson's name among the early contributors and staff members of *The New Republic*, 1914–17. He is an elusive figure. "Notes and News" also specified Johnson's contributions to English magazines. What his British publication might be, I do not know. He wrote six articles between 1910 and 1916 for *Putnam's Magazine, Everybody's Magazine, The World To-Day*, and *System: The Magazine of Business;* e.g., "A Day with the Circus," *The World To-Day*, XIX (1910), 709–15 (ill.). Sometime between 1912–28 he also wrote a play, *Mr. and Mrs. P. Roe* (Drama League of America, n.d.). Henry Goddard Leach to this author (January 27, 1958): "Martyn Johnson was a highly imaginative publisher and published articles of great importance by the philosophical savants of the world. In later years I remember discussing a short story *The Dial* published by D. H. Lawrence in London, in which he explained to me that the story was really a satire. . . . All I remember about Mr. Martyn Johnson was his effectiveness as an editor, his enthusiasm for the best in American thought, and his engaging personality. It is my impression that he died many years ago." In 1919 Mr. Leach had taken a block of stock in *The Dial* on the solicitation of Scofield Thayer and had become "some sort of officer" of the Dial Publishing Company. A stockholder of the period 1916–18, Laird Bell, had no recollections and "could not recall anything about his dealings with the magazine," according to Harley A. Stephenson to this author (December 4, 1957). The only extensive memoir of Martyn Johnson occurs in Harold Stearns' *The Street I Know* (New York, 1935), pp. 145–80 *passim*. Robert Morss Lovett, "George Bernard Donlin," *The Dial*, LXIX (1920), 149–51, merely mentions Johnson in passing. Lovett discusses his editorship of *The Dial* (1919) in *All Our Years* (New York, 1948), pp. 151–56. These three reminiscences constitute the only detailed firsthand accounts of *The Dial* during 1916–19 that have seen publication. Although my account of *The Dial* (1916–20) is in part based on the two books by Lovett and Stearns, these are not accurate in some details and are valuable only when checked against *The Dial* itself and the unpublished papers in the Dial Collection (hereafter noted with a preceding asterisk).

2. *While the information about Scofield Thayer and his purchase of *The Dial* is based on the Dial papers—most importantly, correspondence of Scofield Thayer and Harold Evans (December 9, 15, 17, 24, and 30, 1920)—it also is based on scattered hints in various memoirs of the period and on conversations with Mr. Hermann P. Riccius of Worcester, Mass., and a conversation with Henry McBride on March 11, 1958. Scofield Thayer is not a figure of mystery, despite the statement in F. J. Hoffman, Charles Allen, and Carolyn Ulrich, *The Little Magazine* (Princeton, N. J., 1946), p. 200.

3. Louis Filler, *Randolph Bourne* (Washington, 1943), p. 117.

4. *Scofield Thayer to Harold Evans (December 24, 1920): "As to my desiring to cut short the existence of a liberal magazine, that is the greatest rot I have ever heard. I gave bail for one of the staff of The Masses during the war and most of my friends are socialists. I have always voted the socialist ticket." Also see Scofield Thayer to Maxim Gorki (June 11, 1922): "The Dial was one of the very few journals in America to deplore and vigourously to oppose the attitude of the American and Allied governments to the revolution in Russia."

5. (New York, 1957), p. 66.

6. Paul Rosenfeld, "Randolph Bourne," *The Dial*, LXXV (December 1923), 545–60; in Rosenfeld's *Port of New York* (New York, 1924) and 2nd edn., ed. Sherman Paul (Urbana, 1961), pp., 211–36. For a fuller critique see Louis Filler, *Randolph Bourne*, pp. 76–78, 97–128, with a bibliography, pp. 152–55. Although he treats Bourne's quarrel with Dewey in detail, pp. 97 ff.,

Louis Filler describes inadequately the position of *The Dial* and does not even mention Scofield Thayer's role in this historic and tragically divisive feud among the American liberals. Dewey first contributed a leading article "Current Tendencies in Education" to *The Dial*, LXII (April 5, 1917), 287–89, about five months after Bourne began his association. For a perceptive essay by a friend of Bourne, see Elsie Clews Parsons, "A Pacifist Patriot" (review of Bourne's posthumous collection, *Untimely Papers*, ed. James Oppenheim [New York, 1919]), *The Dial*, LXVIII (March 1920), 367–70.

7. Lovett, *All Our Years*, p. 155, wrote of these Decrees as "the Constitution of the Union of Soviet Socialist Republics," but that document was not promulgated until July 6, 1923.

8. (New York, 1959), pp. 150–51.

9. *Memorandum of a Conference concerning the Investments of Mr. Thayer and Mr. Watson in The Dial* (May 24, 1920), 3 pp. (plus charts).

TWO: The New *Dial*

1. *Only Yesterday*, Bantam Books edn. (New York, 1946), p. 113.

2. "The Decline of the Dial," in the

unsigned column, "A New York Diary," *The New Republic*, LII (October 12, 1927), 211.

THREE: Editorial Attitudes

1. *The two letters quoted from are Scofield Thayer to Gilbert Seldes (respectively July 30 and 25, 1921); brackets indicate lacunae in the ms. "Dickens" was reprinted as one of the essays in Santayana's *Soliloquies in England and Later Soliloquies* (New York, 1922).

2. *Letters of Sherwood Anderson*, ed. Howard Mumford Jones and

Walter Rideout (Boston, 1953), p. 51 (Anderson to Waldo Frank, ?December 1919).

3. *Ibid.*, p. 76 (Anderson to Gilbert Seldes, October 19, 1921).

4. *Ibid.*, p. 81 (after October 24, 1921).

5. *Ibid.*, p. 84 (December 1921).

6. Marianne Moore to this author (May 3, 1958).

FOUR: The Staff

1. *Predilections* (New York, 1955), pp. 103–4.
2. Alyse Gregory, *The Day is Gone* (New York, 1948), pp. 203–7.
3. *Ibid.*, pp. 177–78.
4. *Ibid.*, pp. 181–82.
5. Llewelyn Powys, *The Verdict of Bridlegoose* (London, 1927), p. 115.
6. *The Day is Gone*, pp. 210–11.
7. *Predilections*, pp. 113–14.
8. *Exile's Return*, 2d edn. rev. (New York, 1951), p. 226.
9. Malcolm Elwin, *The Life of Llewelyn Powys* (London, 1946), p. 165.
10. William Wasserstrom, "T. S. Eliot and *The Dial*," *Sewanee Review*, LXX (Winter 1962), 86–87.
11. *The Little Magazine*, p. 200, fn. 13: "Letter, Watson to Allen, May 25, 1943 (unpublished)."
12. *The Letters of Hart Crane*, ed. Brom Weber (New York, 1952), p. 220 (December 1, 1925).
13. "Interview with Donald Hall," *A Marianne Moore Reader* (New York, 1961), p. 267.
14. *Predilections*, p. 111.
15. *A Marianne Moore Reader*, p. 268.
16. *Predilections*, pp. 105–12.
17. *The Day is Gone*, p. 211.
18. *Ibid.*, p. 209.
19. *i: six nonlectures* (Cambridge, Mass., 1953), p. 50.

FIVE: Editor-Contributors

1. Margaret Anderson, *My Thirty Years War* (New York, 1930), pp. 44–45, 188–89.
2. *A Marianne Moore Reader*, p. 266.
3. *The Seven Lively Arts*, 2d edn. (New York, 1957), p. 303.
4. *Predilections*, p. 111.
5. P. 209.
6. *The Little Magazine*, p. 204.
7. Milton W. Brown, *American Painting from the Armory Show to the Depression* (Princeton, N. J., 1955), p. 89.
8. (New York, 1948), p. 24.

SIX: Some Other Contributors

1. As quoted in Wasserstrom, *Sewanee Review*, LXX (Winter 1962), 87–88.
2. *The Letters of Ezra Pound*, ed. D. D. Paige (New York, 1950), p. 180 (July 8, 1922).
3. *The Autobiography of Alice B. Toklas* (New York, 1933), p. 248.
4. *The Letters of Ezra Pound*, p. 346 (October 29, 1940).
5. *Ibid.*, pp. 172–75 (March 18, 1922).
6. *Ibid.*, p. 186 (May 12, 1923).
7. *Ibid.*, p. 213 (October 20, 1927).

SEVEN: And Still Others

1. (New York, 1953), pp. 27–30.
2. (New York, 1959), pp. 149–70.
3. (New York, 1925), pp. 218 ff. See also Kreymborg's *Our Singing Strength* (New York, 1929), pp. 488–90, for his evaluation of Mina Loy's work.
4. *The Little Magazine*, p. 51; Kreymborg, pp. 330–33.
5. Marianne Moore, "The Dial (Part 2)," *Life and Letters Today*, XXVIII (1941), 6.
6. *Predilections*, p. 112.
7. "The Dial (Part 2)," p. 6.

EIGHT: Art, Artists, and Entrepreneurs

1. *The Seven Lively Arts*, p. 292.
2. Charles Norman, *The Magic-Maker*, p. 165.
3. *Troubadour* (New York, 1925), p. 362.
4. William Murrell, *Charles Demuth*, American Artists Series (New York, 1931), pp. 30–31, 36–37.
5. "Dial M for Modern," *The Dial* and the Dial Collection (Worcester, Mass., 1959), pp. 11–12.
6. "The World of Art: Modern Art of One Kind and Another," *The New York Times Magazine* (January 27, 1924), pp. 10–11.
7. "The 'Dial' of America," *Readers and Writers* (1917–1921) (New York, 1922), p. 165.
8. *The Magic-Maker*, p. 151.

NINE: To the End of the Twenties

1. William Carlos Williams, *I Wanted to Write a Poem*, ed. Edith Heal (Boston, 1958), p. 54. The version of the poem here quoted appeared in *The Dial* (March 1927) as the third of "Three Poems."
2. *Ibid.*, p. 53.
3. *The Selected Letters of William Carlos Williams*, ed. John C. Thirlwall (New York, 1957), p. 70.
4. *I Wanted to Write a Poem*, pp. 71–72.
5. *Selected Letters*, pp. 94–95 (April 9, 1928).
6. Hoffman and others, *The Little Magazine*, p. 206.
7. Williams, *Selected Letters*, pp. 103–04.
8. P. 209.
9. *The Passionate Years* (New York, 1953), p. 214.
10. Also see Henry McBride, "Dr. Barnes R. I. P.," *Art News*, L (1951), 16.
11. Marianne Moore to Charles Allen (July 2, 1941), as quoted in *The Little Magazine*, p. 205.
12. *The Achievement in American Poetry* (Chicago, 1951), p. 72.

INDEX

The Dial as a title is not indexed. For specific subjects relating to *The Dial*, see such headings below as "Circulation" or "Format."

Date Due